Willing the Good

WILLING THE GOOD

Jesus, Dissent, and Desire

Paula M. Cooey

Fortress Press Minneapolis

WILLING THE GOOD
Jesus, Dissent, and Desire

Cover image: Cover art by Gerald Bustamante. Photo © Images.com/CORBIS.
Cover design: Brad Norr
Book design: Abby Hartman

Library of Congress Cataloging-in-Publication Data

Cooey, Paula M., 1945-
 Willing the good : Jesus, dissent, and desire / by Paula M. Cooey.
  p. cm.
 Includes bibliographical references and indexes.
 ISBN-13: 978-0-8006-3664-7 (alk. paper)
 ISBN-10: 0-8006-3664-3 (alk. paper)
 1. Church controversies. 2. Jesus Christ—History of doctrines. 3. Dissenters, Religious. 4. Heresies, Christian. 5. Church discipline. 6. Conflict management—Religious aspects—Christianity. I. Title.

 BV652.9.C665 2006
 262'.8—dc22
                    2006010517

The paper used in this publication meets the minimum requirements of American National Standard for Information Sciences—Permanence of Paper for Printed Library Materials, ANSI Z329.48-1984.

Manufactured in the U.S.A.

10   09   08   07   06   1   2   3   4   5   6   7   8   9   10

In honor of my teachers
Dick Niebuhr and
Gordon Kaufman

In memory of my aunt and godmother
Ruth Helen Miller Jack

Jesu, joy of our desiring
Holy wisdom, love most bright;
Drawn by Thee, our souls aspiring
Soar to uncreated light.

Word of God, our flesh that fashioned,
With the fire of life impassioned,
Striving still to truth unknown,
Soaring, dying round Thy throne.

Through the way where hope is guiding,
Hark, what peaceful music rings;
Where the flock, in Thee confiding,
Drink of joy from deathless springs.

Theirs is beauty's fairest pleasure;
Theirs is wisdom's holiest treasure.
Thou dost ever lead Thine own
In the love of joys unknown

J. S. Bach, Cantata 147 (1723)

CONTENTS

PREFACE

What would it mean to love without condition in a world characterized by scarcity? How might we learn to will a good we cannot fully control for another we cannot fully know? What does it mean to desire what God desires as God desires it? What role might the figure of Jesus play in such desire? Does loving what God loves as God loves it necessitate living a life of dissent? What would such dissent look like today?

In this volume I attempt to answer these perennial questions in light of our particular situation today in North America. We live in a fearful time and in ways that have enormous repercussions for the rest of the world. Once accustomed to bounty, we daily encounter scarcity of natural resources like oil, loss of our pension plans (if we once had them), diminished healthcare if our companies provided it, loss of our jobs to outsourcing, erosion of our infrastructure in the face of natural disaster, decline in our social support systems from welfare to education, attack from abroad and from within, and loss of respect from countries once our allies. Whether such events have happened directly to us, whether we have participated directly in the cronyism that produces them, we face the economic and environmental consequences of the greed and corruption of our political leaders, our business communities, and of large-scale economic and geopolitical shifts we can scarcely comprehend. We are left consumed by fear for ourselves and for our families. All this has diminished our vision of a common good, especially a good effected *with*, not just for, those with whom we have little in common.

Cronyism and its fruits come accompanied by a self-justifying ideology. Economic doctrines of individual self-interest, supported by appeals to social Darwinism, and marshaled in behalf of political doctrines of national self-interest, dominate civic life to the exclusion of a common good. Indeed, to speak of a common good is to invite cynicism, derision, suspicion, or at least the caution to be more realistic. In other words, to imagine willing the good for others as well as ourselves, which was once assumed to lie at the heart of good polity, not to mention true religion, is to think outside the box, to go against human nature, to transgress even nature in general. To speak of a common good only partially glimpsed, for another one cannot presume to know, is all the more startling.

In the face of such fear, how are those who seek to serve Jesus the Christ, found in the face of the hungry, the thirsty, the stranger, the naked, the sick, and the prisoner called to live (Matt. 25:35ff)?

I started out in the late nineties to write a theological work on how to address recent scholarship on the historical Jesus of Nazareth, given two thousand years of Christology—that is, doctrinal interpretations of Jesus as the Christ, unique Son of God as Father, second person of the Trinity, truly human, truly divine. I had the idea I would produce a Christology for today that would integrate the efforts of contemporary biblical scholars with the driving concerns of the present time. My Christology would explicitly relate what we have learned about the early Jesus movement to economic problems, environmental issues, and religious pluralism while taking seriously orthodox doctrinal and sacramental confessions—all in one fell swoop. Such an oddly Protestant endeavor!

Circumstances, most especially the circumstance of reading differently Matthew 25:34-46 in light of my own post-9/11 fear, intervened to shift my focus from Christology *per se* to ethics. I realized how deeply I mourned the loss of a sense of a common good among those with the power to effect it. This new awareness forced me to confront the prospect that my fear marked my own participation in the systems of greed and terror that presently pervade the planet. With this awakening came the knowledge that my desire for the good was as narrow, as paltry, as my fear. I have been coming to grips with this failure of desire and the meagerness of imagination it presupposes ever since.

I am now confident that, by grace, we can *will* better, and willing better, we can, by grace, do better than we do, if we just get over ourselves and move on. If, instead of fixating on ourselves, our families, and our misguided sense of national interest, most especially our purported moral superiority as a nation, we fix firmly upon the *other*, the one in whom Jesus, according to the writer of Matthew, tells us he dwells, we will have no time for fear. We will be busily, even joyfully, engaged in and by God's desire. Though we will come into the middle of things and leave before the end without knowing how it all turns out, this joy, by grace, will be enough.

Many thanks go out to a number of people who aided me in the research, writing, and production of this book. Linell Cady, Sarah Ball Damberg, Ann Lewis, Ted Morgan, Rosamund Rodman, and Calvin Roetzel listened carefully and responded thoughtfully to my ideas. Milner Ball, Jeanne Barker-Nunn, Paul Capetz, and Sam

Worley-Ekstrom read various versions of the manuscript, and their comments and suggestions were invaluable; Sam, bless his heart, proofread and did bibliographical research as well. In addition to Sam's help, I was also fortunate to receive student research assistance from Chrissy Blank and Sarah Turner. Gitta Hammarberg and Peter Weisensel aided me in negotiating the ins and outs of St. Petersburg, Russia. The adult education program of House of Hope Presbyterian Church in Saint Paul, Minnesota, kindly invited me to present my work on more than one occasion, where, always, I got thoughtful feedback. A number of medical caregivers, chief among them Tom Thul and Cynthia Myer, kept me going through a protracted and severe ailment. I thank Michael West and Abby Hartman for their patience, their thoughtfulness, and their extremely good listening skills; indeed, I am grateful to everyone at Fortress Press who had a hand in producing this book. I am most deeply indebted to the undergraduate students at Macalester College, who regularly take my entry-level course on history of Christian traditions, "Jesus, Dissent, and Desire," who keep me thinking freshly as time goes by. Last but not least, I thank Phil Nichols, always ready to hop on the next plane, boat, train, or bus with me and go anywhere, laughing all the way.

Several funding institutions provided support for this project: Macalester College and the Mellon Foundation funded research leave for the academic year 2002–03. During this time, the Freeman Foundation funded travel to East Asia that had a totally unanticipated impact on the book. I am also indebted to the Eli Lilly Foundation for funding student research assistance. I am most grateful to the family of Margaret Weyerhaeuser Harmon for endowing the chair that I hold and for the stipend for research and travel that accompanies it; the stipend for academic year 2003–04 supported my travel to Corinth and to St. Petersburg. Macalester College generously supported my research travel to Istanbul in 2004 through its Faculty Development International Seminar as well.

This book is dedicated to three people. I wish to honor Dick Niebuhr and Gordon Kaufman, who taught me to think and to seek understanding beyond the constraints of religious, theological, political, and academic orthodoxy. And I thank Aunt Ruth, who taught me to love what I cannot understand.

An economy of grace confronts an economy of scarcity as demonstrators march on the National Day of Action on Immigrant Rights in Portland, Oregon, April 10, 2005. Arturo Martinez carries the cross. Image © Greg Wahl-Stephens/Stringer/2006 Getty Images.

1

Incalculable Debts and Immeasurable Grace

I want freedom, the right to self-expression,
everybody's right to beautiful, radiant things.
                                                —Emma Goldman[1]

An underground economy exists that operates alongside the various forms of capitalism that presently dominate the globe. In contrast to dominant economies that depend on narrowly defined desires competing over scarce resources, this alternative economy involves neither credit nor debt, neither profit nor loss. Instead, goods of all kinds circulate out of generosity, out of an exuberant attempt of human desire to meet and exceed the needs of an other—needs that are spiritual, esthetic, and ethical as well as material. Standing outside normative economic measures, therefore unrecognized and untaxed, these attempts resist and have the capacity to overturn arrangements of religious, political, and economic power as we normally live within them. As practiced, this generosity constitutes dissent against such powers. Understood as desire, this generosity acknowledges both self-interest and self-denial, but depends on neither and transcends both. As desire, this generosity is love beyond measure. For two millennia, for many who call themselves Christian, this is the good news proclaimed by Jesus as the Christ: Such a love has come to town—unfulfilled and without closure, nevertheless here, now, for us, with us, in us. Given the awfulness of the times in which we live and the ambiguity of Christian history, this good news requires retelling. I begin with a story.

Before she married, Polly Miller Cooey, my mother, was a talented and accomplished dancer.[2] During the late forties, when I was about three years old, she began teaching dancing and baton twirling. She traveled throughout rural north Georgia, holding classes in the public schools—a sort of itinerant dancing teacher. Unlike other teachers who charged much

1

higher fees, she charged $1.00 per student per hour for weekly classes in ballet, tap dancing, and acrobatics. For those who wished to take private lessons she charged $2.00 for half an hour. For baton twirling she charged $.50 for half-hour classes. Every spring, just before school closed for the summer, she held a colossal recital. All students performed at whatever level they were capable of.

My mother believed that every child who wanted lessons should have them and that every child, no matter how poor, should be encouraged to want them. Though highly talented herself, she never let lack of talent exclude a potential pupil. She reasoned that knowing how to dance and actually performing gave one confidence in public, no matter how clumsy and graceless the performance. She also had extraordinary imagination and choreographed elaborate productions, my most vivid memory being her production of the Nutcracker Suite, *performed in the sweltering pre-summer heat of rural Georgia. She spun fantasies of fairies and elves like no one I have known since, and she lured even the most cynical little boy and girl into participating in her illusions. I grew up pirouetting, tapping, tumbling, whirling, and twirling to all kinds of music, while immersed in frothy nets, satins, taffetas, laces, tassels, and feathers. I grew up surrounded by children, some of whom could leap through the air like gazelles and whirl like dervishes, others of whom lumbered and flopped about like beached whales, with big toothy grins on their faces, and with no physical grace whatsoever.*

Most of these children came from lower middle class, working class, and rural families. Until the sixties, all of them were white.[3] The working class and rural kids often came from large families with more than one child wanting lessons. With some exceptions, their parents worked as farmers, mechanics, clerical and secretarial staff at Lockheed, factory workers in Atlanta, school teachers, and support staff for Dobbins Air Force Base. Though most of my mother's students came from families with two parents, single working mothers reared some of them, including my sister, my brother, and me. Contrary to popular nostalgia in regard to "stay-at-home moms" in the fifties and early sixties, most of the mothers, whether with their husbands or without them, worked outside the home. Even at $1.00 an hour, once a week, most parents could hardly afford to pay for one child, never mind two or more. So my mother and the other mothers worked out a barter system, trading homegrown produce, transportation, hair care, and an array of other services in exchange for lessons.

The most elaborate example of this system was Ola Thomas and her four children. Ola was married to an independent truck driver who was often out of work. Ola herself worked as a seamstress on the assembly line for the Lovable Brassiere Company in Atlanta. Ola wanted dancing for all four children and baton twirling for three of them; she further wanted private lessons as well as classes. She and my mother worked out a special deal. Ola fed my sister and me one night a week, supplied us with "seconds" in undergarments, and on occasion made me and my sister absolutely beautiful party dresses from undergarment taffeta and satin out of remnants purchased from the Lovable Brassiere Company. In exchange, Ola's children received both private and class lessons in dancing and baton, and Ola also made many of the costumes for mother's recitals. Incidentally, Ola's three daughters were outstanding dancers and two became highly accomplished acrobats, though Ola's son predictably lost interest once he reached junior high school. Without such a barter system there would have been far fewer, sometimes very talented, students taking lessons.

My mother and the mothers of her students understood clearly that children needed confidence and that this confidence could be acquired through bodily discipline and practice. They knew well that this confidence was much more important than talent. They also valued the experience of enjoying one's physicality for its own sake and sharing that joy through performance with both other performers and an audience of doting parents. So my mother inspired confidence in gawky children and spread joy like an epidemic across north Georgia for about two decades. Some of her students grew up, prospered, and brought their children to her for lessons—still at $1.00 an hour and so forth. And my mother would work out payment with anybody, in some cases just plain giving lessons away—when so-and-so got laid off at Lockheed, was ill and had to quit work, or was wiped out by flood or drought. We ourselves had few flush years economically and mostly a succession of extremely lean years.

My mother was not wild about the poverty, but she loved her work with a passion I often suspected was reserved only for her work, to the exclusion of the rest of us. Now, looking back, I think: So what if it was! So what if she loved her work as much as life itself. Her work was one long sustained act of extraordinary generosity; her imaginary world was one in which every child who wished for it might learn to dance. And all of this work took place against a backdrop of rural poverty, economic instability for working class and lower middle class people, and the personal family tragedy of my father's alcoholism.

What makes this story more than simply a nostalgic memory? There is no doubt in my mind that the collusion of these women around dancing lessons for their children, a collusion of joy, was necessary to their own survival, as well as for the future betterment of their children. Furthermore, this community of women, conspiring to link children's bodies to dance, food, and clothing, in its own small way and in its own small location, temporarily subverted oppressive social structure. It was in its own peculiar way a community of inadvertent, yet deliberate dissenters.

Certainly we learned as students that joy was an acceptable feeling to accompany the discipline and performance of dance. This feeling was driven by and a companion to physical exertion—sometimes quite painful; at the same time performance itself could and often did produce ecstasy.[4] Our parents, mostly our mothers, took pleasure, felt joy, in our accomplishment. For many of us were provided an opportunity that few of our parents had as children, an opportunity that might give us polish, helpful to the upward mobility to which our parents aspired in this heavily classed society, in which class difference was masked by a rhetoric of democracy, but never absent. Both performers and observers cultivated joy, the effect of which was liberating.

This joy and the dance that was its source and effect varied even within the context in which I lived. While the culture in which I grew up for the most part found dancing socially acceptable, some of its communities in fact prohibited dance altogether, never mind taking any pleasure in it. To my Southern Baptist friends, for example, dancing meant the eternal damnation of the immortal soul. Both my mother and I had to contend on more than one occasion with the evangelically exuberant concern of some of my schoolmates and their parents for our future state.

Because much of the culture of the time regarded sexuality at best with ambivalence (and still does), even the appropriateness of joy depended to some extent upon not acknowledging the full implications of the sensuality of dance, especially in regard to the younger children. It further depended upon "gendering" the bodies of the dancers: While the culture accepted teaching dance both to female and to male children, dance itself was feminized and most males moved on to other kinds of physical activity by the time they reached adolescence. Thus, little girls of my generation were taught early on that it was acceptable to want to be ballerinas when they grew up, though this accomplishment was extremely unlikely for almost all of them; little boys, however, were discouraged from pursuing dance as a future calling or career. As a feminized world that accepted but did not go out of its way to encourage male habitation, the world of dance created by my mother and her friends and clients provided its inhabitants with a serious, if not unambiguous, female-centered alternative to the aggression of male sports. One could celebrate femininity, within certain fixed restrictions; one could experience joy with relatively little male intervention and dominance.

This little world of dance, however feminized, was a world where gender definition itself blurred. Though most of the males left as adolescents, some did not. Of those who remained, some later identified themselves as gay, but most did not. Among the female students, relationships with each other and with the male students reflected a highly amorphous sexuality. We touched one another and expressed affection without reservation and irrespective of gender, though not in overtly sexual ways. We openly appraised one another's bodies, yet never engaged in genital relations, at least as far as I know. We were without sophistication, yet erotically aware. That such a world, internally characterized by the blurring of gender distinctions, was culturally marked "feminine" illuminates how power is asserted and maintained by the use of gender distinction to regulate social status.

There were other social implications as well. Ballet, for example, has tended to be viewed in this country as "high art"—in contrast to tap dancing, which owes its origins to folk dancing from a variety of different cultures, both African and European. Acrobatics, until gymnastics, was associated predominantly with the circus—hardly high art. Baton twirling, comparatively new to the world of performance, has never achieved the status of ballet or tap.[5] That my mother put them all together reflected her own class status, rural and working class. That she would make lessons readily available to the rank and file, outside the context of the dance studio, for almost two decades, was remarkable. That the public school system thought nothing of allowing her to pull students out of class to teach them a non-academic hodgepodge of physical movement, for which their parents paid her directly, is a tribute to her astonishing powers of persuasion. As far as I know, it had never happened before, nor has it happened since, in the school systems in which she taught. As she bent these various systems to suit her goals, she extended the context in which students might encounter a range of arts to whole classes of people to whom such advantages had been previously unavailable. At the time, my mother simply didn't know she was transgressing gender and class-defined aesthetic categories in every respect.

I have now, much later, come to conclude that joy is revelatory in ways that are not so much explicitly religious as they are parable-like. By this I mean that the narrative of the dancing lessons works as a parable. The story of my mother's dance classes, for example, though peopled by families that for the most part identified themselves as Christian, has little, if anything, to offer that is conventionally religious in meaning. But then neither do the parables attributed to Jesus in the Gospels, properly apprehended. Taken at face value, the Gospel parables narrate commonplace, ordinary events in a largely agrarian society—farming, cooking, shepherding, losing money, mending, throwing dinner parties, family conflicts, squabbles over labor and wages, even assault and robbery. What makes them revelatory lies not in their reducibility to a single ethical or religious teaching, but consists instead of a constellation of features and interactions. Chief among these features is a characteristic inversion of economic, political power that further subverts conventional expectations. This characteristic of inversion and subversion may produce in the hearer a mature joy, by which I mean a joy that is not innocent of pain.

How does this transaction take place? The inversion of power ("the kingdom of God is like a mustard seed . . .") generates surprise, a surprise that usually depends heavily on foiling the expectations of the hearers (one does not normally associate great power with tiny seeds), compelling them to wonder, creating a disturbance to their conventional ways of thinking about God, the world, and themselves. One could say that good parables turn the hearer upside down, inside out, and backwards. In the case of the Gospel parables, many depend for their richness of meaning upon an inversion of the ordinary relations of power, both secular and religious. So, for example, in the parable of the good Samaritan, rather than working through control from the top down, God takes on the life of a despised ethnic and religious minority ministering to an elite and thus works in and through human life from the bottom up. Similarly, in the case of my mother's dance classes, poor and low-income families get dance lessons for the children that are usually reserved for middle-income and affluent families, because relatively powerless women infiltrate and modify a public school system and organize a bartering economy.

These inversions are disturbing, and as such are not innocent in regard to pain. Consider, for example in the case of the gospel parables, the implications of the seed that falls upon the rocks or the dismay of the prodigal son's good brother. Or ponder the host's rejection of the elite guests who refused to come to his dinner party. In the case of the dancing lessons, consider the backdrop of poverty and personal family tragedy against which the lessons occurred, circumstances for which all the dancing lessons in the world could not ultimately compensate.

Nevertheless, while these inversions no doubt disturb, either because they are so enigmatic as to be incomprehensible or because their full implications are painfully clear, the occasion for such disturbances is also at bottom an occasion for great joy. Thus in parables, hosts throw dinner parties and ultimately invite the outcasts, the maimed, the poor and the reprobate. Likewise a dancing teacher goes out and finds students who want to learn to dance, without concern for whether the children have talent or their parents have money to pay for the lessons. Whether joy over finding a lost coin or a lost sheep, or joy over the discovery that a single seed could grow and flourish, producing shade for birds, or joy over the return of a lost child, or joy over figuring out how to arrange dancing lessons for four children—the joy of a central character or characters of a parable becomes the signifying mark for a hearer that what has occurred, however ambiguous, unexpected, and disturbing, is good.

Far beyond the limits of the pages of the Hebrew and Christian scriptures, one may seek and find parables, not only in a text, but also in a childhood memory, or for that matter, in one's own immediate relationships with others, one's work, a visual image, a film—indeed throughout all of social and natural life. Thus, to my mind, the narrative of my mother's career as a dancing teacher performs as a parable, in that it reveals God's grace at work in the details of mid-twentieth-century white southern U.S. rural and working class life, sustaining an oppressed people, who sought to be faithful to a vision of the future for their children, however limited and immediate—a vision that in its execution subverted, however temporarily, some of the economic and educational structures of oppression themselves. Moreover, this joy, in all its corporeality and generosity, that this transitory band of mothers made, took, and shared in the midst of an otherwise often grim existence, discloses a deep and abiding goodwill and delight that identifies their work as God's ongoing work in and through material, often tragic, human existence. It reveals God making and repairing a world in and through human joy—God's love compounding itself from the bottom up.

Joy is in and of itself ethically ambiguous. It may be generous, selfish, both, or ecstatic, though by virtue of its potential to expand the self, it tends to direct the self outward toward others in some way. Thus, the context in which joy occurs largely determines its ethical implications. In the case of the dancing lessons, joy was born of generosity. The mothers took joy in part because they felt they were giving joy to their children, in part because they simply enjoyed watching their children dance. My mother, the teacher, and Ola Thomas, the seamstress, found great joy in their work of teaching and sewing and the beauty both produced. We children, their beneficiaries, enjoyed learning to dance and to perform in recitals, although practicing was another matter. In short, the mothers' good will toward their children produced a reciprocating delight or joy in the children that refracted back as the further delight or joy of the mothers. Joy born of generosity compounds and reverberates.

What strikes me as curious about this joy is how little focused it was either on self-sacrifice or on self-fulfillment. Surely both were involved, but selves were simply not at the forefront of consciousness. Rather the focus was on the dance—taught, learned, staged, costumed, performed, and watched. Looking back, I now see dance as a profound metaphor for love, both human and divine, for which the language of self-sacrifice and self-fulfillment is impoverished at best.

One of my mother's primary motives was to give dancing lessons to as many children as she possibly could, irrespective of talent. It was so important to her that she went to great lengths, beyond normal human effort, to make dancing as available as possible. Likewise the joy she experienced in seeking to realize this commitment further fueled her generosity. Furthermore, her joy was contagious across its time and place in ways, unforeseen and unpredictable at the time, that would enrich future generations of children and parents.

What my mother refused to take for granted proved to be one of her strongest virtues. She did not, for example, assume that all the children she taught shared the same circumstances. Had she made this assumption, she might have insisted that all families pay for lessons with cash. She did not assume a single definition of good, or she might not have accepted the untalented. She took her students as she found them in their highly varying range of skills and interests, encouraging them to do their best for their sakes. Her aim was to share her own gifts with everyone she could. She further assumed that all of us should share our own unique talents. Her respect for particular differences allowed her to become a particular manifestation of a universally directed love.

I realize now that joy is crucial to survival and carries within it enormous potential to subvert oppressive structures. Shared unconditionally, joy exemplifies one of the most profound manifestations of human dissent, one of the highest expressions of human desiring. So it was for our mothers; so it is now.

DISSENT AND DESIRE

This narrative or "parable" provides a microcosm of how women and some men work together to survive economically and, beyond this, to produce and transmit a culture or ethos for their children against a backdrop of racism, classism, sexism, and homophobia in the aftermath of mass death abroad beyond previous human imagining and in the midst of Cold War political repression at home. Besides the lack of self-consciousness that pervaded the community, the features that strike me most about this process that links survival with cultural production include the transitory and imperfect nature of the community (initially all white), its multiple transgressions (these women and men break the rules—political, economic, and aesthetic, formal and informal), and, above all, extraordinary communal generosity.

We may well be in a transition from organizing global political life in terms of secular sovereign nation states and their relations to one another to an altogether different way of structuring power, one that transforms all social institutions, including religious institutions, and thereby human communal and individual identity. Such a transformation, if it does not result in the demise of secularism, will nevertheless alter it as well. If we are in such a transition, it is too soon to tell what new forms would replace the sovereign state produced by the Western Enlightenment. It behooves us to ask, in any case, how we might sustain religious pluralism and maximize democratic participation in religious and civic life in both our present institutions and whatever ones emerge in the future.

Without knowing what lies ahead, I propose that our institutions will best serve us if we nurture dissent within them. But to honor and cultivate dissent requires a different way of desiring the good from the ways that normally confront us. Affluent white people, the people who are still in charge, suffer an impoverishment of the imagination regarding what we hope for as good on a number of fronts. Among them, we often seek it only for ourselves or for those most immediately related to us. When we extend our efforts beyond the narrow range of self-interest and shared self-interest, we presume to know what the good is for others without their participation in making such determinations. In short, our desire for the good is both too narrowly extended and authoritarian. We do not know how to desire a good that we do not ourselves control. This is true of most of us regardless of our intentions and our political and religious affiliations and values.

I believe that we must not only embrace dissent but must ground our practice and our acceptance of dissent in a desire, a generosity, the future effects of which we can only trust and hope for. In my tradition of faith, such a desire, such boundless generosity constitutes the gift of human participation in divine love itself, a restless love that calls one to a new life. This new life challenges present desires founded on self-interest and narrowly shared interests at their core, even as it permeates and preserves the self and its engagements in the world. This challenge necessarily breeds dissent. Taken seriously, the gift of participation in the love of God embraces human activity in the world, even as it leads to dissonance with human involvement in the very social and personal practices that produce the narrowness and impoverishment of human imagination and desire. This book focuses on dissent and its relation to desire as mediated by the historically ambiguous figure of Jesus of Nazareth, who for his followers became the Christ.

My thesis in its simplest terms is this: White Christians suffer an impoverishment of desire. We who actively resist established structures of injustice, whether these structures are political or religious, suffer this condition regardless of whether, as dissenters, we are conservative, liberal, or radical in our vision of justice. This impoverishment leads us, should our reforms themselves become successfully established, to reproduce authoritarian and unjust systems, albeit in new forms. It is not simply that we want too much or want it only for ourselves, but that our wanting itself is too narrow, a narrowness that we are taught over time by the circumstances of our lives including and especially the institutions we create that recreate us in their image. We learn early and often to presume to know how to want what is good, what this good is, and the other for whom it is good by projecting the particularities of our own desiring and our own finitude on the other for whom and with whom we seek to stand. We forget or we are not taught that we are to love with a love, the full magnitude of which we as finite beings cannot know. We do not grasp the implications of what it means that we are to love those who are altogether alien to our imagination and experience. In this respect, we are no less controlling than those whose actions and visions we oppose. While this narrowness is in certain respects an inescapable condition of our humanity, the good news is that, according to the faith we profess, this love has come to teach us of itself, to invite us to participate in its exercise, to disrupt and widen our desiring and the resistance to narrowness it produces. From a Christian perspective, this love is a gift given through the life, ministry, death, and new life of Jesus of Nazareth, recognized by his companions as among God's anointed. It is present here and now for us to learn and to participate in, however sporadically and feebly we may engage in it.

This love and its embodiment in the figure of Jesus are ambiguous. The history of Christianity is one of prolonged internal conflict and division, concurrent with hostile relations with non-Christians, whether religious or secular in their loyalties. Dissidence at the point of origin notwithstanding, both progressive and conservative traditions of identifying imperialism and nationalism with Christianity, themselves born out of dissent in the name of love, dominate much of Western history, particularly the history of the United States. Today, the figure of Jesus, particularly as construed by politically conservative evangelical Christians, has come to play an increasingly influential role in U.S. political life. Protestant Bible groups meet daily throughout the White House, the Capitol, and the Pentagon. The federal government looks increasingly to religious institutions to take on social welfare programs through faith-based initiatives. School vouchers become a means by which private religious education is federally subsidized. Congress debates constitutional amendments to define marriage "biblically," to ban abortion on religious grounds, and to sacralize the flag. The country grows ever more "Christianized," a process that has major implications for those whose affiliations are not politically conservative, evangelical Christian.

Nationalist forms of Christianity, never altogether absent from the public political arena, have taken on new life in the United States in particular in association with the so-called War on Terrorism. Current cultural rhetoric manifests conflicting messages toward Islam as the country responds to Al-Quaida as an international Muslim guerilla force. On the one hand, the widespread national impulse to dissociate Islam from Al-Quaida and, by association, Taliban violence, has played a central role in attempting to restrain violence against Muslims in this country, though often in paternalistic ways. On the other hand, anti-Muslim profiling, anti-Muslim hate crimes, and anti-Muslim rhetoric flourish at all levels of society, even as the U.S. government hypocritically forms alliances with extremely oppressive Muslim regimes.

Though the old-line Christian denominations, along with liberal Jewish organizations, have worked with Muslim leaders to promote dialogue and religious tolerance (often romanticizing religion in general in order to do so), other Christian groups have resorted to the demonization of Muslim teachings and beliefs.[6] In either case, many of the country's religious leaders, at the level of the local congregation, have avoided serious public challenge to current U.S. foreign and domestic policy and the violence that it has wreaked throughout the Middle East and Muslim Asia. They have rationalized this avoidance in terms of preserving harmony within diverse congregations. All too often, across the spectrum of religious and political diversity, public rhetoric on religion by and large assumes that religion is essentially good, that misguided religious people and cynics corrupt this essential goodness in their dealings in history. This rhetoric also frequently assumes that at bottom all religiosity points to a single ultimate reality manifested in history in various different permutations. Scholars of religion, as well as many devotees across religious traditions, would dispute both assumptions mightily as yet another form of cultural imperialism.

Avoidance of conflict and resistance to challenge characterize any established institution seeking to perpetuate itself, never more so than when the opposition comes from the inside. All the same, making room for dissent, in a variety of forms both conventional and unconventional, whether internal or external, whether religious or secular, is necessary for secular, religiously plural, democratic institutions to survive. Furthermore, one could argue that, if Christian traditions in particular are true to some of their earliest traditions and ethical impulses, dissent is a requisite to their survival as well.

Throughout their history Christian institutions, practice, life, and thought have been internally at odds over what constitutes authority both within their own communities and in their relations with the state or government. Out of such crises important, transforming protest movements have periodically emerged. In the United States the Abolitionists, the Suffragists, and the fundamentalist populists of the nineteenth and early twentieth centuries, as well as the Civil Rights movement, the Anti–Vietnam War movement, and the Women's Liberation movement of the 1960s and 1970s immediately come to mind.[7] Likewise, Christian traditions have historically benefited from critical dialogue and engagement with other dissenting non-Christian traditions, from ancient Greek philosophy to contemporary work with Buddhists, Muslims, and Jews. It seems timely now to explore the theological significance of dissent in the midst of this early-twenty-first century crisis of violence perpetrated by both the state and its adversaries in the name of God.

Dissent, as a historical phenomenon, is fraught with irony. For example, individuals who understand themselves as insiders to a tradition may suddenly find themselves on the outside, as they engage in intellectual debate and political interaction with other insiders. Such was the case with Tertullian and Origen, ancient architects of what was to become Christian orthodoxy, later declared heretics themselves by the very authorities they helped to create. Conversely, dissenting movements that become established as normative provide a second example of irony. Once a movement is established, its leaders may insist that their way is the only way and that those who disagree must be purged. Such is the case within Christianity itself in its struggles over what constitutes a truly "catholic" or universal church.

A pluralistic movement borne out of prophetic, messianic, and wisdom-centered visions of a generous realm of peace and justice with mercy, the various Christian churches have from the beginning repeatedly degenerated into totalistic institutions in ways that have produced external as well as internal violence. Their authorities have insisted, for example, that belief in Jesus as the Christ is the only way to relationship with God—an offense to all other monotheistic traditions, just as monotheistic insistence on one God alone can be an offense to nontheistic and polytheistic traditions. Grounded ostensibly in creedal and biblical authority, diverse churches have proclaimed themselves to be the Church universal outside of which there is no salvation, a similarly problematic claim.[8] Like dissent, this triumphalist self-understanding, ironically exclusionist even as it asserts universality, stands at the core of Christian identity and is indeed sometimes the very result of dissenting groups that have become established. So located, it has made its own contributions to a prolonged history of anti-Semitism, religious warfare, and persecution, both within Christendom and externally with Jews and Muslims.

In other words, dissent and pluralism are inseparably linked with triumphalism, and Christian identity stands at odds with itself. Christianity not only originated out of a plurality of Jewish movements and traditions in the midst of an extremely religiously plural Roman Empire, but also, from the very beginning, its internal structures and beliefs were highly heterogeneous. What we now call doctrinal orthodoxy was not fully established until the middle of the fifth century of the Common Era. Once established, orthodoxy has never reigned altogether unchallenged in the history of Christianity. Furthermore, while Christianity has dominated Western history, it has never been its sole tradition, even when most dominant. Thus with more and less violence in relation to tolerance, Christian institutions have confronted differences within and without from the inception of Christian traditions.[9]

In this respect Christian history is simply part of the rest of human history. I am persuaded by historian of religion Ernst Troeltsch that ultimately Christianity (and for that matter all other religion) has no essence, no enduring core sustained unchanged throughout its history.[10] I do think that as a text-centered tradition it contains within it impulses and themes that recur in response to the material conditions in which Christians and Christian institutions find themselves at any given point. These impulses include contradictory tendencies toward radical anti-authoritarianism and toward extremely authoritarian imperialism.

Technically speaking, Christians and Christian traditions are part of the material conditions, shaped by and shaping global history.

This fluidity and multiplicity likewise characterize political institutions and worldviews like secularism. What we call world religions and the longstanding political institutions of empire and nation state—as well the effects of their interactions in the production of human practice and identity—bear no single, distinguishing, enduring essence. Instead they reflect an amorphous contentiousness of ongoing processes of human construction, as groups of people, multiply defined, work out their internal and external differences in more or less intentional and unintentional, violent and peaceful ways. Terms like *Christian*, *Muslim*, *religion*, *state*, *West*, and *East* are in a sense deceptive photographs, an attempt to grasp water in motion as humans seek to tell their multiple, corporate, highly selective stories.

Put another way, we are constantly making maps to figure out where we are and where we are going; but maps as representations diverge from their intended purpose. In their reification of flux they reveal best the human struggle over the power to define the terrain, even as they represent the only access we have to the terrain itself. The mapmakers and map users thus unwittingly make the terrain as they go, even when looking over their shoulders at where they think they have been. Unsettling as this knowledge is, we can't get anywhere without maps, no matter what the destination, even if it isn't where we expected to end up. The history of Christianity, however told, no matter who tells it, and no matter how often it is told, provides an excellent case in point.

Readers of this book, regardless of affiliation, Christian or otherwise, will find several governing questions that are relevant to anyone who feels overwhelmed, weary, and frustrated with the way things presently are. Given how truly awful life increasingly grows for many on the planet—particularly after the various oppressive responses of the United States government to the events of 9/11 as well as its neglect and ineptitude in response to the events surrounding the destruction of hurricane Katrina on August 28, 2005—what gets us out of bed and back into the midst of the messiness of things every morning? What keeps us going? What heals our wounds? What regenerates us in the face of our own mistakes, failure, and remorse? What gives us joy? Why and how do we keep resisting unspeakable evil and suffering, in spite of our complicity with both, by seeking political and economic changes we will likely never live to see in place? Why not numb out, give up, or simply spend a lifetime indulging ourselves? Many people understandably do precisely this.

I propose to explore the possibility that what drives us is a generosity not our own but is one found in the compelling faces of the "least of these," namely, the most helpless, most vulnerable, most neglected, most brutalized, and most outcast of society. Their unmet need, their invisibility, and their disposability are the price they pay for making human life possible for the rest of us in an economy based on credit, debt, consumption, and profit. Our recognition of their generosity marks the beginning of the transfiguration of an otherwise corrupted desire, altering it so that we might begin to desire the good of all planetary life, however little we may presume to know specifically about what this good might be. To live out of this desire is by definition to live a life of dissent.

I explore this possibility in specifically Christian theological ways for at least two reasons. First, I work as a Christian theologian; it is my job. Second, Christians, as I have just noted, have historically played a double role throughout their history as a people called specifically to minister to the "least of these" and as perpetuators of economic and political conditions that create the very distinctions of "least" and "most." We have lived both as dissenters against and perpetrators of injustice and oppression. All the same, the possibility of such generosity and its effects transcend and challenge all particular affiliations and loyalties. Although I address this generosity in specifically Christian terms, I am assuming a religious and secular plurality of responses, a pluralism that I address later at some length.

In other words, three forces drive me to write this particular book at this particular time to this particular audience: the sheer awfulness of how things are; an incalculable debt that I think anyone who is white and economically privileged can never return in kind; and the haunting and enchanting power of the ever elusive figure of Jesus of Nazareth found in the midst of the ragtag communities of people with whom he worked and lived.

We live in a time characterized by insatiable human greed, a greed that fuels and depends on unprecedented consumerism, a greed that continually threatens global stability and steals the very future of planetary life itself. Even if we do not consider ourselves individually greedy, even if we do not define ourselves in terms of consumption, if we are white and relatively affluent, we depend upon, participate in, and benefit from the systems that promote and reward greed. One major facet of our participation is fear. Resisting greed depends heavily on overcoming fear. Both fear and greed are variations on desire. To overcome them requires nothing less than the transfiguration of desire.

Transfiguring desire depends on a particular exercise of imagination and discipline and leads to a lifetime of dissent against the corruption that presently produces the greed and fear characteristic of this world. Transfiguration occurs daily all around us and through us, though we do not always recognize it as such. This lack of awareness makes us more vulnerable to the fear that saps the energies needed to sustain dissent. I believe that Christian traditions, in spite of the double-minded nature of their history, provide resources particularly suited to transfiguring desire and sustaining a lifetime of dissent. At the heart stands God's grace, mediated by the dissenting figure of Jesus of Nazareth through the communities with whom he continues to live and work.

FEAR'S COLLUSION WITH GREED IN THE TWENTY-FIRST CENTURY

Human greed and fear are hardly new to the twenty-first century.[11] However, in the aftermath of 9/11 and with the economic downturn already then in process, greed that benefits the few who exercise political and economic power has accomplished its ends far more successfully than ever before by getting ordinary people from the upper middle classes downward to buy into fear. We now live consumed by and consuming fear or terror on a daily basis, terror brought to us not only by international guerilla forces, but also on a far grander scale by our own political and economic leaders. Resisting greed requires understanding its dependence upon fear. Gaining such an understanding marks the first step in imagining desire transfigured, a desire grounded in an economy different from global capitalism and governed by a different polity from that of secularism. Understanding the relationship between greed and fear permits us to imagine desire driven by a mediator different from self-interest as constructed by the electronic media and disciplined by nationalist forms of conservative Christianity masked as civil religion. We may thus gain access to daily disciplines and habits other than the cultivation of consumption, including and especially the consumption of fear. In this vein there are resources both christological and practical already at work in history that provide contexts for this transfiguration to occur. I confess at the onset, however, that I have no quick fix or grand plan. I seek instead only to point to a starting place.

While we may differ on the precise meaning we give to the concept of greed, we would probably agree that greed constitutes desire gone amok. At the risk of oversimplifying, I suggest my own working definition of greed as the gratification of my desires beyond meeting my own reasonably sustainable needs, at the expense of meeting your needs or the needs of a common good that extends to the good of all planetary life. Excess and hoarding particularly characterize this gratification of desire. When my desire is governed by and limited to my own self-interests or those of my group, narrowly defined, I am greedy.

When I place the gratification of my desires—what Augustine and other theologians referred to as appetites—first, I reduce other people and other forms of life exclusively to means to accomplish my ends. Because all humans engage in relations with one another, relations of work, family, friendship, and citizenship, each of us is a means to the accomplishment of others' ends or projects. Immanuel Kant defined *person*, however, as one who is not only a means but also an end in herself, one who has projects, engages in the privacy of an interior life, and possesses inherent worth. Scholars presently debate whether personhood can be extended to species beyond the human, but we can at least agree minimally that greed effaces the personhood of those whom it victimizes, never more so than when it depends on their collusion. In regard to nonhuman life, greed at the very least denies its inherent worth.[12]

Said another way, greed is piracy.[13] Its worst crime is theft of the future. Greed is not simply a feature of individual psychology but a socioeconomic phenomenon construed along lines of political power. Although it is systemic and entangles us all, our roles differ according to social location. Not everyone has equal access to the machinations of greed, as witnessed by the disproportionate number of poor Black people stranded on roof tops in New Orleans in the wake of hurricane Katrina, nor do most people and the rest of the planet actually benefit from it, either in the short term or in the long term, as witnessed by the economic and ecological effects of Katrina's devastation of the eastern Gulf Coast on the rest of the country. Greed in the United States maintains and extends itself by means of the cultivation of consumerism, through exploitative labor practices, and by appeals to divine authority characteristic of Christian nationalism. These interactive forces work to construct, regulate, and police the desires of citizens as consumer-workers. In short, greed breeds a culture of fear and then trades upon it. Since the attacks on the World Trade Center and the Pentagon, fear itself has moved to the center of this network of interactive forces. Our capitulation to fear marks in part our own particular collusion in the greed that benefits the few.

Fear that sustains greed represents the distortion of what I consider to be normal desires to meet fundamental human needs for food, shelter, and relative stability. To the extent that fear reigns, it entangles everyone. We collude in the greed of the most powerful not simply for the short-term satisfaction of purchasing beyond our needs and economic means, but because we fear for our future survival and the survival of those whom we love. Our fear has at least three consequences. Fear prevents the possibility of identifying one's interests with those most vulnerable in society. Fear, moreover, has serious, horrible implications for human rights at home and abroad as well as deleterious effects upon all planetary life. Finally the exploitation of fear produces its own cottage industry of additional goods available for consumption.

While it might make sense that people do not wish to be identified with social victimization or the threat of victimization, fear serves in the long run as an obstacle to empathy, sympathy, compassion, and activism for social change dependent on solidarity. Worse still, fear cultivates attitudes of docility, apathy, acquiescence, and deference to those in positions of authority. Fear drives one to preserve and promote the interests of those who hold power and authority out of the mistaken assumption that they will provide security. In addition, fear reinforces authoritarian religiosity, particularly in the service of nationalism. When economic times are relatively good, identifying one's interests with those of the successful and the powerful reinforces the hope that one can change one's situation or that of one's children. When economic times take a downward turn, as more and more people become downwardly mobile, this identification may even prevent despair. Both the hope and the despair rest on self-deception. In addition, misplaced hope and despair deflect energy that might work creatively in concert with others to effect change. Insofar as these interests are in conflict with the basic human well being and depend on human exploitation, we collude, however unintentionally, with the greed that victimizes ourselves and others far more vulnerable.

Fear likewise plays a major role in the shrinking and violation of human rights at home and abroad. The Patriot Act passed by Congress on the heels of 9/11, and soon to be followed by additional repressive legislation, represents a violation of due process and a serious threat to the rights to privacy and free expression of all U.S. citizens, immigrants, and temporary foreign visitors to the United States. Meanwhile, U.S. leadership, employing outright fraud that magnifies fear in order to guarantee support, has thought nothing of attacking foreign soil in the name of liberation from terrorism and in the interests of the energy industry, among others. In addition, the U.S. government has suspended the Geneva Conventions in the name of exceptionalism, a suspension that has set up the conditions for gross abuses of human rights as witnessed by the events at Guantanamo Bay and Abu Ghraib and the slowness of any corrective response on the part of U.S. officials. Although the popularity of the current president has suffered ups and downs, the majority has by and large supported his leadership, largely out of fear for national security. The rhetoric of national security, buttressed once again by appeals to divine authority, has become the discourse of the day for both political parties, as each tries to position itself as the ultimate hawk when it comes to the War on Terrorism. To challenge this rhetoric is to invite social stigma, possible economic repercussions, and even federal investigation; in this respect fear serves as an obstacle to sustained dissent. Fear for both personal and national safety has colluded well with greed to reproduce and extend terrorism around the world.

Last but not least, fear has become a cottage industry in its own right, tied directly to profit and loss. The fairly recent creation of a futures market on terrorism provides the most telling of all examples of how greed quite literally trades on fear.[14] In July 2003, Democratic senators Byron Dorgan of North Dakota and Ron Wyden of Oregon exposed a project developed by the Defense Advanced Research Projects Agency (DARPA), headed by Rear Admiral John Poindexter, a former Reagan appointee best known for his involvement in the Iran-Contra Scandal of the eighties. The plan, based on efficient markets theory, allowed for invited investors to "bet" on future possible political upheaval in the Middle East. Betters could invest in the possibility of assassinations, terrorist acts, and other political disasters in Egypt, Jordan, Syria, and Israel with the idea that they could reap profit from the accuracy of their investing, just as if they were trading on hog futures. The idea behind the plan was to use the betting of the investors to predict future terrorist attacks. Using the model of a futures market, a model developed at the University of Iowa, had already proved more successful than poll taking for predicting the outcome of elections. Why not apply the same model to the assassinations of Osama Bin Laden, Saddam Hussein, or the king of Jordan?

Critics objected to the plan on a number of grounds. Among them, they found the plan morally repugnant in that its success depended on capitalizing in every sense of the word on human tragedy and disaster. While I agree with this assessment, profiting from human disaster is hardly new to the futures market—or to the stock market, for that matter. Investment is, after all, what the weapons industry is all about. Equally disturbing to me is the complete dissolution of all boundaries between government and economic systems. The Pentagon, long known for its corruption and cronyism with the business world, has now internalized big business altogether. Any distinctions between economic and political-military methods, interests, and aims have now disappeared completely. In short, national security and individual profit-making have become wholly identified as a form of intelligence gathering. That the Pentagon cancelled the futures investment project in response to public outcry does not negate this identification, nor does it prevent the project from reappearing in mutated form in the future and under better cover from public view. Economists and journalists continue to debate the plan, with a number of them supporting it.[15]

If I am correct in identifying fear as a partner to greed through misplaced identification with the greedy, the destruction of human rights, and the elevation of terror to a stock in trade, insofar as fear governs our ethical, political, financial, and spiritual practices, then we collude. In short, the logic of the relationship between greed and fear is relatively simple. This human world that we have made is destructive to virtually all life. Much of this destruction arises out of greed, a greed that depends for its persistence on never-ending consumption of unneeded and dangerous products. For the necessary rate of consumption to continue at a sufficient pace to meet the ever-growing greed, the human desire for such products must be continually cultivated. Since 9/11 desire among ordinary people has increasingly taken the form of fear. Our leaders trade quite literally on this fear to drive the production of vast war machines as well as various small-time more local industries (for example, handguns, face masks, duct tape, security systems, etc.) at the expense of meeting fundamental needs. Our infrastructure deteriorates; the quality of our environment declines; our poor, both working and unemployed, have no safety net and are especially vulnerable to any natural, political, or economic domestic crisis. Our fear is our collusion.

In addition to the destructiveness and the misery greed generates, sustained fear has had a devastating effect on the life of the spirit. Speaking for myself, I became depressed and edgy, as I felt increasingly helpless for quite some time after 9/11 as the economy continued its downward spiral and as foreign policy deteriorated. It took the realization that helplessness, edginess, and depression supported the status quo to turn me around. I once was utopian; the aftermath of 9/11 has since made me aware that I had been giving up my utopianism for some time. I no longer believe that the kingdom of God will come on earth (or in heaven) in some final sense. This does not mean that I have given up on justice or a better future for all life on this planet and throughout the cosmos. It does mean that

I no longer think that progress occurs without monumental historical setbacks. Furthermore, insofar as we do progress—whatever that might mean—we do not progress to some foreknown final end.

Rather, I think the work of justice with kindness for all remains always to be done and will never reach ultimate completion. In other words, I have wisely, I think, given up on finality, in part because its underside has become clear to me. Presuming to know absolutely what is good for either the present or the future and presuming its completion transmute quickly into imperialism and totalitarianism. There are other alternatives. Once I realized that I had inherited a rich legacy of resources from my own traditions of practice and belief, I began to regain the energy, steadiness, and passion to face what I now consider to be a historical crisis beyond all previous reckoning. In order to do my job, however small, defined by an altogether different economy, an economy of grace, I had to learn all over again what it means to "live in the world but not of it" in ways I had never imagined before.[16]

A BOUNDLESS GENEROSITY
(OR AN INCALCULABLE DEBT)

In the final chapters I say much more about an economy of grace as an alternative to corrupt, death-dealing economies characteristic of human life today. Here I simply want to point out that within a Christian theological context human life depends on a different ordering and distribution of goods as well as a different understanding of "good"—in short, a different economy. The divine economy defines itself according to generosity, a generosity that begins with God and saturates all existence, most especially suffering—voiceless existence and the corruption of human desire notwithstanding. This generosity is not quantitative, and thus it cannot be measured nor, most importantly, can it be returned in kind. In this respect it represents an incalculable debt. Unable to repay this debt, one can only participate in this generosity in ways limited by human finitude as well as by human corruption. According to Christian teaching God created the world good and meant it for good things. "Good" in this context reflects the inseparability of ethical worth from beauty and usefulness, qualities divinely intended for all forms of life according to the early creation accounts found in Genesis.

Human sin, often understood as disoriented and disfigured appetite, desire, or will, has intervened to corrupt both nature and the social order.

God nevertheless upholds the world, repairs it, and redeems it through ongoing natural and social creativity. Because of the inevitability and inescapability of human sin, however, the world itself is ambiguous. God calls Christians to seek to love the world as God's creation. At the same time, by the power of grace we are not to be conformed to its corruption. Thus we live within and possessed by a tension of sin and grace, often expressed as living *in* the world but not *of* it.

An economy of grace is one based on the gift of generosity itself. Within this economy worth is not determined by success and failure, profit and loss, credit and debt. Worth is given—again, a divine gift. One who begins to live intentionally out of an economy of grace lives not out of fear but from love beyond reckoning. Desire is not mediated by the narrowness of the interests of oneself, one's family, or one's cronies, nor even one's sacrifices. Rather, the figure of Jesus, his own face shaped by the alienation of the "least of these" (Matt. 25:40), mediates nothing less than the desire to love what God loves as God loves it and to act accordingly.[17] Mediated by the figure of Jesus, desire now identifies across, down, and out—not up. To comprehend and to live out of God's love for the good of all life involves risk, for it is ultimately to live in dissent, intentionally or unintentionally, against the corruption of the world as we know it today.

To live out of an economy of grace is to undergo the transfiguration of one's own desires, however slowly, away from the consumption of fear in particular, away from excessive consumption in general, away from appetites that exceed what we can stomach, literally and metaphorically speaking. The demand is heavy. One who lives caught between sin and grace is called to love and to participate in corrupted life in light of divine intentions that are strikingly manifest in human suffering. To live out of this economy, I argue, is to live necessarily a life of dissent.

Before proceeding further, however, I need to clarify the fundamental concepts that frame this discussion of grace in the face of how awful things are in the early twenty-first century. Dissent, desire, and imagination as I am using them here are modern conceptions. Does this make them anachronistic? Although I don't think so, as modern concepts they require brief working definitions with attention to context.

DISSENT

Dissent, in certain respects an invention of the West—whether it takes the form of a social movement, an individual right, or a moral obligation—has fared poorly in Western history. Dissent, even as a highly espoused value in modern times, has a history of being met with ridicule, economic persecution, imprisonment, torture, exile, and execution, a history that continues into the present. This history is ironic. Christianity, the dominant Western religious tradition since Roman Emperor Theodosius I declared it so in 380 C.E., originated as one of several dissident Jewish renewal movements, in protest against the temple cult in Jerusalem and the Roman imperial government.[18]

As an early Jewish renewal movement, the community surrounding the figure of Jesus inherited from their Hebrew ancestors both a prophetic tradition of protest against injustice and a healthy respect for the powers of the human intellect exercised critically in the service of God, both of which play a role in generating dissent. In its earliest manifestations, this movement was highly pluralistic in structural organization, religious practice, and belief. From the beginning to the present its entire history could be written in terms of the internal and external controversies out of which it has constructed itself. Indeed, internal critique, debate, and challenge have on occasion proved to be productive, effecting a transformation for the better. A heritage of dissent notwithstanding, from the beginning, the Jesus movement, so highly variable within, manifested severe difficulty dealing with both internal and external conflict. No longer the object of persecution under Constantine's Edict of Milan (313 C.E.), once Christianity was politically established as the sole legal religion of the Roman Empire under Theodosius I in the fourth century C.E., Christian institutions and Christians themselves have been loath to tolerate critical challenge from within their own communities, not to mention questioning generated by outsiders.

This aversion to self-critique and difference further continues to characterize secularism as practiced within the United States. Whether evolving from Christian traditions or reacting against them, secular forms of resistance to dissent flare up especially in the context of nationalism, in spite of constitutional guarantees to free speech, freedom of the press, freedom of assembly, freedom of religion, and due process. This resistance reflects a prior, deep ambivalence toward multiple points of view and associated practices, especially when they diverge—in short, toward religious and secular pluralism. Regardless of this aversion, pluralism nevertheless characterizes national life in the United States, and political and religious dissent persists in its social environment. Furthermore, dissent itself is not merely the product of Western Enlightenment liberalism. Rather, a tendency to dissent constitutes one longstanding important feature of Christian faith and practice, whether manifested as internal or external critique and activism. This tendency forms the theological focus of this book.

Simply put, dissent means saying no to the way things are. It is one mode of resistance among several possibilities, including rebellion and revolt. Dissent may be intentional or unintentional, active or passive, direct and explicit or secretive, conventional or unconventional. Taken in context, dissent is rarely an act of saying no for its own sake. Rather, dissent usually presupposes assent or consent to an alternative point of view or worldview, which presupposes in turn a desire for change. What we call *dissent* is historically rooted in Graeco-Roman philosophical and political traditions, about which much has already been written. Dissent is also rooted in religious, political, and theological protest movements of ancient Palestine during Late Antiquity, especially movements dominated by Mosaic liberation, prophetic, messianic, or apocalyptic worldviews, and the Maccabean revolts, among other ancient contexts.[19] It is with these less acknowledged contributions that I begin my analysis.

This dissidence, though domesticated and transformed as Christianity into a triumphalist religion, never entirely disappears even within Christian traditions themselves, as witnessed by such "heretical" movements as the Cathari in southern France during the High Middle Ages. The sixteenth century, during the Protestant and Catholic Reformations, marks the beginning of a recognition of dissent as a practice central to Christian traditions themselves and crucial to just government. By the seventeenth century, religious leaders are arguing for the right to overthrow unjust kings, based on a right to dissent.[20] In other words, as I argue later at some length, the sixteenth century serves as a turning point in western Europe in the history of dissent. It marks the start of a process that produces the more modern concept of dissent as a secular right, a right guaranteed to individual citizens without reference to religious or nonreligious affiliation. At this point in history, the twenty-first century, dissent may be viewed as a moral and political obligation as well. The trajectory of the history of dissent has been to become ever more individualized and in its present most rational and rationalized forms assumes that the individual human will exercises at least a relative freedom in making its choices.

DESIRE

Dissent presupposes a desire for change. Whether and how human beings can desire widely enough to will the good for others that would include resistance even to our own established values and practices, our own specific desires, is the ultimate focus of this book. By and large our desires restrict our acceptance of dissent to our own resistance; we limit what we will tolerate to our own particular vision of change, often quite narrowly defined. Given the origins of Christian traditions as a resource, what I propose for today is a transfiguration of desire, where desire is understood in political and economic terms, as well psychological ones.

I understand desire as a culturally produced phenomenon that exceeds simple reduction to individual exercises of choice. The human will, however it may exercise itself through acts of choosing, is nevertheless governed by desires it does not produce. Rather, in profound ways, desire produces the human will itself. Human desire is taught, cultivated, or disciplined through various, often-conflicting sociocultural media that include the religious traditions themselves. If, as I claim, desire is culturally produced, transfiguration requires a different economy, a different ethos, a different set of disciplines—in short a different culture or world located within but not of this highly destructive world. Desire links individual choice to culture. In this respect, desire is inextricably linked to dissent insofar as desire for a different way of living determines one's choices to resist particular features or aspects of culture.

IMAGINATION

Just as dissent presupposes desire, however articulated or inchoate, desire assumes imagination, no matter how faint. The trajectory of the history of the concept of imagination has been in some respects the opposite of that of dissent—a movement from the individualistic toward the more social and communal. *Imagination* gains currency in the West as a philosophical concept during the early eighteenth century in Germany, England, and the United States. Romantic philosophers and poets like Friedrich von Schiller, F.W.J. von Schelling, Samuel Coleridge, Ralph Waldo Emerson, and Henry David Thoreau tied imagination to a preconceptual relation to nature through inspiration, defined as a faculty possessed by individuals, best exemplified in works of artistic creation. In light of the work of philosophers like Ludwig Feuerbach and social theorists like Émile Durkheim, *imagination* has increasingly come to refer to the corporate social and cultural practices that go into the making or production of society as well. In other words, imagination has come to refer to the human capacity, both individual and social, both intentional and unintentional, to make things up and make them real. These practices include producing or making the worldviews that society's members inhabit.[21] In this context the concept is useful for understanding both the relationship of individuals to movements and the relationship of the present to the past, for it points to how humans have shaped as well as been shaped by the social realities within which they find themselves. This reciprocal, shaping activity of the imagination would include not only social realities both past and present, but also the hermeneutical work involved in retrieving the past as well.

Dissent, desire, and the imaginative activity upon which they depend exhibit a quality of self-consciousness on the part of the theorists who use them that contrasts with the movements and individual acts to which they are attributed. In other words, neither Jesus nor his associates explicitly identified themselves as dissidents in a modern sense, nor did the later followers attribute their interpretations of Jesus to their imaginative construction, either individual or corporate. From the early Hebrew prophets on, however, the ancients did concern themselves with the nature of human appetites, yearnings, hunger, and thirsting in relation to human ethical behavior and true worship of God. Although they did not speak of dissent, desire, and imagination in the social scientific terms that we use today, for many early Christian communities speculation—that is, imagining or constructing worldviews—was encouraged, as in the case of the so-called gnostics. In addition, both the early Greek theologians and their Latin counterparts intentionally appropriated philosophical and other forms of speculative thought into theology (for example, Origen and Augustine, respectively).

For contemporary theologians, biblical scholars, and historians of religion, these particular conceptions—dissent, desire, and imagination—have proved especially useful for placing the early Jesus movement in its own historical context, that is, in relation to other concurrent movements, worldviews, and institutions. Equally as important, dissent, desire, and imagination, as I am using the concepts, allow us to understand ourselves in relation to our heritage, regardless of our many different stands on religion in general and Christianity in particular.

THE EVER-ELUSIVE FIGURE OF JESUS

What, specifically, does Jesus have to do with dissent in the midst of ancient religious and cultural pluralism out of which later Christianity was born? The center of contention over authority and right teaching,

Jesus is for Christians the stuff of which dreams, visions, and material reality are made. The shadowy figure who ever eludes those who seek to find him in history has served for believers as the medium out of which to construct a highly diverse, messy, historically problematic, theologically and morally ambiguous tradition, or more accurately, collection of traditions.[22] Throughout this history the believers, understood metaphorically as the body of Christ, comprise an unruly, heterogeneous collection of communities, ever producing new denominations, sects, and religious orders out of struggles over authoritative representations of Jesus and their relation to institutional structure and communal and individual life and practices. Within this mélange coalitions form and dissolve. Covenants are made, honored, broken, and renewed.

Who participates, who is excluded, and in either case on what grounds? Wherein lies ultimate authority? Who has power to determine the traditions and to govern the institutions, what kind of power, and for what duration? What makes for proper relations with external, civil authority, other religious communities, and the wider culture? All of these issues interact with the imaginative shape given Jesus of Nazareth, received by faith as the Messiah or Christ (one anointed by God to usher in God's rule). Be they clerics, preachers, scholars, poets, artists, musicians, or other laity, all who call themselves Christian have a hand, whether intentional or unintentional, in christological imagining. Furthermore, for a number of different reasons, members of other traditions both religious and anti-religious, including Jews, Muslims, Manichaeans, Buddhists, and Marxists have on occasion made their own contributions to the ongoing processes of representation. At the center of contention, Jesus has provided the material for religious and social critique, whether for Mani, the ancient founder of a religion now long dead, or for Friedrich Engels, Marxist political and economic theorist of the nineteenth century, or, more recently, for American playwright Arthur Miller.[23] Jesus, made up and made real by those who follow him and by those who don't, simultaneously remakes the makers in the process, lending whole new meanings to the Word made flesh and the image of God.[24]

At the heart of these processes of christological imagining lies the issue of how to address the multitude of conflicting interpretations or representations, appearing throughout the history of the Christian traditions. Were this issue not so fraught with the exercise of violence as a means of resolution, I conjecture that Jesus himself might find the whole struggle humorous and wondrous in a poignant sort of way.

For, like other Jews within his community of followers and within other Jewish communities at the time, Jesus was, I am convinced, a dissident, albeit perhaps a reluctant one.[25] Like the prophets before him, contemporaneous with him, and subsequent to him, he took issue with established religious and political authorities and institutions. The canonical Gospels, however conflicted on Jewish observance, nevertheless portray Jesus as one who lived his life in accordance with Torah, as he understood it (for example, Matt. 5:17-20; Mark 12:28-34; Luke 10:25-28; Matt. 22:34-40; Luke 26:14-15; Matt. 19:16-30; Luke 18:18-25).[26] They represent him as debating those who understood and practiced Torah differently, for the most part, though not entirely, without anger toward his interlocutors (Mark 2:18—3:6; Luke 5:33—6:11; Matt. 12:1-14). Even more remarkably, the Gospel representations imply that Jesus on occasion accepted challenges to his own views in ways that allowed him to be transformed as well, as in the case of his encounter with the Syrophoenician (Canaanite) woman (Mark 7:24-30; Matt. 15:21-28).

The same materials, along with noncanonical sources, moreover portray him as possessing a sense of humor. He is the laughing savior of the gnostics (*The Sophia of Christ* 92).[27] He is also the Torah-observing exorcist of demons, whom he sends into unclean swine to plunge headlong over a cliff, thereby removing two forms of uncleanness at once (Mark 5:1-43; Matt. 8:28-34; Luke 8:26-39). These materials likewise depict him as someone who enjoyed celebrations—when, for example, he converts the water to fine wine at the marriage of Cana (John 2:1-12). In the apocryphal Acts of John he sings and dances.[28]

The parables and sermons attributed to him also indicate a sense of wonder. According to them he possessed an acute sense of the extraordinary revealed in and through the ordinary, whether exemplified by the bounty of a single seed (Mark 4:30-32; Luke 13:18-19; Matt. 13:31-32) or the mystery of a parent's love for a runaway child who finally returns home (Luke 25:11-32).

His earlier followers saw him as prophet, king, and divine man; his later ones saw him as God. While the gnostic materials dispute his death, the canonical Gospels emphasize his opposition to authority that resulted in his crucifixion, an execution by the Imperial Roman State reserved for those who commit blasphemy and treason. If Jesus, not only a dissident but also a distinctively Jewish dissident, did possess a sense of humor and a sense of wonder, he would surely find Western history subsequent to his crucifixion ironic and strange.

However troubling, strange, or sometimes humorous this history is, it is not my purpose to write it, nor is it my purpose to propose some kind of ultimately definitive representation of Jesus. To do either would in the last analysis defeat the purpose of trying to grasp the theological significance of dissent as it took place within a pluralistic context in relation to Jesus, to begin with. To capture a sense of the complexity of dissent, the multitude of desires it reflects and shapes in a pluralistic context as it surrounds the indefiniteness of the figure of Jesus is the point. To accomplish this task requires looking at history, knowing that it too is constructed, and trying to discern how various patterns of christological imagining emerge, to find processes of imagining, not so much content itself, that might be helpful to us today. The purpose then is to try to capture a kaleidoscope in motion and the ever-moving place of dissent and the desires from which it is born.[29]

OVERVIEW

With the foregoing in mind, Chapter 2, "Jesus in Late Antiquity," focuses on Christian origins as a dissident Jewish tradition and its transition to a gentile religion dominant in the Roman Empire.[30] As I have noted, present-day New Testament scholarship views the early communities who claimed Jesus as their teacher as one of several Jewish renewal movements flourishing at the time. It was a dissident movement in relation to the Roman Empire and also with regard to the Jerusalem Temple cult. Within four centuries this dissident renewal movement had achieved the status of state religion of the Roman Empire. This shift in status from countercultural movement to established state religion took place neither necessarily nor merely by chance—nor was it by the design of a supernatural power. Rather, the movement was internally plural and subject to political and economic contention from the start. Like other renewal movements, it historically faced several possible futures at the time of its birth.

I propose in the next chapter to illustrate how the internally plural traditions that we now call Christianity survived to become a major "religion" by deploying various strategies, including the destruction of minority traditions and competing traditions both within and without the movement itself. Driven by desires that were both more and less generous, these often conflicting strategies were inherent in the movement's plural teachings and practices as far back as scholars can get to the point of origin itself. No single internal logic or external force drove the processes by which this history unfolds, except that those who became followers, whatever their social status, appropriated and recreated the figure of Jesus to authorize their responses to their particular material circumstances, a pattern that continues on into the present. This pattern, in its earliest development, took place in the midst of a political and economic struggle that involved the making of the Roman state, and the citizens who populate it. I propose to examine three moments that illustrate in motion this ongoing struggle over religiopolitical authority. Among them, I draw on selected Pauline epistles, early gnostic documents, and the adversarial relationship between Christians and Manichaeans as exemplified in selected texts by Mani and Augustine.

Context is everything. Regardless of significant parallels between late antiquity and the present, the modern period and its postmodern critique differ drastically from the first five centuries C.E. The sixteenth century, the focus of Chapter 3, marks a major turning point for the long journey to what we now recognize as a formal right to dissent that depends on tolerance of religious and secular differences. As a result, it requires extended attention. By the sixteenth century, western Europe had witnessed the invention of the printing press and the revolution it produced in the form of new approaches to knowledge and multiple religious reformations. This same century saw previously unprecedented global expansion and the emergence of capitalism as an economic system. Three centuries later, with new technological advances that produced the industrial revolution, capitalism, understood not only as an economic system, but also as a whole culture and politics, becomes the air we do not even realize we breathe. By the twenty-first century capitalism in multiple forms dominates the globe. Early in this overall process of globalization, in the United States, dissent becomes a constitutionally guaranteed right through the First Amendment. In this context religious traditions in general proliferate and become commodities in certain respects, if not entirely.[31]

The third chapter, "The Complexity of Dissent," articulates a richer conception of dissent than we normally assume. I examine four "moments" of individual and social dissent, deliberately chosen from the sixteenth century, because this century marks the beginning of a shift in the status of dissent from religious apostasy and capital crime to legal right, though completion of this shift to a constitutionally guaranteed right would take some time to come. The sixteenth century also represents an era marked by a renaissance, indeed a revolution, in learning, contemporaneous with various religious struggles that produced the Protestant, Radical, and Catholic Reformations of Christianity. I argue that dissent is a form of negotiation that may not be intentional, does not always take place in recognizably conventional ways, and may turn out to be morally and politically corrupt, particularly when dissenting traditions become established as normative. For Christians, dissent and the traditions that sustain it constitute highly fluid practices that include drawing on equally fluid construals of Jesus as the Christ for their authority.

Chapter 4, "Disciplines of Desire," begins an analysis of the characteristics of our own time in history that both connect it to and distinguish it from previous times. It focuses first and foremost on the social production of desire in a modern and postmodern context, in other words, a secular context. I first explore two different economies or orderings of desire that conflict with each other—desire grounded in an economy of scarcity and desire grounded in an economy of grace. I then examine how an economy of scarcity generates and sustains U.S. secularism as the means by which identity as "American" is produced. I further argue that this identity reflects a thinly disguised religious nationalism, fueled politically on both the Left and the Right by Christian triumphalism. I conclude with a critique of secularism's most recent, far more transparent entanglement with Christianity manifest in the ascendance to political power achieved by the Christian Right.

I am, in other words, looking at the processes of the formation of identity as "American." These processes reflect Christian teachings and practices, especially a penchant for the apocalyptic, even as they mask their Christianity. These processes also blur the specificity of racial whiteness, ideological individualism, and economic privilege by representing them as universally human characteristics. These processes, themselves born out of histories of dissent in which the figure of Jesus plays a central role, inevitably produce authoritarian domestic and foreign policies that are self-reinforcing as truth and righteousness, regardless of whether they are instituted by liberals or by conservatives, in spite of their substantive political and religious differences. I conclude with a christological critique of our present U.S. regime.

Chapter 5, "The Other-Shaped Face of Jesus," focuses on my own constructive understanding of the significance of Jesus of Nazareth for this particular historical context. I do not propose a definitive picture of Jesus—either the historical Jesus or Jesus as the Christ. Instead I propose a starting point that I hope sustains multiple and diverse images. Christians have been taught that, if they desire to see God, they must look first to the figure of Jesus. According to Matthew 40:25, however, to find the figure of Jesus they must look into the faces of others. I propose to explore what it means to seek Jesus in the faces of others, particularly dispossessed others.

The restructuring of desire within an economy of grace constitutes my central organizing focus. Drawing on resources from the past, taken with innovative imagining in the present with an eye to the future, people captured by the figure of Jesus may continue the work of perpetual reformation. Our hope for an unknown future lies with sustaining an ongoing revolution within our institutions, as well as within our hearts, even as we stand as multiple communities in critical relation to a world of which we are a part, but with which, in its impoverishment of desire, we cannot be entirely identified. It is a world we are called to serve. In light of religious and political pluralism and the actuality of global catastrophe, how should this service manifest itself? What constraints do our own traditions and practices place on transforming outside our own communal boundaries? I propose a different starting point from one focused on christological doctrine or any other single image of the figure of Jesus. I suggest an inversion for apprehending the figure of Jesus through multiple human faces and responding with nothing less than God's own desire, God's love. This inversion transfigures individual and communal responses to the outrages now perpetrated by forces claiming to be authorized by God that steal freely lived lives in the name of human freedom—a gross distortion, yet one hideously logical conclusion, of our religious traditions themselves.

LOCATION

Last but not least, a word on my own relation to the issues addressed in this book is in order. In honest recognition that no human being enjoys the luxury of a totally objective perspective, it has become customary for scholars to state clearly their own locations with reference to their work, especially when this work is heavily constructed, as is the case in theology and theological ethics. Over time, however, I have grown less sure what real information I am giving out when I identify this location. For one thing, we know better now that our locations reflect multiple, sometimes contrary impulses, affiliations, aspirations, experiences, and identities, all of which further change rapidly over time and circumstance, and many of which are unknown as well as known to us.[32] For another, we also know that people sometimes rattle off their locations as if this meant that they were not called in certain profoundly ethical ways to exceed the limits of their individual and social experience. To me "location" can connote property, real estate; I find such a proprietary conception of identity misleading.

Rather than thinking of myself in terms of location as if that were somehow permanent, I prefer to speak in parables of the others who have nurtured me into my present existence, as witnessed by the beginning of this chapter. Anything I have to say about myself is necessarily self-selected. Others see me differently. At least two people I can think of know me better than I do. In any case, whatever the givens and gifts by which I understand myself, they are circumstances and features over which I have little control, especially in regard to their origin, but for the ethical exercise of which I am nevertheless accountable.

In this highly fluid vein, I write from the perspective of an academic theologian, a white feminist whose specific theological heritage is Reformed Protestantism.[33] I write as a secularized Christian who feels ambivalent toward this piece of self-knowledge. On the one hand, I seek as a Christian to affirm a radical democracy that is thoroughly plural, one that preserves and nurtures dissent—all secular values, though with religious historical roots. On the other hand, I am as critical of secularism as currently produced by the nation state as I am of evangelical Christianity, a phenomenon that I think threatens democratic values. I think that statism and the privatization of religion as produced by secularism reinforce Christian nationalism as it cultivates and authorizes totalitarian impulses. Furthermore, the Christian Right did not create this situation; it results in no small part from the interactions of liberal Protestant traditions with Enlightenment philosophy and capitalist economics from the colonial period to the present. Current historical processes, ranging from international resistance to "Westernization," to U.S. imperial efforts in the creation of and response to international guerilla war (also known as "terrorism"), to the emergence of the European Union and the economic development of the Pacific Rim, lead me to believe that I may be watching the demise of the nation state or at least its transformation into something radically different. I have no idea what this new creature, or possibly creatures, will be. I do think that one of the most important contributions humans can make to the human future is to preserve and extend dissent and the generosity in which it is best grounded.

Within this context I consider myself a philosophical materialist of sorts in that I take sentience and the production and distribution of material goods as fundamentally real. In this respect, however, I think that word and flesh interact reciprocally and that human desire forms the nexus that relates them to each other. I am preoccupied most especially with the cultural construction and performance of difference—gender, race, ethnic, class, age, religious, and sexual difference—and its theological significance. In this society difference is never neutral; rather, it is construed and practiced in subordination to a dominant "same" that reflects a cluster of particularities assumed by default as normative. In this present culture these particularities, masked as universally human, include "white" and heterosexual male of a specific socioeconomic status, one who is an unspecified age that is nevertheless adult and measured mainly in terms of public productivity. At the global level, this dialectic of same and different plays out through binaries constructed as center and margin, West and East, Europe and Asia, developed and developing/underdeveloped/undeveloped, global and local, universal and particular, secular and religious, "have" and "have-not," native and foreigner, "white" and "color." Difference and sameness and the other binaries with which they reciprocate at bottom have no essence; nor is their dialectical tension static, nor are agency and victimization within their configuration clear-cut. Nevertheless, given their dynamic and diffuse power relations and the inescapable violence they produce, the nurture and sustenance of dissent is a necessity, not a luxury. Dissent and a grim sense of humor may be the only weapons we have available at present, as we seek to live our faiths.

My trust in and loyalty to dissent goes all the way back to dancing with my mother in the face of Southern Baptist opposition. As you have gathered from the initial parable, I grew up at the intersection of rural, working class, and lower middle class existence in the mid-twentieth-century, still racially segregated southern United States, heavily defined by evangelical Protestantism. My earliest memories of political events are dominated by the Cold War. I recall snippets of investigations by the House Un-American Activities Committee shown on television, as my mother, bless her, gathered us around the TV to watch Edward R. Murrow take on Joe McCarthy. When I was in grammar school at the height of the fifties' "Red scare," I was required to read John A. Stormer's *None Dare Call It Treason*. It succeeded in scaring me so much that for years I prayed that God not let the Russians bomb us. Nevertheless, I matured during the protest movements defining the sixties and seventies and lived to see these movements change human existence for the better, though not enough, not for nearly enough people, and all too often only to be assimilated into commercialism. I also lived through Watergate and one dirty little war after another in Latin America. This history has taught me well that all successes, personal and social, are gifts dependent on the work of others, and furthermore, gifts that are highly tenuous, relative, and fleeting at best. I know that political and social progress can be difficult to recognize and reversed quickly and easily. I also know firsthand that, difficult as is it to practice dissent, it is harder still to tolerate it, never mind to encourage it, when it is directed toward one's own community or one's own personal values and desires, even for people possessing the very best of intentions.

In light of these experiences, this knowledge, and the impetus to exceed their limits, seeking ways to nurture and sustain dissent becomes for me personally all the more urgent. I feel this urgency especially as a middle-aged white woman who has enjoyed the benefits of upward mobility and moderate vocational success, due largely to the efforts on behalf of all women made by so many other women and men, both known and unknown to history. Such efforts exemplify yet another instance of that incalculable debt I can never repay in kind.

What I cannot repay in kind, I can at least pass on. This book is a reminder of a heritage that deserves to be cherished that it might help to create a future I cannot know and ultimately will not inhabit. My proposed alternative, though not new, may seem strange even in its familiarity, insofar as we forget our pasts and because the human future requires new ways to address today's crises. There is unfortunately nothing in what I propose that immediately resolves the horror that greets us now every day. If, however, participation in an economy of grace, as that transfigures our own desires, enables us to get out of bed and greet the day by responding creatively and with justice, however partial, to the figure of Jesus in the face of all life, but most especially in the faces of "the least of these," then perhaps it is a good beginning.

The journey from the early evangelical Jesus movement to the imperial religion known as Christianity, ultimately centered in Constantinople and symbolized by the Hagia Sophia, took over three centuries. Built on the site of a temple to Athena, the church was later converted to a mosque by conquering Muslims who renamed the city Istanbul. Turkish secularists have since transformed the building into a museum and have set about to restore previously covered mosaics to their original condition. Images of Mary Theotokos (the Mother of God), holding the baby Jesus in her arms, particularly abound.

2

Jesus in Late Antiquity

The journey between Corinth and Istanbul, once Constantinople, and before that, Byzantium, takes about two hours and a half by airplane and taxi. It took more than three centuries to make the same journey from the early evangelical Jesus movement, preached beyond Palestine to gentiles as well as Jews, to the imperial religion known as Christianity, centered at the great church of Hagia Sophia (Holy Wisdom) at Constantinople, then the seat of the Roman Empire. For me, now making the journey from one to the other in the twenty-first century, the contrast between the two sites is filled with enigma, subject to multiple and contradictory impressions and readings.

Ancient Corinth is striking in its compactness in the midst of startling natural beauty. Once a major, thriving Greek city, it is now a village defined by ruins and a rash of summer vacation houses for upper-middle-class and wealthy Greeks and foreigners. A tourist industry has grown up around the ruins. The ruins attract scholars as well. I seem to be doing double duty, the difference between scholar and tourist not altogether clear to me. The attractions are many.

As we walk several times a day from our inn to the center of the village, we pass a small Orthodox church. Its bells mark times and services. In its parking lot stands a monument on which 1 Corinthians 13 is carved in several languages, among them English. "Though I speak with the tongues of men and angels and have not love," that most famous and cherished passage on how humans are best to love one another, now appropriated into the service of Christian wedding ceremonies, a romanticizing of Christian ethics!

Founded by the ancient Greeks, Corinth once ranked with Athens and Sparta in its economic, political, and cultural significance. Burned to the ground by the Romans in 146 B.C.E., Corinth was rebuilt by Julius Caesar roughly one hundred years later. It was to Roman Corinth that the Apostle Paul came to preach, presumably in the public forum. The ruins that center the town represent the Roman version of the city. Above the city on Acrocorinth stands a fortress dating from the Middle Ages. Formerly established to protect the city below, it too is a ruin. Not that far from the city lie the remains of the cemetery of Cenchreae, yet another location where Paul preached. My husband and I have come to Ancient Corinth to spend time with Macalester College students and faculty who are there to study the cemetery. In addition to trying to get a sense of Corinth in the time of Paul, we seek to learn a little bit about digging around for artifacts among the bones of corpses. Though learning more about Paul and digging among the corpses are obviously related, digging around in the dust constitutes a new and different kind of reading for me. Meanwhile we also take pictures of the Temple of Apollo and the forum in Ancient Corinth; we shoot digital images of the city from the fortress on Acrocorinth; we photograph the painted walls inside the tombs.

The day we grub around in the dirt inside the tombs is particularly hot. By afternoon the sun beats down pretty fiercely. The nearby sea radiates a range of blues I have never seen before, especially the brilliant teal near the shore. We ride back and forth to the cemetery in a small van with the windows down. The wind blows in my face, stinging my skin as the heat melts my consciousness. My mind sizzled and burned, my body covered in dust, I feel as though I were a pot baking in a kiln, then scoured by the wind. I grasp briefly once again why ascetics retreat to the desert to stare at the sun. All those ruins. Two millennia and more of dead people whisper in the breeze, beckoning from the past.

The journey from Corinth to Constantinople, now Istanbul (which is the Turkish version of the name "Constantinople," and still called Constantinople by the Greeks), requires a shift in scale and density of activity. Though the ruins of Ancient Corinth stand magnificent against the Greek landscape, the village around them slumbers in the sun except for the occasional herd of tourist buses retracing the steps of Paul. By contrast Istanbul, vast in size and still growing at a rapid rate, teems with activity in a bit more temperate climate. The sheer torrent of humanity pouring through the streets of the old city is overwhelming. So many living people!

The great church of Hagia Sophia or Ayasofia (depending on one's preference for ancient or modern Greek), constructed from the ruins of pagan temples, built on the site of a temple to Athena in what was then called Byzantium, was burnt to the ground and rebuilt by architects Isidoros of Miletus and Anthemios of Tralles in 537 C.E. in the city renamed Constantinople. Muslim conquerors converted it into a mosque and again renamed the city Istanbul. Now transformed into a museum by twentieth-century Turkish secularists, Hagia Sophia is hardly just another building. The Roman emperor, fully Christianized by 537 C.E., had his own private entrance where, upon entering with his wife, he would remove his armor.

While the empress made her way to her own balcony, he, joined by the patriarch, entered the sanctuary (no separation of religion and state here). Muslims later painted over the mosaics depicting Jesus' life and hung huge calligraphies in tribute to Allah and Muhammad. They left the fish and the crosses because they were not images of humans. Much to my secularized Protestant surprise, I experience a fleeting moment of offense that they would cover the face of Christ. Where did that feeling come from? Meanwhile, the Turkish secularists have set about to restore the mosaics to their original condition. Images of Mary Theotokos (Mother of God), holding the baby Jesus in her arms, particularly abound.

The Blue Mosque stands across the street from Hagia Sophia, dwarfing it to some extent, a tribute to the talent of its architect Mehmet Agha, who completed it in 1616. Absent any human representation, the interior is tiled in blue from floor to the top of the dome—austere and grand. It is a working mosque; people enter and pray. I enter without shoes, head covered, out of respect. Both buildings dwarf the ego and force the gaze upwards.

Our tour ends at the Grand Bazaar. The sound of the guide's voice transforms circles, squares, and triangles into four dimensions, as hawkers of wares mark every site by the buying and selling of beautiful things, regardless of prohibitions against idolatry across the Jewish, Christian, and Muslim traditions.

What does it mean to go, look, listen, wander about, and buy? To remove my shoes and don the headscarf, yet without performing ablutions or prayers? I promise myself that someday l will write an article titled "When Religious Site Becomes Theme Park, How Do We Tell the Scholars from the Tourists?"

But I am distracted; our guide is giving us history, here, now. Whose history? God's? I am losing all sense of personal possessive pronouns, all sense of "here," "there," and "when." I have undergone the temporary dissolution of time and space before, the loss of "me" and "mine." But now "ours" and "theirs"—whole families, tribes, communities, groups, nations— blur. NOT into a single universal "one." Rather, particularities pile one upon another in a jumble, their borders fuzzy yet remaining, huddling, shimmering without end. From Corinth to Constantinople, now Istanbul, it is the near-death of each and every distinctiveness blurring into the birth of another—not some final, complete whole, but a never-ending rhythm or series of rhythms, wound around one another, pulsating in the orthodox church bell, the muezzin's call, and the cargo ship's blaring horn along the Bosphoros. I seek to capture the enigmatic quality of those early bits and pieces, those fragmentary corpses layered one upon the other that dot the way from Jesus' time to the present teeming life, through the centuries as dissident Palestinian Jews morphed into gentile Christians.

According to most New Testament scholars, the early communities who claimed Jesus as their teacher made up one of several Jewish renewal movements flourishing at the time. Whether intentionally or inadvertently, the movement comprised a dissident movement in relation to the Roman Empire and the Jerusalem Temple cult. There being no clear-cut separation between religion and politics at the time, a modernist self-deception at best, the movement was countercultural with respect both to the empire and to the local government. Within four centuries this dissident renewal movement had achieved the status of religion of the Roman Empire. I think that this shift in status from countercultural movement to established state religion was neither by necessity nor merely by chance, nor was it by the design of a supernatural power. Most importantly, it was not some four-century fall from a pure origin. By this I mean that what we now call Christianity did not start out as some essentially "good" or "pure" movement, only later to fall into apostasy. Rather it was internally plural and subject to political and economic contention from the start. Like other renewal movements, it historically faced at least four possible futures: First, religiopolitical countercultures get destroyed by the states they challenge. Second, they become marginalized as relatively separatist communities by a sort of tacit agreement with the host state. Third, they accommodate the host state and assimilate to it while modifying its structures. Or, fourth, they invent new states. Regardless of which future befalls them, however, they are always subject to developing new forms of religious, political, and economic tyranny that elicit in turn new forms of dissent, driven by conflicting desires.

I propose in this chapter to illustrate how the internally plural traditions that we now call Christianity survived to become a major "religion" by deploying all of these strategies, including the destruction of minority traditions and competing traditions both within and without the movement itself. Virtually all of these strategies were inherent in the movement's plural and often conflicting teachings and practices as far back as scholars can get to the point of origin itself. These teachings and practices, these disciplines of individual and communal identity, were driven by desires that were both more and less generous. No single internal logic or external force drove the processes by which this history unfolds, except that those who became followers, whatever their social status, appropriated and recreated the figure of Jesus as the authorization for and reflection of their responses to their particular material circumstances, a pattern that continues into the present. This pattern of making a world around the figure of Jesus, itself a continually remade image, additionally takes place in the midst of political and economic struggle that involves the making of the state and the citizens who populate it. It is not my purpose to write this history but to present select moments that set in motion this ongoing struggle over authority.

HISTORICAL CONTEXT: PAUL TO AUGUSTINE

Though the dominant culture of late antiquity was Hellenistic, the Roman Empire sustained extraordinary cultural diversity and, at the turn of the millennium, a relative peace—relative, that is, to the well-being of the power elite, which depended on oppressive military enforcement and a slave economy. Hellenistic culture was cosmopolitan, polytheistic, and world affirming. For example, Stoicism, one of the dominant philosophies of the time, identified God with the cosmos or nature as its "all soul." The Stoic world was an ordered cosmos with which humans could stand in harmony, a place where humans could belong. Egyptian cults, Greek mystery religions, Roman practices surrounding the hearth, and Epicureanism easily coexisted in practice, if not always in conceptual agreement, with this comparatively optimistic worldview. As we shall shortly see, other existing traditions and newly emerging ones reacted against Stoicism's monism, its materialism, and its this-worldly optimism.[1]

Given the cultural diversity of the empire, the *Pax Romana* depended heavily on supportive local governance and religious tolerance, so long as religious life and practice did not challenge Roman authority. Loyalty to the Roman emperor trumped all other loyalties. The emperor himself stood at the center of civil cultic practices; all who served in the military swore allegiance to him as a god. Appeals to religious authority that challenged or appeared to challenge local religious and political rulers in the service of the emperor constituted by association threats to the sovereignty of the emperor and the imperial government. Those who made such appeals were subject to charges of sedition or treason. If convicted, they were often executed by crucifixion. Survival of a province, a country, or a religious community could depend heavily on assimilation to the dominant culture and collaboration with Roman authorities. In this context there simply was no serious distinction made between religion and politics and thus no separation of religion and state, as we understand it today. Within this milieu, cultural and countercultural forces alike were to serve simultaneously as sources of contention and resources for development for what was to become Christianity. Judaism and gnosticism constituted two of the most powerful countercultural forces at work.

PLURALISM IN JUDAISM

Within this extreme diversity, Judaism, as practiced in Palestine or beyond it, was internally plural.[2] No particular group escaped the influence of Hellenistic culture altogether, simply because Greek was the dominant language. Nevertheless, communities formed in reaction against the Temple cult of Jerusalem, which they viewed as corrupted beyond repair by the dominant culture. By Jesus' time, Palestine had been the source of repeated violent confrontation between the Roman military and various rebel Palestinian groups, and the Roman government considered it to be a source of ongoing disruption. Tensions eventually mounted to the point that the Roman army invaded and destroyed Jerusalem (70 C.E.) and, later, drove the Jews from Palestine (110 C.E.).

At the time that Jesus began to attract followers, several groups contended over the claim to represent the true chosen people of God, the true observers of Torah. These groups included, among others, the Pharisees, the Essenes, and the followers of John the Baptist. Such groups stood as dissident communities in relation to the Temple cult, regulated by the Sadducees as the established representatives of Judaism. These dissident communities also competed to some extent with one another. A brief analysis of some of their major commonalities and differences will help to clarify the nature and level of their dissent.[3]

All three groups shared with Jesus and his earliest followers the centrality of Torah, though they differed as to the precise extent of its observance and role in Jewish life. For all these groups, *Messiah*, the Hebrew term for which *Christ* is the equivalent, meant the human one anointed by God to usher in God's kingdom on earth. These groups, including the followers of Jesus, further shared an apocalyptic worldview in contrast to the dominant Greek worldview assimilated by the Sadducees. This vision minimally included the hope for the Messiah (though they disputed whether Jesus himself was the Messiah), the ushering in of the kingdom of God on earth, and a general bodily resurrection of the dead at the end of time. All four groups were critical of the Temple cult, either intentionally or by default; the most explicitly critical among them was the Essene community at Qumran.

Their differences are as significant as their commonalities. In contrast to the followers of Jesus, the Essenes and the followers of John the Baptist formed ascetic communities. Both practiced fasting, and the Essenes practiced celibacy. The practice of celibacy in particular reconfigured the significance of the family by challenging the value placed on biological reproduction. At the same time, one did not have to practice celibacy to produce familial reconfiguration; Jesus, who may or may not have been celibate, challenged family structure by calling on his followers to leave their conventional families and form a new family with him. The establishment of this new family leveled class and gender differences as well. This reconfiguration in effect challenged some of the ritual observances of the Levitical codes and the reigning conception of holiness among the Pharisees in particular, setting the two communities at odds with each other. Like the Pharisees, the Essenes also were concerned with ritual purity, though they employed different strategies to sustain it. In contrast to the Pharisees who remained within the dominant culture, the Essenes appear to have built separatist communities; so, for example, Essenes established themselves at Qumran near the Dead Sea to avoid cultural contamination. Whether a group remained within the culture or separated from it affected to some degree the group's relations with civil authority. Unlike the Essenes, the Pharisees do not appear to have been considered a religious or political threat to the Temple cult. At the same time, the Gospel accounts of the beheading of John the Baptist carry undertones of political tension between local Roman governance and John's followers. Likewise Jesus' crucifixion for blasphemy indicates that his crime was tantamount to treason; his male disciples' initial abandonment of his cause suggests that they assumed that they too would be pursued and prosecuted.

In short, neither Christianity nor Talmudic Judaism existed as such.[4] On the contrary, Judaism was highly fluid, and Jesus and his followers, like the Pharisees whose traditions were to transmute into Talmudic Judaism, emerged from the flux as one Jewish sect among several dissident groups at the time. Before the followers of Jesus took their message on the road to the gentiles, the Jesus community stood in contentious relation with some of the other Jewish groups, particularly the Pharisees, concerning what God required of God's people. As the number of gentile converts increased to the point of dominating the Jesus-centered communities, the relationship of the movement to its Hebrew heritage, as well as to other coexisting forms of Judaism, became less clear and more contentious. The movement's status as Jewish sect shifted by degrees to a new, distinctively gentile collection of traditions, just as Talmudic Judaism, rooted in the Pharisaic tradition, became the dominant form of Judaism. The relationship between the two traditions became more formalized, often in ways that were in the long run devastating to all communities involved.

What began as essentially an in-fight between the two groups was to become tragic in its consequences throughout subsequent history, tragic especially for Jews, as Christianity grew to dominate the West. A subsequent, disturbing history notwithstanding, Jews and Christians, once differentiated as such, also continued to share a history in which they intermittently interacted peaceably as well.[5] Records exist from as late as the fifth century C.E. of the two groups praying together in Minorca and of a religious festival shared by Jews, Christians, and pagans alike at Mamre. A Palestinian historian records one such festival in which

> The inhabitants of the country and the regions round Palestine, the Phoenicians and the Arabs, assemble annually during the summer season to keep a brilliant feast. . . . Indeed, this feast is diligently frequented by all nations: by the Jews, because they boast of their descent from the patriarch Abraham; by the pagans, because angels there appeared to men; and by Christians because He who has lately revealed himself through the virgin for the salvation of mankind once appeared there to the pious man. . . . Some pray to the God of all; some call upon the angels, pour out wine, burn incense, or offer an ox, or he-goat, a sheep or a cock . . . [and] all abstain from coming near their wives.[6]

This brief example indicates, at least to me, that antagonistic relations were not a historical necessity. Meanwhile, to return to the first century, in addition to the various forces within Judaism, gnosticism made its own indelible impact on the followers of Jesus.

GNOSTICISM

Never officially a discrete religion in its own right, gnosticism refers to common practices and beliefs held by otherwise divergent groups throughout the Near East during late antiquity.[7] Gnostic communities predate Christianity and appear to have existed within both Jewish and pagan religious frameworks.[8] The central feature of gnosticism that bound otherwise disparate groups together was the notion of a special, secret, saving knowledge, available to a select few. This knowledge—grounded in any one of a number of mythological variations on the Neoplatonic philosophy of Plotinus—represented an absolute rebellion against the world, one that yielded freedom from its constraints as the realm of the flesh.

These mythological appropriations varied. Though all groups were dualistic in their effects, gnostics differed over the origin of the dualism, evolving into two different types. Gnostic monists considered the event of creation itself as the result of a tragic flaw or episode within the life of the divine *pleroma*, a plural godhead or hierarchy of divine energies, so to speak. By contrast, gnostic dualists construed the episode as emerging from a dualism between Light and Darkness. Because the monists most influenced Christianity, I shall focus on their characteristics for the moment. (I turn to a modified dualist conception of gnosticism in the discussion of Manichaeism, below).

Monists characteristically suffered a deep sense of human alienation from the world. This alienation usually entailed an adamant rejection of matter, a tripartite anthropology and sociology of matter, soul, and spirit, and a realized eschatology (the view of the end of time as present in the here and now). At the center of a monist vision stood the ultimate unknowability of God. Appropriating Neoplatonic thought, monists conceived God as a Godhead or divine pleroma. This plurality articulated itself as paired, gendered emanations from within a single Source, itself sometimes construed as a monad, sometimes as a gendered dyad. Though precise accounts of the origin of evil vary, monists generally mythologized that a demiurge or, for lack of better words, an incompetent, ignorant, and brutish force, was its cause. An abortive offspring of the divine wisdom—Sophia, one of the several feminized dyadic aspects emanating from the Source—this demiurge morally subverted the rest of the pleroma. By and large, monists viewed the creation of the world as the product of this ignorant, if not altogether malevolent, deity or demiurge. In opposition to the demiurge's ignorance, his mother Sophia made secret wisdom available to the elect within select human communities. This wisdom would restore the unity of the divine pleroma through human self-realization, understood as fulfilling the divine spark of this knowledge within them. This wisdom was thus salvific both for humans, and ultimately for the Godhead itself.

Within this cosmogony, humans themselves fell into three categories. They might be born as *sarkic* or fleshly beings, for whom there was no hope of escape from the world. They might be born as *psychic*, en-souled beings, who possessed the potential for escape in some future life. They might, more desirably, be born *pneumatic* or en-spirited beings, who possessed a divine spark, a part of the Source, within them. These last formed the elect, the ones who might be saved by a secret knowledge, available only to them—a mystical knowledge of their divine origin and ultimate destiny in relation to the Source or Beginning of all things, itself wholly other and thus unknowable. The disciplines and practices that produced this knowledge might take an ascetic form or an antinomian, libertine form, depending on the group. In both cases, the practices provided a Way that ultimately released the spark of the divine within the practitioner so that the spark might be reunited with the Source. Once all the divine sparks were restored to their rightful place, the world would cease to exist.

Such a conception of reality lent itself well to assimilation into other religious and theological frameworks. Some scholars have suggested, for example, that kabbalistic Judaism represents the development of an earlier infiltration of gnostic mythology and theology into the flux of Judaism during late antiquity. Infiltration would not have been difficult. The wisdom traditions of the Hebrew Bible personify and feminize (*hokhmah*, like *sophia*, is a feminine noun) the wisdom of God (for example, the book of Proverbs). While Hebrew conceptions of a good Creator who makes a good creation are on the face of it incompatible with a demiurge Creator, the wisdom tradition could have nevertheless been modified to accommodate and assimilate a more gnostic conception of the divine Wisdom or Sophia.

Given that gnosticism migrated into many different existing and emerging traditions, the earliest converts to the Jesus movement, whether Jewish or Gentile, could have subsequently brought gnostic influences with them to contribute at the very beginning to what was to become Christianity. For example, in some of the early gnostic christologies, Jesus the Christ mediates salvation as the embodiment of divine wisdom or Sophia (for example, *The Sophia of Jesus the Christ* and *The Gospel of Truth*).[9] The wisdom tradition of Hebrew scripture, found also in the apocryphal and pseudepigraphical writings of both Jewish and Christian traditions (for example, The Wisdom of Solomon and The Odes of Solomon), continued in sublimated form in some of the Christian canonical materials. For example, in earlier Pauline texts, Christ becomes the Wisdom of God (1 Corinthians 1:28—2:16). Later, in the Gospel according to John, the Word of God takes on the function of the Wisdom of God (John 1:1-14, compare Wisdom of Solomon 9:1–3).

Both explicit and sublimated forms are in turn congenial to subsequent gnostic interpretation, appropriation, and modification, even if not historically interactive with some form of gnosticism. In any case, the earliest followers of Jesus appear to have drawn upon different strands of gnosticism from both Jewish and pagan directions in the formation of the earliest communities. As we shall shortly see, these beliefs and practices, whether Jewish or gentile in origin, would, like the other different strains of Judaism, become not only formative but also sources of contention.

The pluralism within Judaism and the gnosticism of otherwise diverse and disparate religious traditions indicate just how fluid, interactive, interdependent, eclectic, and nonmonolithic actual religious beliefs and practices really are, especially at their point of origin. Furthermore, the activity going on at the beginning is both more and less than intentional. Just as dissent is not always clearly identifiable as such or clearly distinguishable from established beliefs and practices, so the earliest participants in the development of religious traditions are likely unaware of the full implications of their activities. Indeed, their motives and goals may be altogether different from the actual historical results.

Such, I think, was the case for the early followers of Jesus. Whether they sought to be true to God's covenant with them, or to escape the prisons of their bodies and release the spark of divinity within them— or some combination of these—they brought with them their various heritages to leave as fingerprints on something new to them at the time. What seems to have bound them together was some sense of renewed or, in the case of the gentiles, altogether new communal and individual relation to God, associated somehow with the figure of Jesus, in ways that were to have dramatic political and religious consequences for subsequent history. They also brought a vast array of differences, some of which were to become internally irreconcilable and to remain so even into the present. At the heart of the social process of christological imagining lies the issue of how to negotiate the multitude of conflicting images or construals of Jesus and thereby God, arising out of such diverse heritages and mutating throughout the history of the many Christian traditions. How these differences were addressed in the first five centuries set in motion both troubling and promising patterns for internal and external relations with which we today, whether secular or religious, continue to live.

The first five centuries following Jesus' crucifixion thus witnessed both great turmoil and creativity within the Jesus movement. This turmoil manifested itself internally over the significance of the figure of Jesus, the relations between Jewish and gentile converts, the establishment of governing ecclesiastical structures and authorities, and the regulation of the lives of the converts. At the same time, as the prospect of the kingdom of God on earth faded into the horizon, the status of the developing communities in relation to the Roman government shifted slowly from countercultural sect, subject to persecution, to the official religion of the Roman state itself. This shift in power required major theological rethinking of eschatology, christology, and believers' relations to civil order. Equally importantly, rivalry with other traditions, both established and emerging, kept theologians at work justifying the desirability, not to mention superiority, of Christian life in preference to other options, for example, Manichaeism. In short, the early Jesus movement transformed from a countercultural collection of loosely affiliated Jewish communities with both commonly held and disparate traditions and practices into a relatively well-organized gentile institution with fairly coherent governing doctrines, namely the Church universal, the religion of the Roman Empire.

The earliest texts evidence a pluralism of christologies. Depending on their presuppositions regarding the kingdom of God, the earliest ones are provisional and address highly specific situations. This is not to say that they are incoherent. On the contrary, they narrate stories. There is no monolithic single story, however. Nor is there an essential, single story to which the multiple stories can be reduced. Rather they comprise a family of stories rotating around the central figure Jesus the Messiah or Christ, where even "Messiah" or "Christ" is itself apprehended in a variety of different ways.[10] Unlike most families, this one begins as a genealogical family and transmutes into a voluntaristic or adoptive one. As with most families, however, so with this one in the extreme, there are dramatic differences among the various members, due no doubt to its voluntaristic nature. These differences produce serious disruptions. The early controversies manifest these disruptions and the attempts to resolve and regulate them, as well as the attempt to manage Christian relations with the Roman state and with other religious traditions. It is to these artifacts that I now turn.

The Pauline Epistles

The earliest extant texts we have are the Pauline epistles.[11] Biblical scholars disagree on which letters are authentic, though most agree that Paul minimally wrote all or most of 1 Thessalonians, Galatians, 1 Corinthians, 2 Corinthians, Philippians, Philemon, and Romans.

Most also agree that Paul wrote these letters in the decade of the fifties. Regardless of other differences, most Pauline scholars also emphasize the provisional, situational, apocalyptic qualities of Paul's letters and by implication his theology and ethics. This can be seen also in his christology. Paul's thinking, however, was not utterly fragmentary and without coherence. His encounter with the resurrected Messiah or Christ, apprehended as a call to become an apostle to the gentiles, provided him a coherent sense of identity and work which stood as a unifying force in dialectical tension with the diverse circumstances he encountered in his mission work. Paul's vision was theocentric, and within this vision Jesus the Christ initiated a new, yet to be completed order. For Paul, Jesus was born, Jesus suffered and was crucified for human sin, he arose from the dead, and he would come again—in the near future. Meanwhile, within the Pauline epistles Jesus as the Messiah performed differing roles, depending on the context in which Paul found himself as an apostle.

Building on this scholarship, I propose that the provisional, situational, and apocalyptic qualities of these various images of Jesus as Christ evidence pluralism in the service of dissent. I will focus particularly on his letter to the Romans taken with Galatians, on 1 Corinthians, and on his letter to the Philippians to illustrate this claim. These letters register three areas of tension. Romans, taken with Galatians, addresses the issue of Jewish identity in relation to gentile converts, both for those Jews who accepted Jesus as the Messiah or Christ and for those Jews who did not. In 1 Corinthians Paul focuses on divine wisdom in ways that reflect possible gnostic influences on his own spirituality and at the same time take issue with what might loosely be called gnostic tendencies within the Greek community. In his letter to the Philippians Paul responds at least implicitly in opposition to the absoluteness of the authority over human life claimed by the Roman government. I treat these letters out of chronological order because I think that understanding Paul's sense of his Jewish identity informs the wider context for addressing his view of divine wisdom and his relation to the Roman government as its prisoner.

Scholars have argued heatedly over Paul's understanding of his relationship to Judaism in light of his call to be an apostle for Christ to the gentiles. Certainly much that Paul wrote, or that has been attributed to him, when taken out of context, lends itself readily to legitimating anti-Judaism and later anti-Semitism.[12] I am persuaded, however, by those scholars who argue quite to the contrary that Paul never rejected his Jewish identity. Furthermore, though he dissented against some of the traditions of his origin, his transformation to his new life in Jesus as the Messiah must be understood as Paul's modification and expansion of Jewish traditions rather than his repudiation of them. These modifications nevertheless placed him in opposition not only to his traditions of origin, but also to the Jewish Christian community in Jerusalem as well.

This way of viewing Paul's Jewish identity depends first and foremost on understanding that there was no normative Judaism during the first century. As I noted earlier, Jesus was an observing Jew, and the earliest followers were likewise practicing Jews, Paul himself among them. Indeed, the disputes among various Jewish groups, including the followers of Jesus, were over the very nature of Judaism. The introduction of gentiles into the equation forced the issue of whether Jewish identity would remain genealogically defined. Put theologically, the issue was whether the covenant made between God and the ancient Hebrews, marked by the circumcision of Hebrew males, extended to gentiles and, if so, what this required of the gentiles, particularly gentile males. That gentiles converted to Jewish communities was not new. When they did, however, the males apparently underwent circumcision, symbolizing the significance of a genealogical connection. Thus the traditions remained genealogically defined.

Paul as Saul of Tarsus appears to have understood his own Jewish identity in genealogical terms. With his encounter with the resurrected Messiah, however, Paul's vision of the covenant, the promises of God, and the people of God underwent a dramatic shift. This shift does not mean that he gave up his Jewish identity; rather he extended his distinctively Jewish view of election, grace, and covenant to gentiles without requiring them to undergo circumcision or to observe Torah strictly. In short, as Daniel Boyarin points out, Paul universalizes Jewish traditions by eliminating crucial aspects of particularity as required of gentiles.[13] In so doing, he not only takes issue with the Judaism of his past but also with the Jewish Christians of his present; hence his extreme anger at Peter and other leaders for what he considered to be their meddling in the Galatian community as usurping his authority. To legitimate his own authority, he ultimately appeals to the authority of the Christ of the preexisting baptismal hymn of Galatians 3:28: "There is no longer Jew or Greek, there is no longer slave or free, there is no longer male and female; for all of you are one in Christ Jesus." The universalizing impulse is overwhelming; all differences, even distinctions, appear to be obliterated by the figure of Christ.

ROMANS

The significance of difference nevertheless remains an issue for Paul, one that he takes up again in his letter to the Romans. Calvin Roetzel notes that Paul's epistle to the Romans is the only one of his extant letters that does not address a specific contention or need of the community to which it is directed.[14] Instead, Paul appears to have taken the occasion as an opportunity to reflect on the status of Jews in relation to that accorded gentiles. In my opinion, the salutation in Romans is particularly noteworthy in that it contains a christology that he will employ to work out what might be called a theology of interrelations among converted Jews and gentiles on the model of an adoptive family. The first six verses read:

> Paul, a servant of Jesus Christ, called to be an apostle, set apart for the gospel of God, which he promised beforehand through his prophets in the holy scriptures, the gospel concerning his Son, who was descended from David according to the flesh and was declared to be the Son of God with power according to the spirit of holiness by resurrection from the dead, Jesus Christ our Lord, through whom we have received grace and apostleship to bring about the obedience of faith among all the Gentiles for the sake of his name, including yourselves who are called to belong to Jesus Christ.

Paul's christology in Romans is distinctively Jewish. While the preexistence of Christ before Jesus' birth is not precluded, Paul makes no reference to it here, in contrast to other letters, notably Philippians. Jesus is the Jewish Messiah of whom the prophets spoke in scripture. Jesus' historical reality is emphasized by his genealogical connection to David. It is through the resurrection that he is declared the Son of God, one who is granted the spirit of holiness. His resurrection from the dead warrants his lordship. This lordship effects mercy upon Paul and authorizes his apostleship. It is Paul's job as an apostle to bring about obedience among all the gentiles. Obedience is required, for the gentiles who are called by God belong to God. Thus Paul introduces a distinctively Jewish Jesus, whom he connects immediately to Hebrew scripture and history. For Paul the resurrection extends the domain of Christ as well as holiness and election to the gentiles. Paul's own special task is to effect this extension.

Who declares Jesus to be the Son of God is unclear. One could read the passage to mean that the resurrection causes the followers to recognize and so declare that Jesus is indeed the Son of God. Alternatively one could also read the passage that the resurrection itself marks Jesus as the Son of God. The absence of reference to a preexisting Christ, as well as the lack of reference to Jesus as Son of God at his birth or by virtue of his life on earth, allows the text to be read as if Jesus becomes the Son of God by virtue of his resurrection. According to this latter reading, one could infer that the resurrection effects Jesus' adoption by God as God's son, so to speak.

Regardless of the way one reads the text, adoption becomes for Paul a metaphor for establishing a new, mixed family of both Jews and gentiles who benefit from this relationship as children of God and brothers and sisters to Jesus the Christ and to one another. In this respect, Jesus the Christ is first among equals. In Romans 8:15-17 Paul writes, "For you did not receive a spirit of slavery to fall back into fear, but you have received a spirit of adoption. When we cry, 'Abba! Father!' it is that very Spirit bearing witness to our spirit that we are children of God, and if children, then heirs, heirs of God and joint heirs with Christ—if in fact, we suffer with him so that we may also be glorified with him." Bound by present identification with suffering and future glorification rather than blood, this newly established, adoptive family takes on cosmic proportions (Romans 8:19-23). It further stands in a relation of both connection and disconnection with genealogically defined Judaisms.

Romans 9–11 registers a series of perspectival shifts. Chapter 9 marks a shift from a discussion of intracommunal relations (the adoptive family of chapter 8) to a discussion of interrelations with Jews who reject the lordship of Jesus as the Messiah or Christ (the genealogically defined family). Paul takes issue with this rejection explicitly from his location as apostle to the gentiles. From this location, the differences set the families at enmity with one another, due to Jewish resistance to Paul's view. From this location, Paul never resolves this issue in a way that would allow for amicable relations across the two families. In chapter 10 he shifts the discussion to a universalizing motif. In the long run, the lordship of Christ obliterates differences (Romans 10:12). Chapter 11 then shifts abruptly to the significance of Jewish resistance to the gospel from God's perspective. Within this context, Paul locates himself clearly as "an Israelite, a descendant of Abraham, a member of the tribe of Benjamin" (Romans 11:1). He poses the question: Will God reject the Jews who reject Christ? He answers with an emphatic no. It is now God who is universal in God's righteousness and actions—particularly God's mercy and God's election or calling. In other words, God calls *all* to repentance that they might receive mercy. The gifts of God are irrevocable (Romans 11:28). For Paul, whatever enmity exists between the new mixed communities of Jews and gentiles and the exclusively Jewish communities, God's loyalty extends to both. All share in common their disobedience to God; all share in common God's mercy extended to them. This part of the discussion excludes all mention of Jesus. Disobedience and mercy shared alike by the adoptive family and the genealogically defined family override any claims to special status in God's eyes made by either family. Moreover, by implication the differences between Jew and gentile within the new communities remain distinctive even as their significance is relativized by membership in the new adoptive family.

Paul's theocentric impulse to relativize his own work, placed side by side with his tendency to universalize his outreach, does not resolve the serious differences between the two families. At the same time, these devices, taken together militate against any claims to special favor or to supersessionism by either party. In chapter 12 Paul returns to the adoptive family and exhorts it to focus on God's grace and its practical, ethical impact on their lives. The implication is that in the long run intrafamilial and interfamilial differences are subordinated in priority to lived human relations with God and one another.

1 CORINTHIANS

Paul's tendency to relativize differences by formally equalizing them in the face of a transcendent reality characterizes other epistles as well. What he later assumes as a theocentric perspective in Romans, he earlier assumes as a christocentric perspective in one of his earlier epistles to the Corinthians, what we now refer to as 1 Corinthians. This epistle addresses differences among Greek converts in Corinth.[15] At the time, religious enthusiasm, manifested among members of the community as speaking in tongues, antinomianism, libertinism, idolatry, and claims to superior wisdom, apparently threatened to destroy the community. Reports of these activities motivated Paul's correspondence. Paul's aim is to reconcile differences in this context, in contrast to his attempt to address their irreconcilability in Romans. The letter is eloquent and rich in christologically driven imagery. Familial imagery, this time more specifically biological, abounds. God is, of course, Father, and the followers are brothers and sister. At the same time, transcending gender distinctions, Paul himself takes on familial roles both as wet nurse and as father (1 Cor. 1:3, 3:3, and 4:15, respectively). Paul also uses an economic language of treasures and riches of the Spirit and divine ownership of the human in Christ, who in turn belongs to God (1 Cor. 3:21-23).

To reconcile contention, Paul employs the metaphor of the body to organize yet distinguish differences within the community. The Lord's Supper effects an interrelation of differences and dynamic participation of the members of the community in Christ (10:16-18). Paul writes that he has heard of heresies or, more accurately, divisions, among the Corinthians manifested in the way they observe the Lord's Supper (11:17-20), a passage that at the hands of Augustine of Hippo three centuries later would authorize drawing hard and fast lines between heresy and orthodoxy in terms of absolute truth. Paul writes in verse 19, "Indeed, there have to be factions among you, for only so will it become clear who among you are genuine." At the time he is writing, Paul is making an apocalyptic statement; he views "factions" or "divisions" as a sure sign that the end times are near. He himself clearly draws a line as to how much difference in practice he is willing to tolerate. He defines his limit in ethical terms however. For him the factions present a violation of social ethics, grounded sacramentally. To celebrate the Lord's Supper in "an unworthy manner" is here identified with drunkenness and gluttony, while letting others at the table go hungry (11:21). Such behavior violates the body of Christ present in the bread and the wine. This violation condemns the celebrant (11:27-34).

Factions or divisions notwithstanding, Paul's ultimate point of reference is nevertheless reconciliation. At this point Paul turns abruptly to the issue of spiritual gifts. Members become metaphorical body parts of the body of Christ, differentiated according to different gifts, in non-hierarchical relation to one another, although, taken together, all are subordinated to Christ as both the whole and head (12:1-31). Paul juxtaposes his discussion of the body of Christ celebrated in the bread and the wine with his use of the body as a metaphor for relating different spiritual gifts. Communion becomes community, rendering the members of the community God's own. By virtue of God's ownership of Christ and Christ's ownership of the elect, human participation in Christ through the Lord's Supper and the exercise of spiritual gifts constitutes participation in the divine life.

Paul's earlier use of the cross to transvalue wisdom (1 Cor. 1:17—4:1) sets up this human participation in God. For Paul the suffering and death of Jesus on the cross reveals God's wisdom by relativizing human wisdom. An inversion occurs. God's power to save is revealed in the message of the cross.[16] The cross *is* the message. Accepting the message saves one from perishing. That God would reveal God's power to save in a crucifixion appears foolish to the world but constitutes true wisdom for those who are called by God. As God's gift, it is a wisdom of which no one can boast. Paul reminds the congregation where it came from and to what end. By human standards the congregants were not wise or powerful or of high social status; yet God chose them to shame the wise, the strong, and the noble so that "no one might boast in the presence of God" (1:29). God is indeed the source of life in Christ "who became for us wisdom from God, and righteousness and sanctification and redemption. . ." (1:30).

This wisdom is only the beginning. Paul goes on to add, "Yet among the mature we do speak wisdom . . . God's wisdom, secret and hidden, which God decreed before the ages for our glory" (2:6-7). Those who have received the cross as God's wisdom may mature to a love for God (2:9) and receive God's wisdom through God's Spirit speaking with and to the human spirit. God's self-revelation extends beyond the wisdom of Christ crucified to a communion with the Spirit of God. What God reveals is that love itself is the most valued of all activity, human and divine (1 Corinthians 13).

Paul's letter to the Corinthians may very well simply reflect a conflict between Paul's countercultural values, practices, and beliefs and those of the dominant culture, imported into the new, struggling countercultural community in Corinth. However, the passages on wisdom, human and divine, as well as Paul's later application of the gnostic conceptual distinction between the fleshly and the spiritual to the resurrected body (1 Cor. 15:35-58), lend themselves easily to a gnostic framework. The enthusiasm, antinomianism, libertinism, and claims to superior wisdom within the community can likewise be seen as the effects of gnostic tendencies. One cannot help but wonder to what extent Paul as gnostic might be attempting to temper the excesses of a gnostic group. Paul would later state in Romans that, as an apostle, he became all things to all people. Conversely, he certainly did not view the God of Abraham and Sarah as a demiurge, nor did he assume a realized eschatology. Furthermore, though he is at the very least ambivalent toward the flesh, he does not reject the created order out of hand, for the whole creation desires human redemption (Romans 8:22). All the same, divine wisdom, indeed secret wisdom revealed only to those mature in their love for God, awaits those who receive Christ crucified as a wisdom that appears disguised as foolishness to the world. Thus he inverts wisdom as associated with power and transvalues it in the process. Whether and to what extent Paul was gnostic remains unclear; nevertheless, it is easy to see why later gnostic Christians would consider Paul one of their own.

Other Pauline Letters

Paul's strategy of inverting hierarchies to explode ordinary assumptions about power, a legacy of his prophetic heritage, carried over, at least by implication, into the realm of civil relations in addition to spiritual ones. On the whole, Paul tends throughout his letters to exhort the various communities under his care to avoid conflict with civil authorities, though he clearly subordinates all earthly power to God's authority.[17] His letter to the Philippians takes a subtle, different turn, however. In this epistle Paul appropriates a christological hymn as the centerpiece for his challenge to the Philippians to continue to take on the mind of Christ in the face of strong opposition. He exhorts:

> Let the same mind be in you that was in Christ Jesus,
> who, though he was in the form of God,
> did not regard equality with God as something to be exploited,
> but emptied himself, taking the form of a slave,
> being born in human likeness.
> And being found in human form,
> he humbled himself and became obedient to the point of death—
> even death on a cross.
> Therefore God also highly exalted him
> and gave him the name that is above every name
> so that at the name of Jesus every knee should bend,
> in heaven and on earth and under the earth
> and every tongue should confess that Jesus Christ is Lord
> to the glory of God the Father.
> —Philippians 2:5-11

Looking back through the lens of two thousand years of Christian history, a contemporary reader surely finds the unintended validation of slavery, as well as the triumphalism, deeply troubling. The readers at the time and Paul himself, however, did not expect there to be subsequent millennia, nor would they find the triumphalism of past and present-day tradition even recognizable. Moreover, at the time this letter was written and read, Paul was imprisoned (it is not clear where), and the community at Philippi was marginalized and opposed by local authorities. Both Paul and the Philippians faced persecution and possible death. In this context the hymn takes on both a heartening and revolutionary power.

The Christ Jesus of the hymn relinquishes all claims to deity, clinging to humanity, indeed slavery, and thereby upending established relations of power, including all enslavement to human authority. Obedient even to a hideous and shameful death on the cross (a political death reserved for the seditious), Jesus merits God's exaltation as Lord over all. The universalizing impulse recurs. The humility and the triumph of Christ are to be mirrored in the lives and deaths of his followers to the glory of God. Present opposition, persecution, and even death cannot prevail (3:20-21). Meanwhile, Paul seeks converts among the imperial guard (1:13; 4:23). In this context, conversion, baptism, and the celebration of the Eucharistic meal would have been acts of dissent inviting charges of sedition. In short, Christ Jesus' identification with enslaved humanity disestablishes and deauthorizes slavery, along with worldly hierarchical distinctions and associated power; all are equal to one another as subordinates before the lordship of Christ. Contemporary readers may find the prospect of falling upon one's knees and confessing anyone else as Lord disturbing, if not altogether distasteful. For the earliest followers of Jesus it was an egalitarian and revolutionary move.

Paul's repertoire of christological strategies or discursive practices includes universalizing, interrelating parts to whole, gender bending, power inversions, and relativizing his own communities' interests from christocentric and theocentric perspectives. He emphasizes God's gifts to gentile and Jew alike, particularly the wisdom, bestowed initially by Jesus the Messiah or Christ, manifested as love of God in both senses of God's love for humans and human love for God. It is an inverted wisdom that transfigures human desire within an economy of grace. The children of God, through Christ, participate in the divine life. This participation challenges all earthly power and the hierarchies that manifest it. Many of these same discursive practices and themes, as well as the conflicts they addressed, characterize the later canonical and noncanonical materials that appear during the first two centuries. Like the Pauline epistles, they represent the multiple interests and concerns of various different communities of followers or audiences. Like the epistles, they exhibit contention with the Temple cult, other Jewish groups and the imperial state. In both genres, Jesus becomes a disruptive force that challenges established ways of conducting life in the world as regulated by established religious and governmental authority.

THE GOSPELS COMPARED WITH PAUL'S LETTERS

Paul's epistles differ in form and in content from the Gospels. Unlike the epistles, the Gospels in particular focus on Jesus' ministry as witnessed by parables, miracle stories, and sermons attributed to Jesus.[18] The parable was particularly significant as a vehicle for disrupting its hearers' ordinary assumptions regarding power and its distribution. Its defining discursive practices were numerous. They included, among others, an apocalyptic focus on the kingdom of God, the embedding of the parable within a context of dispute or contention, relative brevity, the inversion of structures of power and social status, the use of the ordinary to convey or reveal the extraordinary, hyperbole, a sense of drama or surprise, the use of irony and ambiguity, the intention to teach through indirect speech, and a sense of generosity and abundance as characteristic of the kingdom itself. Likewise the miraculous healings attributed to Jesus often reflect inversions of social-class distinctions and produce conflict over the proper observance of the Levitical codes. To touch an unclean person, to heal on the Sabbath, and to raise the dead was, for Jesus, to transgress established social and religious taboos; to claim God as his authority for doing so only further compounded his sedition and blasphemy.

Christological representations within these genres, employing various devices, differ substantively among themselves. For example, the Synoptic Gospels (Mark, Luke, and Matthew), probably written between 70 and 85 C.E., assume an imminent, proleptic eschatology, in contrast to the Gospel according to John, dated between 90 and 110 C.E., which assumes a realized eschatology. Each of the four canonical Gospels represents in turn a different christological agenda. The Markan account, the most apocalyptic of the four, begins with Jesus' baptism by John the Baptist and stresses Jesus' mission as the herald of the impending kingdom of God on earth. In its earliest extant form it concludes with the empty tomb rather than appearances of the resurrected Jesus. The omission of reference to Jesus' birth and resurrection as supernatural tend to emphasize Jesus' humanity and to subordinate his person to his role as the initiator of God's kingdom. For the author of Matthew, from birth story to resurrection Jesus constitutes the fulfillment of the Torah. His family's flight from Herod at his birth, from Palestine to Egypt and back, parallels the story of the Israelites from their flight from famine to Egypt, to God's giving of Torah through Moses, to the Israelites' return to Canaan. During his life Jesus fulfills the requirements of Torah as summed up in the commandments to love God and neighbor. He furthermore shows special care for children. Moreover, he instructs his followers shortly before his death to minister to him in service to the dispossessed. Rather than imitate Christ, the followers are to seek and find Christ in the very faces of the dispossessed and serve him there, registering a shift in ethical priority from the moral quality of an agent's acts to the material, ethical, and spiritual needs of others. For Luke, Jesus fulfills the ancient prophecies of the one who will bring justice, conceived as an inversion of the present oppressive structures as power. For the author of John, Jesus is the cosmic Christ who preexists as the very Word of God at creation.

Such differences in christology erupted into contention within a particular community or set of communities. The Gospel of John serves as a case in point. Daniel Boyarin argues, persuasively in my opinion, that this Gospel originated out of a distinctively Jewish form of mysticism. As a form of Jewish mysticism it represents one side of a controversy among Jews over the status of Torah in relation to God's Logos (also of Jewish, not Christian, origin, according to Boyarin), as well as the nature of the Logos itself.[19] According to Boyarin, what specifically makes John's Gospel most controversial among Jews is neither the identification of the Word or Logos with divine Wisdom or Sophia, nor the identification of the Logos as God, but the claim made by the author of the Gospel in 1:14 that the Logos takes on flesh. What becomes anti-Judaism in later times begins as a contention among Jewish communities, erupting over the claim that Jesus is the Logos in the flesh.

Other biblical scholars have argued, less persuasively to my mind, for a historical relationship between the Gospel of John and the noncanonical Gospel of Thomas. Elaine Pagels suggests, for example, that the two Gospels, taken together, represent a contention among communities over a gnostic understanding of the significance of the figure of Jesus (found in Thomas), to which the comparatively more universalistic christology found in John is a response.[20] For example, one aspect of the controversy consists in whether the believer is to do as Jesus did in order to find the way back to God the Father or to believe in the person and work of Jesus as the Son of God the Father as the only way to salvation. Are followers to bring forth that which they have within themselves to save themselves (Thomas, saying 70) or to worship Jesus exclusively as "the way, the truth, and the light" (John 14:6)? This contention represents two very different understandings of salvation—the salvation of the few who have access to knowledge of what is required in their self-realization and those who quite simply believe in the person of Jesus as their savior. Those who take on the task of their own salvation in imitation of Jesus constitute an elect few to whom this knowledge of this particular way has been revealed. Belief in the person of Jesus as the exclusive way to God requires comparatively far less rigorous self-discipline and the surrender of self-reliance; in this respect it is open to a larger number of possible adherents and subject to external authority. Placing these two texts together gives one entry to what was to erupt as a major controversy between gnostic and universalistic Christians.

While I think Boyarin makes the better case, both Boyarin and Pagels agree on one very important point. The Gospel of John provides an example of one response in the midst of a multifaceted contention, a contention that reflects an underlying plurality of views of Jesus, his authority, and his status in relation to those who claimed him as central to their lives. It was this response with its claim on Jesus as exclusively the way to God that was canonized. This christological exclusivity became authoritative even over other canonical views such as Paul's more theocentric and pluralistic view of Jewish-gentile relations in Romans. Whatever the original context, the claim to exclusivity served to buttress hierarchical authority and religious supremacy for subsequent history.

VALENTINIAN GNOSTICISM

At the time these early materials circulated in oral and written form, the disparate communities possessed no single agreed upon scripture, governing structure, universally shared creed or doctrine, or single definitive representation of Jesus. That there exist what we now designate as canonical and noncanonical materials, both of which emerge within close temporal and geographical proximity to one another, points to one of the earliest in a series of controversies that would beset the new communities, the issue of what constituted authoritative scripture. By the second century, the early communities disagreed strongly over whether to include a Greek translation of the Hebrew Bible. They also disagreed about what to include as authentic of a vast number of materials floating around at the time that claimed to be authoritative accounts of the life, acts, and teachings of Jesus and his disciples. Marcion and his followers sought to include only an expurgated version of the Gospel according to Luke with select Pauline epistles. By contrast, Jewish-Christians and other groups sought to include the Hebrew scriptures translated into Greek (the Septuagint) and a wider range of materials focused on Jesus' life and on acts attributed to the disciples as well as non-Pauline epistles to some of the earliest communities. The canon, as contemporary Western Christians know it, was not formalized until the sixteenth century when some Protestant Reformers removed what are now referred to as the Apocrypha of the Old Testament and Roman Catholic Reformers relegated them to secondary status while keeping them in the canon. Subsequent emerging groups claiming Christian identity continue to contest the canon. The Church of Jesus Christ of Latter-Day Saints, for example, claims subsequent revelation to have occurred, known as *The Book of Mormon.*

The early communities also did not agree on how they should structure themselves individually or in relation to one another. Would the governing structure be egalitarian or hierarchical? Would the communities led by bishops enjoy relative autonomy and stand in equal relation to one another, or would they be subordinated to Rome? This controversy revolved theologically in part around the authority, status, and role of the Spirit of God in the lives of the believers. In the mid-second century, Montanus, Prisca, and Maximilla became leaders of an egalitarian, apocalyptic, ascetic, ecstatic Christian community in Phrygia. The movement grew rapidly. Though Montanism was condemned as early as 160 C.E., the movement made its way to Rome, spread throughout Asia Minor, and persisted well into the fifth century.

The early communities moreover disagreed over how to understand Jesus and the Spirit he dispensed in relation to God as Jesus' Father. In addition, they were at odds over how to articulate Jesus' relation both to God and to humans, particularly believers; indeed, they disagreed over the origin, nature, and status of Jesus himself. These controversies were ultimately to produce the doctrines of the Trinity and the two-natured Christ, articulated respectively in the Nicene Creed and the Chalcedonian Formula. Affirmation of these two doctrines would become the ultimate test for orthodoxy.

In short, controversy flourished, and the disputes grew bitter. There was no established force against which clearly defined groups dissented. At this historical moment we glimpse, however dimly, the making of orthodoxy and its necessary dialectical twin, heresy. According to historian Walter Bauer, what was later to be declared heresy—Marcionism, Montanism, and Valentinian Gnosticism, for example—actually dominated the emerging traditions at earlier points in their development as majority, normative perspectives. What we now call orthodoxy emerged as a subsequent minority movement that ultimately defeated the majority traditions.[21] Some, notably the orthodox themselves, would view the ultimate success of this one-time minority voice as the operation of the Holy Spirit, the third person of a triune God. Others, however, viewed it as a distortion and contamination of the early Jesus movement. Though defeated, these dissenting views were never totally silenced; they have continued to make themselves heard throughout subsequent history, as we will see from an analysis of dissent in Chapter 3. In any case, by dint of better institutional organization, cultural accommodation, wider accessibility to converts, and in some cases dirty politics, this minority voice assumed majority status. Theological thinking, particularly christology, both reflected and shaped the power struggles at play in these controversies. The making of orthodoxy and heresy through the temporary defeat of Valentinian gnosticism serves as a case in point.

Little is known about Valentinus, the leader of a gnostic form of Christianity that flourished in Rome from about 135 to 160 C.E., who claimed to be a student of Paul.[22] Born in Egypt and educated in Alexandria, he headed a school of disciples, of whom many were formidable speculative thinkers and theologians in their own right. Much of what we know of Valentinus and his school comes from his disciples and from their detractors, particularly universalistic theologian Irenaeus,[23] rather than from Valentinus himself.[24] From these extraneous materials scholars have gathered that Valentinus fostered a plurality of expressions of gnostic thought among his disciples. Hans Jonas notes at least eight divergent views on the development of the pleroma alone and sees this as evidence that diversity and independence of thought were encouraged. Irenaeus's complaint at the time that "every day every one of them invents something new, and none of them is considered perfect unless he is productive in this way" lends support to Jonas's view.[25] The diversity of views, the relatively few extant texts, and scholarly dependence on the opponents' responses to Valentinian gnosticism render it exceedingly difficult to give an overview of Valentinian thought and practice. Nevertheless, as a school of thought Valentinian gnosticism flourished, evolving into distinctively Eastern and Western forms and providing one of the major sources of contention in the second- and third-century battles to define the limits and scope of Christian institutional structure, teaching, and identity. Where did Valentinian gnosticism come from and what was at stake in the contentions with the emerging universalistic communities?

Though no one can be sure, Valentinus's gnosticism and that of his followers may be Egyptian in origin. It is possible to trace a line of influence from *Eugnostos the Blessed*, a non-Christian proto-gnostic document dated in the first century B.C.E., through its appropriation and modification as *The Sophia of Jesus Christ* as early as the last half of the first century C.E.[26] *The Sophia of Jesus Christ* appears to be a proto-Valentinian document. It depicts Jesus as a divine savior figure within a quasi-gnostic framework. What makes it a gnostic document is the focus on secret knowledge or insight granted to an elect few that saves them from Error and restores them to right relationship within the divine pleroma.

What distinguishes *The Sophia of Jesus Christ* (as well as its source, *Eugnostos the Blessed*) from other gnostic documents is the author's comparatively benign view of the creator of the universe and the created order itself. Though inescapably enmeshed in error, identified with both ignorance and matter, the created order reflects inferiority in relationship to the divine pleroma rather than its evil opposite. For example, the metaphors of contrast are those of waking to reality as opposed to sleeping in ignorance, implying a realized eschatology rather than apocalyptic visions of an ongoing, violent battle between good and evil or light and darkness. Furthermore, the Christianized document's teaching on salvation allows for two classes of individuals to be saved rather than one: those who are restored to pure knowledge of the first principle or Father; and those who possess a defective knowledge, who will be consigned to an outer realm within the pleroma. This comparatively more generous view of matter and more accessible soteriology (doctrine of salvation) distinguishes some forms of later Valentinian gnosticism from other more dualistic forms of gnosticism. *The Gospel of Truth*, a second-century document ascribed by some scholars to Valentinus himself, reflects similar tendencies.[27]

Generosity and relative accessibility notwithstanding, Valentinian gnosticism fell within a wider range of gnosticisms with which non-gnostic groups contended. The central points in dispute were numerous. They included ecclesial structure, the place of martyrdom in spiritual life, and the status of women. Across the board the figure of Jesus served to justify positions held on either side of any given dispute. Elaine Pagels notes that gnostics in general tended to minimize or reject the humanity of Christ by denying a biological or literal resurrection of Jesus from the dead; for them the resurrection was symbolic.[28] At stake in the claim for literal interpretation, according to her reconstruction, are the authority of the bishops and the further centralization of ecclesial power in Rome. Those texts that insist on the literal appearance of a clearly recognizable Jesus reinforce the authority of Peter and ultimately the centralization of power in Rome, where tradition held that Peter, the "Rock," had died.

Pagels raises other issues as well. The insistence on a literal bodily resurrection reinforced the courage of those persecuted and undergoing martyrdom. Martyrdom itself was a source of conflict between those who risked persecution and death by publicly acknowledging their loyalty to Jesus the Christ, some of whom were gnostics, and those, also often gnostics, who remained secretive about their beliefs and practices and even ridiculed those who accepted martyrdom. Those who rejected martyrdom tended to justify their rejection by claiming that Christ, by virtue of his divinity, only appeared to suffer during his passion and crucifixion. In short, in contrast to the apostle Paul, for many of the gnostics Jesus simply was quite simply not human.

In addition to issues of centralizing ecclesial authority and ongoing persecution, gnostics differed from their opponents on the significance of difference in gender. Gnostic theologies and cosmogonies, as well as ritual practices, were more inclined to support egalitarian structures of governance than the more patriarchal and hierarchical structure of the universalistic communities. Gnostic readings of texts, particularly from Hebrew Bible, tended to run counter to non-gnostic readings precisely because of the view that an ignorant demiurge had created the world. Gnostics thus read such texts as the creation story from Genesis 2 as a rebellion against the demiurge and therefore a "fall" into freedom, rather than a fall into sin.[29] Lastly, Pagels claims that the knowledge offered by the gnostics was a self-knowledge, a proto-mysticism, so to speak, that by definition undermined any attempts to regulate knowledge made by a centralized, hierarchical authority.

The christology of *The Gospel of Truth* and other Valentinian gnostic material both confirms and challenges Pagels's view. This christology, while ambiguous on the post-crucifixion life of Jesus, unambiguously affirms his passion and death on the cross as a divine revelation, a feature that distinguishes it from other gnostic and apocryphal tracts. In an obvious allusion to the creation story of Genesis 2, the author writes of Jesus' passion, crucifixion, and death that he "was nailed to a tree (and) he became the fruit of the knowledge of the Father" (18.25). The author regards the tree of the cross and its fruits as a reversal of the knowledge produced in the Genesis account of creation by claiming that the knowledge produced by the crucifixion does not lead to destruction. Though the author does not pursue the issue, the allusion to Genesis appears to presuppose a more conventional reading of the text. At this point the metaphors shift. In order to reveal saving knowledge, Jesus, knowing that he would be slain, takes or becomes the book of the living, the book with the names of the elect written within. For this reason "the merciful one, the faithful one, Jesus, was patient in accepting sufferings until he took that book, since he knows that his death is life for many" (19.10–15). Of the significance of Jesus' death the author writes, in a language reminiscent of Paul, "having stripped himself of the perishable rags, [Jesus] put on imperishability, which no one can possibly take away from him" (20.30–35).

There is no mention of a resurrection as such, either literal or symbolic. Omission of an event so central to the identity of so many followers at least implies a stand against those who insisted on a literal interpretation. Irrespective of the lack of attention to a resurrection, the focus on the sufferings and death of Jesus could easily have served to encourage those facing martyrdom. In regard to the issue of gender, *The Gospel of Truth* assumes a gnostic cosmogony rather than narrating it to the reader. The metaphors tend to be gender neutral (ointments and jars), gender inclusive with respect to believers (children of the Father), and biblical (Jesus as a shepherd for whom the believers are sheep). At one point the author identifies Jesus as the revealer of the "Word," a word of wisdom and love that goes out into the "totality" and brings it back "into the Father, into the Mother, Jesus the infinite sweetness" (24.1–9). This use of feminine with masculine language for the pleroma stands in stark contrast to the exclusively masculine language of those who opposed gnosticism.

Pagels also identifies gnostic cultivation of and reliance on self-knowledge as opposed to knowledge of God as a major source of contention. This is true in some cases. Certainly for some gnostic sects and the later Manichaean movement, the saving knowledge was that "Man" was above all things. Jonas notes that this claim is made by or attributed to the Ophites, and the Nassenes, and that it appears in *The Apocryphon of John*.[30] Whether this is a claim made about the relation of humans to the created order or to the pleroma itself, however, remains unclear. Furthermore, the statement may be anagogical rather than literal.[31] If intended or taken literally, then the claim registers an early expression of religious humanism that would have struck Jewish followers and gentile non-gnostic followers in the early movement alike as idolatrous, only further fueling contention.

Even if intended and taken literally, however, the claim did not characterize all forms of gnosticism. In various gnostic texts, including *The Gospel of Truth*, knowledge of God and knowledge of the human are not set in antithetical relation; rather they imply one another or are, if anything, identified as one and the same. This holds true for non-gnostic traditions as well. I think that the real points of contention were who had the power to define what constitutes knowledge and who had access to it. Gnostic and non-gnostic alike shared the claim that, in Christ, true knowledge of God and self were revealed. Where they disagreed was on the content of knowledge, the nature of God, the relationship between Christ and God, and the place of the knowing self within this schema.

For the non-gnostic, God was the one and only Creator of a world that was initially good and the Redeemer of this same world, now fallen and corrupted by human sin. Jesus the Christ effected the redemption of the world in his material suffering, crucifixion, and resurrection. As the one who atoned for human sin through his crucifixion, Jesus reconciled humans to God. One had only to repent and to accept this reconciliation to participate in it, to be saved. The saved might or might not experience this relationship as a mystical communion with God or Christ in God. In either case, reconciliation and participation were made real through the sacraments, initially through baptism and repeatedly through the Eucharistic meal. The effects were to live one's life in a progressive state of holiness, thus fulfilling one's true calling.

For the gnostic, by contrast, salvation lay in right knowledge proffered to an elite few, the "totality" to which the author of *The Gospel of Truth* refers. These elect possessed, unbeknownst to them, sparks of the divine pleroma within them. Cast into an inferior and alien world, dominated by suffering and ignorance, they lived as in a disturbing dream, separated from their true home (29–30). Jesus the Christ revealed to them the way home, a place of repose and blessedness (42.35–40). This revelation consisted in awakening them from their slumbers in ignorance to a new life. The author of *The Gospel of Truth* announces at the beginning, "The gospel of truth is joy for those who have received from the Father the grace of knowing him, through the power of the Word that came forth from the pleroma, the one who is in the thought and the mind of the Father . . . the Savior" (16.34–35). Self-knowledge, realized at the human level, in turn strengthened and restored divine self-knowledge (33.9–10). This knowledge, though it required formal initiation that took place over time, did not depend on periodic reception of the sacraments.[32] Moreover, the saved, foreknown and foreordained as such, differed ontologically from the rest of humankind by virtue of the spark of divinity they possessed within themselves. Knowledge and knower alike thus circumvented the regulatory power of centralized and hierarchical authority.

Clearly, the contention between gnostics and non-gnostics reflects tensions already present in the epistles of Paul between election and universalism, between ecstatic knowledge and humbly assenting faith, between those of a mature wisdom and those of a fledgling wisdom. This contention further echoes earlier conflict over the status of outsiders brought into the fold, as well as conflict regarding who has the ultimate authority over newly formed communities (members within the group, the apostles who founded them, or a more centralized authority located elsewhere). From a twenty-first-century perspective it is ironic that the choices were between a more activist, inclusive, materialist, patriarchal, authoritarian set of institutions, beliefs, and practices and a mystical, exclusive, anti-materialist, egalitarian, anti-authoritarian counterpart.

Paul himself left unresolved certain conceptual problems in his epistles (for example, a universal invitation to a particular election as the people of God). Yet, he sustained a religious activism with mysticism, inclusiveness among Jews and gentiles, a relative affirmation of the created order, a comparative egalitarianism, and a theocentric anti-authoritarianism. Over the ensuing four centuries, gnostic and non-gnostic alike still taught an ethics of care for the dispossessed. Nevertheless, the radical, political edge, that prophetic focus on utopian justice that held conceptual tensions together, lost its hold as the gnostics turned inward and the universalistic communities finalized their hegemony. The universalists ultimately either assimilated the gnostics and other groups who disagreed or drove them out by condemning their views as heresy, thus maintaining and perpetuating their authority. In regard to their relations with the imperial state, the universalists first sought, like other Christian communities, simply to survive the Roman Empire. With the emperor Constantine's deathbed conversion to Christianity, the faith of his mother, the universalists essentially effected a merger of mutual self-interest and benefit with the State itself. Once Theodosius I became emperor, he officially declared Christianity the sole religion of state in 380 c.e., thus solidifying a clearly recognizable authority against which insiders might dissent and with which outsiders might compete.

Manichaeism and Augustine

As universalistic or catholic Christianity and Talmudic Judaism developed in relation to each other and in relation to internal conflicting forces, Manichaeism, a syncretistic religion, also began to emerge. Founded during the second century c.e. by Mani, a Persian visionary, Manichaeism represented a successful, conscious attempt to integrate a variety of religious impulses from Zoroastrianism, Buddhism, and Christianity within a modified, dualist vision of gnosticism.[33] It spread throughout the Roman Empire and into Asia, where, in China, it lasted as late as the fourteenth century. Attacked by Christian theologians and persecuted by the Roman State, Manichaeism died out in western Europe by the sixth century, though it reappeared from time to time as a strong influence among various heretical groups such as the Cathari and the Albigensians of the eleventh and twelfth centuries. Mani himself wrote down his teachings, canonized them, and encouraged their translation into other languages. Fully seven volumes are attributed to him. Engaging in missionary activity, he traveled widely throughout his life. Between 274 and 276 c.e., he was attacked by Zoroastrian priests in Persia, where he was imprisoned, tried, and crucified. Manichaeism is by Mani's intention a religion in its own right, distinct from Christianity; nevertheless, it appropriates the figure of Jesus for its own purposes, among them to attract converts from Christianity. This appropriation makes its interaction with Christianity especially suitable for a discussion of dissent within the context of religious pluralism.

Manichaean dualism differed from monist conceptions of gnosticism in a number of ways. First, Manichaeism represented an intentional founding of a discrete tradition rather than a school of thought simply mingling with or assimilated to other traditions. It was further a tradition in which Jesus played a major role, but one that differed significantly from Christian views. Second, Manichaean conceptions of the status of evil differed greatly from both monist forms of gnosticism and non-gnostic Christian construals. Third, and most importantly, the gnosis or knowledge Manichaeism proffered was available to all, though not realized by all in the same way. Each of these differences, but especially the universalism of Manichaeism, made it a major competitor with universalistic or catholic Christianity, as well as a source of serious contention.

As mentioned earlier, the monists considered evil as exemplified in the event of creation itself to be the result of a tragic flaw or episode within the life of the divine pleroma. By contrast, dualists assumed a preexisting dualism of a realm of Light equated with good and a realm of Darkness equated with evil. Whereas for the monists evil was a deprivation of the good and could be overcome by the transformation or restoration of reality to its initial goodness, for the dualists evil stood in direct positive opposition to the good and could be vanquished only by containment in its own realm. In short, for the Manichaeans evil was unredeemable. For the monists, the creator of the cosmos, the demiurge, an abortive offspring of the divine wisdom, Sophia, was mythologized as ignorant of its Source, symbolized as light. By contrast, for the dualists the creator of the cosmos, symbolized as a preexisting darkness, caught sight of the light and desired to possess it. This desire produced aggression on the part of darkness as it sought to invade and capture the light. A great battle between the forces of good and the forces of evil ensued. Creation of the cosmos occurred after the darkness stole some of the light and became mixed with it. Furthermore, cosmic creation was a strategy on the part of the forces for good for recapturing the light from the darkness and restoring it to its source. The cosmos itself thus became the battleground for an apocalyptic struggle to the end of historical time, in contrast to the realized eschatology of the monists.

In parallel with the monist classification of human beings as fleshly, ensouled, and enspirited, Manichaean anthropology classified them as elect, hearers, and sinners. Unlike monist constructions, for the Manichaeans all humans possessed light within them, light that would finally be returned to the source for all light. The elect, who practiced a strict asceticism, celibacy, and vegetarianism, found release from cosmic existence within their present lifetimes. The hearers served the elect and enabled them to sustain their practices. Though the hearers themselves were initially unable to sustain such rigorous asceticism, they underwent reincarnation until they eventually achieved the status of the elect. The sinners, meaning those who remained unconverted, would ultimately be purged by fire in a great final conflagration that would restore the last remnants of light remaining within the cosmos to their source. In the end, darkness would collapse in on itself in repose, hence no longer aggressive, while light, now restored to its original purity, would dwell eternally in its separate domain

Within this framework, Mani regarded himself as the last prophet in a succession of four, the other three being Buddha, Zoroaster, and the historical Jesus. Mani as the fourth prophet proclaimed a final revelation, a complete gnosis, one that integrated and augmented all prior gnosis. While prior prophecies were partial, all four prophets shared the status of representing a pre-cosmic figure known as the Luminous Jesus. Jonas notes that the Luminous Jesus is a redeemed-redeeming principle, "his own self cast into all things" (228). Jonas explains:

[I]n addition to being the source of all revelatory activity in
the history of mankind, he is the personification of all Light
mixed into matter; that is, he is the suffering form of Primal
Man. . . , the passible Jesus who "hangs from every tree," "is
served up bound in every dish," "every day is born, suffers and
dies." He is dispersed in all creation. . . . Yet at the same time
with the active aspect of his nature he is the transmundane
Nous [Mind] who, coming from above, liberates this captive
substance and continually until the end of the world collects
it, i.e., *himself,* out of the physical dispersal. (228–229,
emphasis added)

It was the task of the Luminous Jesus to persuade Adam to eat from
the tree of knowledge and to urge him to withstand Eve's attempts to
embroil Adam in sexuality. He succeeded in the first instance, though
he failed in the second. For the Manichaeans, procreation, resulting
from lust, perpetuated the hideous admixture of light and darkness that
constituted human beings on earth.

Like other dualist gnostics, particularly the Ophites and the
Nassenes, Mani read Genesis 2–3 as the first act on the part of physically
bound human beings to discover the knowledge or gnosis that would
release them from the prison of cosmic existence. He further viewed
Eve as the result of a fall from androgyny, perpetrated by the forces of
evil to perpetuate the entanglement of light with matter or darkness
through sexual lust leading to procreation. While this view might have
been compatible up to a point with some of the monist construals
of Genesis, earlier Jewish Christians would have found unacceptable
Mani's association of a preexisting Christ figure with the serpent of
Genesis 2–3, along with his rejection of procreation and family life.
For all their misogyny and ambivalence toward sex, the same would
hold true for many of the later universalistic or catholic bishops as well.
Augustine, the Bishop of Hippo, a Manichaean hearer for ten years, led
the fourth-century church's response to Manichaean teachings.

Augustine, preacher and theologian as well as bishop, was arguably
the single most influential thinker and leader of the Western church
from the fourth century until the late Middle Ages. Catholic and
Protestant theologians, along with philosophers of all stripes, continue
to this day to study his writings as resources for their own work, and
secular historical and psycho-biographical scholarship on Augustine is
somewhat more than a cottage industry in its own right. From the late
fourth century C.E. well into the fifth, he produced countless sermons

and theological works. He is probably best known for the *Confessions*, an account of his conversion to Christianity during his youth, considered to be one of the first autobiographies in Western literature, if not the first. Another of his classics is *The City of God*, a central building block in the architecture of church-state relations in the late Roman Empire.

Many of his writings are polemical attacks on various theological positions flourishing at his time that, in part due to the skill of his refutation, were declared heresies, among them Pelagianism (the notion that sin is acquired after birth and can through free will be overcome) and the Donatist controversy (the notion that the efficacy of the elements of the sacrament of Communion depends on the moral and spiritual purity of those who distribute them). Because Manichaeism and Christianity shared symbols, most notably the figures of Jesus and Adam, Augustine considered Manichaeism particularly noxious. He disagreed with the Manichaeans on many grounds, among them: their conception of God as capable of change; their panpsychism (the attribution of soul or consciousness to all life); their views of matter, the human body, and sexuality; their determinism in regard to the human will in embodied form; their trust in astrology; their strict vegetarianism; and their rejection of the Hebrew Bible or Old Testament. That he produced several volumes written against Manichaeism over his lifetime testifies to the success of Manichaeism as a competitor with Christianity.[34] (It may also evidence an extreme defensiveness on Augustine's part in regard to his own past. Not only had he been a hearer before converting to Christianity, his religion of birth, but he also had converted friends to Manichaeism.) I will examine briefly one small selected text to get a sample of how christological thinking works itself out in relation to non-Christian traditions.

On Genesis against the Manichees, two volumes written within two years of Augustine's baptism as a Christian, reflects the first of Augustine's many interpretations of Genesis 1–3.[35] What concerns me particularly is his argument for identifying Adam with Jesus as the Christ and Manichaeism with the serpent. In so doing he aims to refute the Manichaean view that argued that the Luminous Jesus persuaded Adam to eat of the tree of the knowledge of good and evil, thereby implying an identification of Jesus with the serpent. As he proceeds from what he calls a historical (literal) interpretation to what he calls a prophetic (typological) interpretation of Genesis 2–3, Augustine allegorically identifies Adam as the Christ and correlatively Eve as the church. By extension this identification through Adam to all subsequent humanity within the church makes Christians the bearers of Christ in accordance with Augustine's interpretation of Matthew 25:40. Augustine distinguishes the true fruits of all the other trees of the Garden of Eden as the fruits of the Spirit, in contrast to the fruits of the tree of knowledge. These fruits, comprised of virtues and affections, include "charity, joy, peace, patience, kindness, goodness, faith, gentleness, continence" as opposed to a knowledge of good and evil, the acquisition of which would make one "as gods" (134 and 135 respectively). In making this contrast Augustine notes that Catholics come to the knowledge of good and evil through their experience of the difference between "simple Catholic faith and the deceit of the heretics" (124). He writes:

> For we have in this way come to the knowledge of good and evil. For he [the apostle Paul] said, "It is necessary that there also be heresies so that the approved among you might become manifest" [1 Cor. 11:19]. For that serpent taken prophetically signifies the poisons of the heretics and especially of these Manichees and all those opposed to the Old Testament. . . . In general, all heretics deceive by the promise of knowledge and find fault with those whom they find believing in all simplicity. (135)

Two features make this passage particularly intriguing—the appropriation of the Pauline text and the epistemological role played by heresy in relation to orthodoxy.

The Pauline text makes no reference to heresy in the more formal sense of false doctrine, as Augustine uses the term. Rather, as I have noted, heresy in Paul's time refers to divisions or factions surrounding practice within and across the early communities. The distinction between orthodoxy and heresy in this latter sense had yet to develop historically. The Vulgate text transliterates the Greek *haeresis* to the Latin *haereses*, which Augustine takes to mean heresy in the formal sense. The text in transliterated form reflects how the act of translation itself is never culturally neutral, therefore always subject to possible, serious distortion.[36] Furthermore, Augustine, albeit a master of literary analysis, takes the verse completely out of context to suit his own immediate purposes. As I noted in the previous discussion of 1 Corinthians, Paul is addressing division within the community over the celebration of the Lord's Supper as an act of gluttony while letting poor communicants go hungry. As it occurs in context with other verses, the passage more accurately reads:

For to begin with, when you come together as a church, I hear that there are divisions among you; and to some extent I believe it. Indeed, there have to be factions among you, for only so will it become clear who among you are genuine. When you come together, it is not really to eat the Lord's supper. For when the time comes to eat, each of you goes ahead with your own supper, and one goes hungry and another becomes drunk. What! Do you not have homes to eat and drink in? Or do you show contempt for the church of God and humiliate those who have nothing? What should I say to you? Should I commend you? In this matter I do not commend you! (11:18–22)

The extended passage (11:17–34) includes a commendation to believers to place themselves under God's judgment rather than their own because their own self-judgment would be insufficiently self-critical (11:31–32). As I noted earlier, Paul is addressing internal differences surrounding the attitude and practices associated with the celebration of the meal. In context, in verse 19—"Indeed, there have to be factions among, for only so will it become clear who among you are genuine"— Paul is making an apocalyptic statement; he viewed "factions" as a sure sign that the end times were near. Likely unaware of the context for the passage, Augustine has stood this passage on its head as a justification for asserting the genuineness of his position over against those of a distinctively different tradition. (One could have spiritualized the passage in the opposite direction, for example, by interpreting it as a philosophical claim that truth arises dialectically out of ongoing contention from a number of different perspectives.) Worse still, he has authorized this inversion by a spiritualized and exclusivist reading of Matthew 25:40, the culmination of Jesus' injunction to his followers to minister to him by ministering to the dispossessed who make up his family. Rather than minister to Christ by feeding the hungry, welcoming the stranger, and clothing the naked, Christians, according to Augustine, are to become Christ by cultivating certain virtues and affections that distinguish them in their faith from the Manichaeans in their knowledge. In short, in Augustine's hands identification with the outcast shifts to identification with established power.

It is not the case that Augustine should have somehow exercised modern literary and historical-critical skills. Furthermore, he did not know Greek and had available to him only the Vulgate. Rather, Augustine's interpretation reflects the solidification of and theological justification for the distinction between orthodoxy and heresy, its further extension of applicability from intrareligious conflict to interreligious conflict, and the spiritualization of ethical, political activism that had characterized the earliest communities. By Augustine's time and with his aid, a hard and fast distinction between heresy and orthodoxy, its application to both internal and external opposition and competition, and the spiritualization of ethical meaning in scripture had become so deeply embedded in ecclesial identity that any attempt to think outside them was all but impossible. Difference from standardized church teaching had become valorized as heresy by definition—a far cry from the diversity of the earliest communities. Though the earliest communities fought among themselves over what constituted true practice and teaching, Paul fought for a zone defined as "things indifferent" which tolerated relative diversity in practice; for example, he argued for tolerance of difference in practices or observance between Jews and gentiles. Just as importantly, he relativized even his own position, in relation to others, before his God. Likewise, some of the groups now labeled gnostic sought to create space for individual autonomy in relation to one's spiritual development. They further encouraged difference in theological speculation and doctrine. While hardly pluralists in the sense of total relativism of all practices and beliefs, some of the early leaders and their communities clearly tolerated, and in some cases positively valued, a relatively high level of difference in opinion and practice.

By the fifth century, for the universalists, in contrast to the earlier internally pluralistic movement, heresy had become formalized and logically necessary in order for orthodoxy to be recognizable as such. The one and only acceptable faith depended on its contrast with heresy in order to shake out or make manifest those who held to approved teachings, to the truth. Those who promised knowledge, as opposed to simple faith, ironically produced truth by standing as false in relation to it. Those who produced truth could judge it to be so only by contrasting it with presumed falsity. This dialectical irony generated a substantive one as well. In this case the choices were between two universalistic traditions—Manichaeism as a dualistic, anthropocentric, rigidly ascetic, matter-despising tradition that evolved out of an openness to integrating a number of different traditions, and universalistic Christianity as a monistic, theocentric, comparatively less ascetic and more matter-affirming tradition that identified all differences with heresy. In the case of Manichaeism, Jesus as the Luminous Jesus promised liberation to an a-cosmic existence. In the case of Christianity, Jesus—understood by Augustine as the inner Teacher and the Word of God, internalized as certain virtues and affections in all believers—led believers to right relation with God within cosmic existence first and only later beyond it.[37]

CHRISTOLOGICAL IMAGINATION, INSTITUTIONAL PRESERVATION, AND DISSENT

We learn how the human imagination works by examining its practices and its products or artifacts. This is no less true in the case of christological imagination. From early antiquity, particularly from the letters of the apostle Paul and the various canonical and noncanonical materials, we learn at least the following: Christological formulae initially emerged to meet practical, liturgical needs—baptism as expressed in the hymn of Galatians 3:28 and the fellowship meal as formulated in 1 Corinthians 11. Within the first four hundred years, creedal formulation and theological argument morph into means of establishing orthodoxy, and as such, the ways to construct and preserve hierarchical authority by regulating, indeed eradicating, difference. As the established institution and later religion of the empire, the Church universal lost all distinction from the very powers and principalities that the earliest communities, for all their internal strife, rejected or sought to transform.

Christological themes, particularly in the letters of Paul, address highly specific, varying situations, with ethics as well as theology uppermost in mind. The early writers wrote in an overall context of eschatological expectations; their cosmological assumptions, while not overly systematized as metaphysics, differed drastically in comparison to ours today. They did not draw fine distinctions between fact and fiction, religion and politics, or piety and activism. They often wrote in a historical context of great social depression, fear, and malaise in regard to the events of the time, and this overall depression took a world-rejecting, inward, anti-materialist turn for many.

The earliest followers were dissidents, albeit possibly reluctant and inadvertent dissidents. The early movement experienced serious differences with other Jewish groups, with the Roman government, and within the movement itself. As members of a highly diverse Jewish community, they stood at least in tension and sometimes in direct opposition with other Jewish sects and the Temple cult. The imperial Roman government persecuted them, as well as other Jewish groups, for their vision and practices, which the government viewed as seditious. Evangelizing gentiles was one particular way this early movement survived and flourished in spite of persecution; the decision of its leaders to extend the good news beyond the people of God who observed Torah created enormous stress within the various communities in regard to determining the expectations for gentile converts.

The early followers' orientation toward practical needs, their eschatological expectations, their historical context, their conflicts within and across religious communities, and their persecution by the Roman state produced a number of strategies informing how they conceived and understood the figure of Jesus. The Pauline epistles in particular are exhortatory, situational, provisional, and ambiguous about relations to and with the world. Dependent on Hebrew scripture, oriented toward the future, and eclectic in relation to non-Jewish traditions, the epistles reflect communities internally at odds over the relations between the particular concerns of the group and the universality of its ethics, as manifested in its invitation to outsiders. This tension later transmuted into conflict between universalistic communities and elitist ones.

While the later communities continued to experience theological creativity in the extreme, they also had to confront both the pluralism and the conflicts of the first half of the first century. They thus contended with one another, the conflict between gnostic elitists and universalistic or catholic Christians serving as a prime example. They further contended with other emerging traditions—notably Talmudic Judaism and Manichaeism—and with the Roman imperial cult and various pagan groups.

In short, from its inception the figure of Jesus manifested many faces. It was characteristically pluralistic in its internal workings. It emerged as a cacophony of oral and textual images. The apostle Paul, among others, drew upon a wealth of material in creative ways to respond to varying circumstances without the need for systematizing according to consistency. Whether one's eschatology was imminent or realized, time worked in favor of emphasizing the situation at hand over planning for an enduring historical future. By the time of Augustine a major shift had occurred. In the Western church Augustine's theology makes official the shift of the kingdom of God, from both a hope for the immediate future on earth and an internalized eternal present, to a life after death in heaven. What began as an internally plural, dissident movement now takes shape, on paper at least, as a monocultural, established religion of an imperial state. In spite of this shift from a plural to a monolithic structure, the writings of Paul, Valentinus, Mani, and Augustine represent what were to become characteristic features or ways of imagining that continue into the present as modified by continuing, changing circumstances. Some of these strategies bear further critical scrutiny.

As a Jew called to extend the promises of God in Christ to the gentiles, Paul works at the margins of multiple religious traditions, Hellenistic culture, and the Roman State. In his epistles he consistently opposes the dominant authorities, whether they represent the Judaism of his origin, the Jewish Christians of Jerusalem, the dominant culture in which the struggling community of Corinth finds itself, or the imperial state. His dissent against these various authorities costs him dearly. At various points he notes that he has suffered poverty, hunger, disease, and beatings. He writes to Philippi from prison. Later tradition holds that he was transported to Rome, tried, and executed there.[38]

As a dissident working at the margins of religious and political power, he employs a number of christological strategies to persuade, exhort, and uphold the communities in his care and to stand against the authorities who would challenge and impede his work or persecute him and those under his care. As one who becomes all things to all people on behalf of Christ, he exhibits a deep sympathy for and identification with the particular circumstances of his various audiences. He characteristically bends gender both with respect to his own call and with respect to the figure of Jesus. As midwife, nursing mother, and father he calls forth a new family centered in God through Jesus the Messiah. Coming from a tradition rich in the personification of wisdom as a feminized feature of the divine life, Paul identifies Jesus the Christ as the very Wisdom of God. Jesus, thus transgendered, becomes the epistemological lynchpin, so to speak, by which God's power is revealed and by which the possibility for an ever-deepening wisdom of God opens up for those who mature in their love for God. The epistles thus pose through the figure of Jesus as Christ an alternative reality to the imperial world in which Paul lived.

This reality is grounded in an economy of grace within which human desire undergoes restructuring as a love of God that transforms human beings into participants in the divine life itself. His participation in this love sustains Paul's ability to live without certainty, to relativize, insofar as he is able, his own varying christologies to a wider theocentric vision, and to be self-critical on the one hand and confident on the other.

In addition to gender-bending and the use of a language rich in metaphor, Paul deploys a number of discursive strategies to fit the specific conflicts he addresses. He challenges opposition directly and with furor and, polemics aside, first and foremost on substantive grounds. On some occasions he reduces or obliterates differences by universalizing them; on other occasions he sustains differences by incorporating them as distinctive parts dynamically related to a greater whole.

Where differences appear irreconcilable, he relativizes even his own perspective and loyalties by standing in solidarity with his opponents in the conditions of shared sin and shared mercy before God. Though initially involved in violence as a persecutor of the followers of the new movement, as one who has joined them, Paul never resorts to violence again as far as we know. Instead he urges patience and the endurance of suffering as a christology of the cross in ways that revolutionize conventional Hellenistic conceptions of power. Participation in the divine life begins with participation in the crucifixion by identifying one's own sufferings and the sufferings of others, including the earth as a whole, with those of Christ. Taken out of context, an ongoing interpretive practice throughout Christian history, this christology could be and has repeatedly been read as an accommodation to oppressive external political and economic powers and institutions. At the same time, placed in context, Paul's christological inversions of hierarchical relations relativize all earthly authority and disestablish its power in revolutionary ways.

Some of Paul's strategies of christological imagining stand in tension with one another. His universal invitation to join the elect certainly challenges any genealogical notion of election; it is on the face of it conceptually confusing even in the framework of adoption. One way to resolve his use of the discourse of election in conjunction with his tendency to universalize, however, is that he quite possibly understood the new order that Christ ushered in to be open to anyone, though clearly not acceptable to everyone. Even so, his erasure of differences by universalizing would seem to contradict his preservation of differences by connecting them as parts related to a greater whole. Moreover, Paul's tendency to universalize logically contradicts the relativization of his own previously universalized position. Thus the deployment of a strategy clearly depends on the circumstances Paul addresses. In short, context, and particularly the configuration of power relations, is everything.

In sum, for Paul, a God of boundless generosity chose to call all people to a radically new life that restructured and fulfilled the very nature of human yearning, a new life present but not fully realized, one that challenged reigning authorities. Though not all would accept the invitation, those who did lived in the present with a focus on a future only dimly seen, though longed for. The Son of this God by virtue of his resurrection, Jesus as first among equals—sisters and brothers who likewise took up the cross—mediated this theocentric vision. Paul portrayed the figure of Jesus as mediator from a number of different angles, depending on the needs of the occasion. He focused most squarely on the transfiguration of desire that it effected—to give up the status of God and cling in solidarity with others to the humbleness of what is human. Though the figure of Jesus mediated Paul's theocentricity, in the last analysis it was God as God who called the shots, relativizing Paul himself, if need be. While we may not share Paul's cosmology, his eschatology, or his view of the resurrection, we can surely appreciate his vision of love as a disruptive, relativizing, humanizing force that frees one to desire the good even here and now. We can also appreciate Paul's willingness to accept seeing into a future only dimly, not yet face to face. Trusting in God, he lived in hope without closure.

Later materials, particularly the parables, and later doctrinal and political conflicts within the movement exhibit some of these same tensions and contradictions, though they fail to sustain the energy. Whether Valentinus actually studied with Paul and whether he wrote *The Gospel of Truth*, we may never know. Whoever wrote the Gospel in any case continues in the same vein as Paul to emphasize a theology of the cross. Like Paul, the author also connects the figure of Jesus to the Hebrew Bible, employs gender-bending in the context of familial metaphors, identifies Jesus as the Wisdom of God, and stresses election. As a sort of introductory text to Christian gnosis, it would appear to be an attempt to persuade any reader, rather than a more specific audience. Nevertheless, the author departs from Paul. Focusing on gnosis without reference to faith, the Gospel stresses that the elect are known before time as named in the book of life that Jesus himself becomes. While election is no longer genealogically defined, Paul's universalistic impulse is altogether missing. In short, the writer was an elitist.

Meanwhile, the universalistic communities gained ascendancy. In addition to their effective, albeit authoritarian, organizational skills, as well as political maneuvering, they emphasized accessibility to salvation for all through faith, wisdom having been subordinated or restricted to an elite few. Though ambivalent toward the world, they retained at least a residue of Hebrew and possibly Stoic affirmation of the created order. Like Paul they emphasized participation through Christ in the divine life, the connection to Hebrew scripture, and a theology of the cross. Like Paul they focused on the resurrection. Unlike Paul, universalists tended not to invert hierarchies of power; rather they eventually grew to identify their interests with those of the state. The universalists further did not relativize their own positions and communities in relation to other traditions before God. Rather, they insisted on eliminating them by pronouncing them heretical, using Paul against Paul. With the first such pronouncement christological imagination became reduced to the struggle to find the single, definitive representation of Christ, no matter how pragmatically conducted, no matter how ambiguous in its effects. While obviously no such standard could be found, nevertheless, creedal formulae evolved for preserving institutional hegemony hand in glove with civil authority. The Christianity that proclaimed a universal love became simultaneously the epitome of the very forces that the earliest Jesus movement initially challenged. As such, it would fuel the very desires that drove the dissidence that it produced.

All of this is not to say that theologians should not draw upon past resources. Quite the contrary, Paul and the writers of both canonical and noncanonical materials did precisely this in fresh and exciting ways. Furthermore, these early appropriators of Hebrew scriptures, gnostic texts, Greek philosophy, and pagan thought and practices did plenty of their own appropriating and distorting in quite creative ways. The difference between Paul's time and that of Augustine lies in part in the difference between an apocalyptic countercultural worldview and a worldview of established power seeking to preserve itself, though the tendency to demonize the other erupts quickly out of apocalypticism in almost any context throughout the history of Christian traditions. Equally as important, many who were not apocalyptically disposed seemed to see multiple interpretations within certain very loosely defined constraints as a virtue. These early speculators did not seek once and for all a final definitive creed or set of creeds by which to abide. Instead, it is as if they thrived on variety and difference; certainly this was true of many of the Christian gnostics and the Manichaean thinkers. Even in spite of past attempts to reduce differences through canonization, counsel, and the assertion of heresy, this diversity continues to this day to show up everywhere, particularly throughout the canon itself.

Later theologians of antiquity more often than not abstracted the substance of earlier christological work from its various contexts without recognizing the dynamic tension in which the texts held different discursive practices or strategies. Instead of critically apprehending the patterns and processes of such thinking in relation to their own similarly specific contexts, however, later theologians, unlike their predecessors, picked and chose in ways suited to support not only their own intellectual positions, but also authoritarian and absolutist structures of power in the face of dissent. Augustine's distortions of 1 Corinthians 11:19 and Matthew 25:40 serve as excellent examples of such maneuvers.

In addition, when they did not simply pick and choose, theologians tried to make these materials consistent with one another without reference to any specific context at all. Subsequent attempts to resolve rather than preserve the inherent tensions and contradictions within the various texts, themselves disengaged from their contexts of origin, conspired with institutional structure to produce among other things a triumphalist, anti-Judaic, sexist, racist tradition, easily appropriated later in history to support colonization, slavery, and ecological devastation. In contrast to Talmudic Judaism, which retained diversity of opinion as a positive value and therefore left room for relative internal dissent, Christian tradition frequently sustained itself by co-opting or annihilating the opposition. This now dominant tradition of self-preservation through opposition to dissent still dominates within most Christian denominations in the United States today. Even so, the canonized texts themselves, inherently plural and contentious in their christological imaginings, continued throughout the next two millennia to produce the desires that inspired dissent, not only within Christian religious institutions, but most importantly against particular civil authorities as well. Therein lies the resurrection of the body.

The slaughter of peasants at Landsknechten bears witness to how dissenters like Luther and Calvin privileged their own individual and communal memories of suffering, their own outrage, their own righteousness, their own vision for the future. Such memories, the energy of the outrage they produce, and the vision of an alternative future may be creative and precisely what a particular community needs in order to thrive. Nevertheless, privileging the elements of one's dissent, along with the demonization of the other on which it depends, reproduces the oppression and the violence of the dominant group. Image © Foto Marburg / Art Resource, NY.

3

THE COMPLEXITY OF DISSENT

The sign in front of the white, clapboard house read "Insight House, An Experiment in Community." Located on South Lumpkin Street in Athens, Georgia, the house stood next to one of its sponsors, Westminster House, the on-campus Presbyterian Center for the University of Georgia. The university had desegregated in the early sixties with the admission of Charlayne Hunter, later of public television fame, now a media maven in South Africa. Her registration as a student elicited major protest across the campus. The Dixie Redcoat Band had led a shirttail parade in front of her dormitory without the slightest shame. The story has it that only the Dean of Men and an art professor publicly stood with her against the onslaught. By contrast, Insight House would challenge white racism by providing for male college students the first and, at the time, only off-campus biracial student living quarters.

Hardly just a dwelling place, the house allowed the six men who lived there at any given time to become a nucleus that attracted other men and women who, with the leadership of on-campus pastors across the mainline denominations, struggled to live faithfully in accordance with their understanding of scripture; together they sought to love their neighbors in service of their God. Black and white, Presbyterian, Methodist, Disciples of Christ, Baptist, Anglican, and Roman Catholic, the students who lived together joined with others, male and female, every Wednesday for weekly communion services. At the ungodly hour of seven in the morning, like Jacob wrestling with God in the Genesis story, we wrestled with scripture and tried to hear what we were called to do in the midst of what was quite literally war in the streets at home, as well as war abroad in Vietnam and war all over Africa and Latin America. The local constabulary, the local Ku Klux Klan, the local churches, the school administration, and many of the white students who knew about Insight House regarded it, and along with it Westminster House, with open disdain at best and hatred at worst. Nevertheless, the community quietly continued its work of eating, sleeping, worshiping, and studying together.

None of the inhabitants took to the streets, though some of their associates did. Their protest—their dissent—consisted simply in trying to make the community work. It was, like many of life's best experiments, one that in the long run failed. By the time I left town in 1970, married to one of those young men, both Insight House and Westminster House had fallen into disarray. The inhabitants had graduated and scattered around the country; the on-campus pastors had with few exceptions been driven out of the ministry by the belligerent opposition of the local churches to their political involvement. We all moved on, though some of us still remain close.

Today, thanks to the Internet, my neighborhood association in Saint Paul, Minnesota, can turn out seven to eight thousand people for a legal demonstration in less than forty-eight hours. One particular demonstration, a march for peace, took place on March 22, 2003, in protest against the U.S. invasion of Iraq. At the time, students were on spring break and away from local nearby college and university campuses. I mention this detail simply to stress that the marchers were almost exclusively locals. Veterans from World War II, Korea, and Vietnam, wearing their medals and in some cases their uniforms, carried flags and marched with young mothers and fathers pushing baby carriages, gay couples, clergy, local politicians, and Native Americans dressed in full regalia, dancing, drumming, and chanting. The demonstrators convened at the pavilion in front of the Student Center on the Macalester College campus. We wove our way about a mile and a half down Summit Avenue and then across to Grand Avenue to return back to the campus. That day marches took place all over the country and around the world. One of my friends in Denver marched in the streets, as she told her son, in hope that he would not have to march into battle. We all knew what to do. We'd been disciplined to dissent, and we were passing the tradition on. Yet this same generation, so schooled in the practice of dissent, has produced what is perhaps the most dogmatically conservative, politically repressive, anti-democratic government in the history of the country. Protest notwithstanding, war in Iraq continues.

Participation in a community that originates as a dissident movement carries no guarantee that such dissent will be tolerated by outside individuals and groups. From the time of the earliest followers of Jesus to the present, communities have regulated themselves by exclusion through more and less subtle means. Imagine for a moment: What if a utopian society—or what is more traditionally designated in a Christian context the "kingdom of God"—really appeared on earth in some complete, material sense today? What would it look like in a religiously plural, secular world? Would an invitation to participate be extended to all humankind? If so, what form would such an invitation take? What if not everyone wanted to participate? Would there be insiders and outsiders? How would insiders treat outsiders? Within the community, how and by whom would decisions be made regarding governance and the distribution of goods? What if the charter participants disagreed over the nature, the structure, and some of the fundamental values of such a realm? What would happen to those participants whose ideas and practices were ultimately rejected? How would later generations of citizens be reared? Would they be encouraged not only to adopt the ideas and values of the community but also to bring their own new and different ideas and values to the table? What if they challenged their elders' ways of doing things? What would happen should newcomers arrive with different ways of doing things and different, perhaps conflicting values? How would conflict in any context be negotiated? What would happen to anyone who sought to overthrow such an order, either from the inside or from the outside? How would such a community negotiate individuality in relation to communality? How would such a community, country, or world adjust as circumstances changed? How might such a community sustain itself over time?

Indeed the kingdom of God has already put in an appearance from time to time, spiritually within individuals and materially among various communities from monastic orders to mixed-gender, lay communities consciously self-identified. Nevertheless, such manifestations have rarely endured for very long. From a sacramental perspective of reality, God always governs invisibly in and through visible reality. Nevertheless, such a rule in material form remains to be fully realized in any sustained sense of peace with justice and mercy for all involved. Moreover, were it to manifest itself materially, albeit by the grace of God, such a commonwealth would require the work of humans to nurture and sustain it. So far, human beings have shown a marvelous ineptitude at sustaining peace with justice and mercy, with genuine economic equity, and with political and religious liberty for all, especially for those who disagree with the dominant constituency. Western history, particularly Christian and Christianized history, lies scattered with failed efforts, as well as works perpetually incomplete.

In those few instances where small utopian communities have enjoyed measured success, they have tended to separate themselves, at least spiritually and culturally, often geographically, from a dominant culture, viewed as antithetical and invidious. To the extent that they have resisted assimilation by the dominant culture, they have been at least threatened and sometimes altogether destroyed by both overt and subtle forms of violence from outsiders. More often than not, however, the project has broken down due to internal strife. The problem lies in part with the tyranny of the majority. For example, Francis Parkman, a historian of the nineteenth century, wrote of the colonial Puritans:

> Children are taught that the Puritans came to New England in search of religious liberty. The liberty they sought was for themselves alone. It was the liberty to worship in their own way, and to prevent all others from doing the like. They imagined that they held a monopoly of religious truth, and were bound in conscience to defend it against all comers. Their mission was to build a western Canaan, ruled by the law of God, to keep it pure from error, and if need were, [to] purge it of heresy by persecution; to which ends they set up one of the most detestable theocracies on record. Church and state were joined in one. Church members alone had the right to vote. There was no choice but to remain politically a cipher or embrace, or pretend to embrace the extremist dogmas of Calvin. Never was such a premium offered to cant and hypocrisy; yet in the early days hypocrisy was rare, so intense and pervading was the faith of the founders of New England.
>
> It was in the churches themselves, the appointed sentinels and defenders of orthodoxy, that heresy lifted its head and threatened the state with disruption. Where minds different in complexion and character were continually busied with subtle questions of theology, unity of opinion could not be long maintained. . . .[1]

As Parkman emphasizes, and as the historic case of the witch trial of Anne Hutchinson exemplifies, groups that separate from a dominant culture in rejection of its values and institutions frequently fail to make sufficient room for internal dissent and ensuing conflict as normative within the community. Particularly if they understand themselves to be besieged by outsiders, such communities at their worst have difficulty seeing internal dissent as anything less than seditious. Furthermore, even when such communities explicitly make room for dissent, they have serious difficulty sustaining dissent as a value, especially when they perceive themselves threatened by external forces. This difficulty has historically held true with respect to most communities, whether the community is self-consciously religious or secular.

The history of the United States serves as a prime example. While hardly to be confused with the kingdom of God, it was born by revolution out of a mixed heritage, reflecting a combination of Christian and European Enlightenment values, beliefs, practices, and concerns enmeshed in economic circumstances. Visions of the kingdom of God inform its Christian heritage, while visions of Plato's *Republic* and British philosophical liberalism reflect the influence of the Enlightenment. As a historical succession of experiments in republican democracy, it is still a work in progress. Its founding documents seek to insure, among other things, a right to dissent. The U.S. Constitution in particular guarantees through the First Amendment the rights to free speech, free press, free assembly, freedom of religion, and due process. Even today, though Americans in general and American Christians in particular pride themselves on a constitutionally guaranteed right to dissent, in actual practice much remains the same since the founding of the Boston colony as portrayed by Parkman.

We no longer burn heretics at the stake, nor do we drown witches. We have grown more subtle. We may medicalize dissent, by construing it as individual disease or pathological deviance, rather than religious and political protest. We may criminalize dissent when, under perceived risk to national security, we suspend civil liberties. Within the United States we more often simply brand the opposition as disloyal, often at great economic, political, psychological, and spiritual cost to those so designated. We spy upon allegedly suspicious individuals and groups in the name of national security. We discredit the intentions and vilify the character of those who disagree, rather than addressing the substance of their disagreements. As for those profiled as potential threats to security, we are not above employing torture to extract confessions to crimes that, as it all too often turns out later, they did not commit. As for what our government views to be external threats, we are not above military invasion and assassination and, failing these activities, subverting democratically elected governments of sovereign states by supporting anti-democratic, oppressive forces with values totally antithetical to the Constitution by which we claim ourselves to be governed. We simply have not yet realized in practice what it means to agree to disagree, or by extension, what it means to depend on a loyal opposition as a positive, creative force in the work of making human and wider planetary existence more humane. This failure gets re-enacted at every level of human intercourse, from our most personal interactions to our professional or vocational lives, from our religious practices to our national life.

Yet dissent persists in a wide-ranging variety of forms, both intentional and unintentional, in spite of both conscious and unconscious attempts to suppress it. For those who cherish dissent, two questions thus emerge: On the one hand, how is it that even those polities that seek to insure dissent fall prey to its suppression, sometimes knowingly, sometimes unwittingly? On the other hand, how does dissent persist, in spite of what are often overwhelming obstacles to it? Common sense suggests that fear of difference and the loss of security that difference poses, along with the threat of a loss of power, perceived or real, play key roles in the suppression of dissent. I propose that, within Christian contexts, dissent persists in spite of suppression in no small part because of the lure of the figure of Jesus, recognized however inchoately as himself a dissident born of a divine generosity.

To address these questions sufficiently, however, requires a sustained exploration of the nature of dissent. This exploration must begin with attention to the forms of dissent as actually practiced or manifested; otherwise our conception of dissent will become overly rationalized and voluntaristic. Dissent is a negotiation of power, usually by way of deliberately or inadvertently contesting it. Power, as I understand it, refers to social networks or arrangements of intentional and unintentional interactions circulating to produce, sustain, and dissolve society. Though such systems may alter gradually or radically, nothing accessible to humans exists outside some kind of system of power. Metaphorically speaking, the distribution of power, while it may be unequal, more accurately resembles energy circulating through electric circuitry rather than a simple, clear-cut exercise of control by one individual or group over another. By implication, at no point within a system can any single person or group be altogether powerless or absolutely powerful. Rather, power is relative to social position within a given network. At the same time it is always in the process of negotiation, as distinguished from fixed and quantifiable. In this respect humans are both the effects of power relations and responsible for their production, reproduction, and dissolution.

I am obviously indebted for this construal of power to French theorist Michel Foucault.[2] Nevertheless, I inject more intentionality into the system than Foucault would allow. Furthermore, this injection stands in direct tension with his deliberately non-personalistic language of circuitry and circulation. In my opinion, we are caught in the paradox of being morally and politically accountable co-producers of a world that produced us, including our views of agency, a world over which we have no ultimate control. It is my aim, among others, to convey this paradox throughout this discussion of dissent. In other words, dissent in the context of this conceptualization of power is not simply intentional, rationally expressed disagreement with established intellectual positions, norms, and institutions with the aim of taking, shifting, or changing the structure of control, though this is one of its definitions. Rather, it is far more complicated, particularly when the "establishment" is either in the making or about to dissolve.

To capture more of the complexity of dissent, I will draw on examples from the sixteenth century. The sixteenth century in particular represents an era marked by the simultaneous dissolution and re-establishment of the central institutions of Europe at the time, the effects of which still reverberate through the late modern period and indelibly define contemporary characteristics of the dominant society and culture of the United States.

SIXTEENTH-CENTURY EUROPE

The sixteenth century saw tumultuous change in Europe. With the Christian defeat of the Muslims in Spain and the ascension of Ferdinand and Isabella to the Spanish throne at the end of the fifteenth century came widespread colonial expansion by virtually all western European countries into Africa, Asia, and what are now known as the Americas. With colonialism came Christian evangelism. Meanwhile, the corruption of Christian institutions accelerated. Exposure to non-Christian and pre-Christian cultures, along with the invention of the printing press, the use of vernacular tongues as written language (particularly the translation of the Bible into the vernacular), and the extension of literacy, produced an explosion in knowledge and its transmission. Scholars of the time began to employ philological methods to approach antiquity, both Graeco-Roman and Hebrew, an approach to the past that was to begin the intellectual journey that ultimately produced what we now call historicized consciousness. This explosion, of course, had its roots in earlier shifts in thought and activist movements. The philosophical theologies of William of Occam and Duns Scotus, along with earlier movements protesting Roman Catholic hegemony like those of the Cathari, the Waldensians, and the followers of John Wycliff and Jan Hus, had previously set the scene for generating what was to become successful, widespread protest. Dissident movements further resulted in religious schism and ultimately in internal reform within the Roman Church. Colonialism, technology, corruption, and protest together produced a time both filled with promise and fraught with terror.[3]

To be more precise, the sixteenth century, the time of the Protestant Reformation, was an age of several religious reformations within European Christian traditions. In addition to the Protestant Reformation, these included the radical reform movements of Anabaptists and Unitarians, among others, and the reform efforts within the Roman Catholic church marked especially by the Council of Trent and the founding of the Jesuit order. Without question the upheaval of the times resulted from a variety of material conditions including new technologies, colonial expansion, and disrupted patterns of labor due to emerging capitalism. At the same time, this period also saw great public theological debates over human salvation in relation to human freedom. Are humans free to choose between good and evil, a freedom that makes sin inevitable and requires a human role in salvation? Or is the inevitable sinfulness of such choices the very antithesis of freedom? Does salvation lie instead in release from the bondage of bad choices, a release that depends on God's grace alone? What are the origin, status, and role of ethical action or works within the religious life? What is the significance of ritual and spiritual formation in the economy of salvation? Posing and addressing such questions shifted how humans came to understand their ethical, political, and spiritual agency. This shift redefined their relations to their immediate communities, to religious and political authority, to the cosmos, and to God. We live today with the legacy of this redefinition. Furthermore, the process of redefinition continues. Indeed, we may well be in the middle of another historical shift of at least the same magnitude of what we now call the Reformation.

Such a time, then, provides a laboratory for witnessing how theological ideas and religious institutions, practices, and identities are both the product and co-producer of human culture and society. Studying the primary texts in their historical context allows a glimpse of the growth, if not the birth, of both capitalism and socialism, of democracy, of individualism, and of literacy among laity in the midst of colonial expansion, institutional deterioration and corruption, fanatical apocalypticism, and religious and political torture and massacre. Brief specific examples, negative and positive, will suffice.

One witnesses, as a negative example, the birth of anti-Catholic bigotry, as reflected in Protestant theological polemic. While there was plenty of religious bigotry on both sides, this particular form finds its roots in a polemic grounded in an already existing anti-Semitic discourse. One may read almost any theological or conciliar work of the time, from essays by Catholic humanists like Erasmus and Sadoleto, to the theologies of Protestant Reformers Luther and Zwingli, and find anti-Semitism saturating the texts. As the division between Protestant and Catholic deepened, Catholics became the new Jews. Protestants increasingly identified Roman Catholicism with negative interpretations of the practices of the early Hebrews or Israelites of the Hebrew Bible or the Christian Old Testament, as well as with anti-Judaic readings of Paul and John. Polemic against Jews and Judaism, once the exclusive domain of Catholic polemic, transformed in Protestant hands into a vilification of Catholicism and Catholics that pervades right-wing Christianity even today.

Fundamental ambiguities, the effects of which continue to be felt throughout modern Western society, emerge at this time as well. For example, with the rise of colonial expansionism came the enslavement of indigenous people, particularly in Africa and the Americas. At this time slaves did not carry the legal or religious status of human beings, that is, possessors of souls. In response to the abuse of the indigenous people of the recently discovered New World, Bartolome de Las Casas, a Spanish Roman Catholic priest, argued legally and theologically for their humanity and sought to end their exploitation. In making his argument in their behalf, however, he suggested as an alternative labor force the use of African slaves—a position he was later to regret having taken. Nevertheless, his earlier position legitimated the already existing and growing practice of importing African slaves to the plantations of the Spanish-held colonies of the Americas.[4] What is tantamount to a racial caste system determined by blood continues to haunt both American continents today.

On a more positive note, the Reformed churches emphasized educating the laity. Taken in conjunction with the translation of the Bible into the vernacular and aided by the invention of the printing press, this emphasis spread literacy and generated a tradition of valuing humanistic education that endures to this day. In addition, Anabaptist and Unitarian insistence on religious tolerance, while initially viewed as heresy by both Roman Catholic and Reformed Protestant authorities alike, later made their way into the ideals, if not always the practices, of the United States as a secular, pluralistic democracy.

At a more conceptual level, the theologies of both Reformed Protestants and Radicals redefined the concept *religion* by restricting it much more narrowly to belief and attributing much more intentionality to individual persons. This narrowing shifted the meaning of the concept *secular* to connote religious neutrality, giving rise to the distinction we now take for granted between religion and secularity. Sixteenth-century theological debate thus actually marks a turning point in the historical development of the concept *religion*. The works of Luther, of Calvin, and most especially of Zwingli argued for the separation of church and government. Their various arguments marked a growing tendency on the part of Reformed Protestants in particular to distinguish a something called "religion" that, although it stands at the heart of identity or one's soul, exists in a meaningful way separately from one's worldly obligations and activities.[5] Thus the popular conception of religion as a system of belief, without necessary reference to practice or to material reality and altogether distinguishable from civic life, was born. This concept continues to underlie judicial decision making on First Amendment issues at the highest levels in this country—a particularly Protestant spin pervading an ostensibly religiously neutral branch of government. While this way of construing religion in relation to secularity emphasizes individual choice and belief, it often does so at the expense of recognizing the authority of communal institutions and practices. Though it succeeds fairly well as a strategy for negotiating religious differences, it does so by ultimately shifting regulatory control over religion to the state by subordinating religious interest, now defined individually, to the state's interests in self-preservation.

In retrospect, the tumult of the sixteenth century and its legacy for the twenty-first serve as a laboratory for studying dissent in particular. I have chosen four "moments," so to speak, from a vast number of possibilities to serve as case studies. I intend with these to capture group as well as individual dynamics, configurations of class, age, and gender, religious differences, religious and secular dimensions, and differences in education at work in the practice of dissent. Because I focus on the significance of the figure of Jesus in the midst of controversy, I have sought to be especially attentive to the christological dimensions involved. Jesus stands no less at the center of sixteenth-century dissent than he stood at the center in late antiquity.

ERASMUS AND LUTHER

Born in Rotterdam in the late fifteenth century, Desiderius Erasmus represents the quintessential insider who seeks reform within an institution through rationality and compromise, in effect, a liberal in the broader, nontechnical sense of the word.[6] Erasmus's accomplishments and their effects on later history cannot be overestimated. He learned Greek in his thirties, by reading the letters of Paul and the theology of Origen, who was himself an insider, although the establishment condemned him ostensibly for his universalism.[7] Erasmus's application of philological methods to the interpretation of the Christian Bible and patristic theology helped set in motion what was later to become the historical-critical study of the past. Nevertheless, the universities of Louvain, Oxford, and Cambridge banned his writings. In particular, his translation and critical edition of the New Testament, as he himself acknowledged, "laid the egg that Luther hatched."[8] With his close friends Thomas More and John Colet, he was one of the forebears of Christian humanism. Though a critic of the church, he nevertheless remained closely allied with the powerful within the church until his death. As a critic from within he sought reform first and foremost through education.[9] The scholar's scholar, he preferred the study and the approval of those in power to the public arena of contention and dispute. Even so, he spoke out against the excesses of pope and prince alike, particularly regarding the entanglements of self-interest within relations between church and state and the rush to violence to settle religious and political disputes.[10] Though the unity of the church numbered among his highest priorities, he opposed the use of religious persecution to sustain it.[11] Sympathetic to pre-Tridentine critiques of church corruption, Erasmus ultimately found himself caught between the extremism of Catholic conservatism and the radicalism of Martin Luther.

Erasmus's reluctance to engage in conflict and his characteristically conciliatory and rational approach are revealed most clearly in his relationship to Martin Luther. Fourteen years his junior, Luther could hardly have differed more from Erasmus. If Erasmus epitomized the even-tempered, civil humanist scholar, Luther represented the brooding, existentially struggling man of God. Prior to Luther's posting of the *Ninety-five Theses* in 1517, the two men enjoyed a relatively collegial relationship. They subsequently became estranged, and finally broke altogether over their debate on the nature of the human will.

On the one hand, in regard to anti-clericalism and the abuse of the laity, they shared similar views. Moreover, aspects of Erasmus's approach to scripture heavily influenced Luther, though Luther rejected Erasmus's tendency to spiritualize texts. On the other hand, the two could not have been further apart in regard to theology and temperament. Whereas Erasmus's theological concerns were primarily anthropological in focus, Luther was driven by a radically theocentric vision. While Erasmus sought to avoid conflict, valued the opinion and approval of others, mingled gracefully and sociably with the powerful, and enjoyed the ambiguity inherent in meaning, Luther was by comparison bawdy, coarse, ill-tempered, contentious, not concerned with social niceties, and intolerant of multiple points of view. Their debate over the freedom of the will exemplifies their characteristic differences as well as the nuances of Erasmus's dissent against both Luther and the church.[12]

Not only the dispute itself, but also the events leading up to and following the publication of the debate, throw light upon Erasmus as dissenter (that Luther was a master of dissent is self-evident). Erasmus entered into debate with Luther most reluctantly. Blamed by conservatives for having inspired Luther, he at one point told his publisher, Johann Froben, to stop publishing Luther's works, lest their positions be conflated into one. His wish to be dissociated from Luther notwithstanding, he found much with which to agree in Luther's writings, particularly Luther's critique of clerical abuses. In any case, he went to great lengths to avert direct encounter with Luther. At one point, December 21, 1521, he went so far as to relocate from Brabant to Basel in order to avoid a request from the emperor to write a book against Luther. Once Clement VII assumed the papacy, however, Erasmus could no longer avoid confrontation. Clement, a personal friend of Erasmus, requested that he respond to Luther on what was one of the central points of theological controversy dividing Catholic from Protestant, the nature of the human will and its role, if any, in salvation. Erasmus could not decline, though in a letter to Zwingli he wrote that he intended to attack Luther's position in a fashion that would not fuel the fires of Luther's opponents. In short, his intention was to seek a compromise. He subsequently published *De libero arbitrio* (*The Freedom of the Will*) in 1524.[13]

Luther, caught up in the middle of peasant uprisings, nevertheless responded quickly with *De servo arbitrio* (*The Bondage of the Will*).[14] Both pieces were fairly unsystematic. Luther's response, four times longer than Erasmus's, was communicated in a polemic reminiscent of the prophet Amos, a response that took no prisoners, altogether opposite in tone to Erasmus's witty, ironic, and mildly condescending rhetoric. Erasmus, stung to the quick by Luther's fierceness, responded with a lengthy two-volume, much more carefully thought out work titled *Hyperaspistes Diatribae adversus servum arbitrium M. Lutheri*, published in 1526 and 1527, charging Luther with the destruction of peace and order. Had there been any possibility of compromise prior to the debate, it was now lost. The battle raged on. Erasmus's later pleas for mutual tolerance would go unheard not only by Luther and his followers, but by the conservative wing of the church as well.[15]

Regarding the debate itself, Erasmus begins *The Freedom of the Will* with a very disarming disclaimer:

> Let no one misinterpret our battle. We are not two gladiators incited against each other. I want to argue only against one of Luther's teachings, illuminating . . . the truth, the investigation of which has always been the most reputable activity of scholars. There will be no invective, and for two reasons: it does not behoove Christians so to act; and moreover, the truth, which by excessive quarreling is often lost, is discovered with greater certainty without it.
>
> I am quite aware that I am a poor match in such a contest; I am less experienced than other men, and I have always had a deep-seated aversion to fighting. . . . In addition, so great is my dislike for assertions that I prefer the views of skeptics whenever the inviolable authority of the Church permit—a Church to which at all times I willingly submit my own views, whether I attain what she prescribes or not.
>
> . . . I must confess that I have not yet formed a definite opinion on any of the numerous traditional views regarding the freedom of the will; all I am willing to assert is that the will enjoys some power of freedom. (*Discourse* 6)

These opening remarks set the tone for what is to follow, namely, an exploration, so to speak, of how Erasmus comes to his minimalist view of the freedom of the will. Throughout the debate he positions himself as a moderate, seeking a third alternative to the extreme position of the Pelagians, on the one hand, and Luther's position, on the other hand. The will is neither totally free to effect its own salvation (as Pelagius and his followers claimed), nor is it totally passive in response to God's grace (Luther's position). Rather the human will, while totally ineffectual without grace, nevertheless plays a cooperative, albeit minimal role with grace in effecting its salvation. To support his position he defines his central terms, states briefly his theological anthropology, and turns to scripture for supporting texts, translating from the Greek. Where texts would appear to disagree, he spiritualizes them or argues that they are to be understood as hyperbole rather than taken literally.

Erasmus's underlying christology is that of Jesus as moral enabler and exemplar. Outside the grace of Christ there is neither salvation nor morality. The grace of Christ, however, does not preclude the cooperation of the human will, for without free will, however small the role it plays, there can be no real morality as exemplified by Christ himself and required of Christians (for examples, see *Discourses* 58, 67). Indeed his chief concern throughout the treatise is to preserve the human capacity and responsibility for moral action.

In addition to drawing on scripture, he looks for support from patristic theology. As he proceeds, he peppers his argument with classical allusions and philosophical examples. He clearly rejects not only Luther's position but also the position that Luther himself rejects—namely, the transfer of merit, the marketing of indulgences, and various other clerical abuses. His point all along the way is to compromise or, as he put it, to define the will "so as to avoid overconfidence in our own merits and other disadvantages Luther shuns, and still not lose the advantages Luther admires" (*Discourse* 85).

As already noted, Erasmus's tone is erudite and, at times mildly condescending. In his rejection of invective early on, his highly narrow focus ("I want to argue only against one of Luther's teachings") and his strategy of affirming his interpretation of Luther's intent and goals almost seem to protect Luther, even as he attacked Luther's position. At the same time he also telegraphs his desired response from Luther and the reader while shielding himself by disclaiming expertise in the matter. In regard to his lack of expertise, the argument he makes belies his self-effacement. Furthermore, the response he drew from Luther was the very antithesis of what he desired.

Luther's response reflects an altogether different type of dissent from an altogether different christological framework, admirable for entirely different reasons. Luther rejected any compromise that he saw as a fundamental denial of the efficaciousness of God's grace in Christ or a threat to the divine attributes of omniscience and omnipotence. For him, human morality was itself a presumption, an attempt to effect human salvation, and in that respect a mark of human sin. Humans were called to seek Christ in the neighbor rather than be Christ to the neighbor.[16] He turned venomously on Erasmus, attacking not only his position but also his intelligence. While noting Erasmus's elegance, he accused him of ignorance (*Discourse* 98), rejected Erasmus's pleas for peace and harmony (108), and decimated Erasmus's argument, along with Erasmus's exegesis of scripture, with a vengeance. The conclusion of Luther's response captures well his passion for the absoluteness of God's will, upon which God's grace toward humans depended. It also exhibits a rare moment in the text of civility toward Erasmus:

> Man, before he is created to be man does and endeavors nothing toward his being made a creature. And after he is created, he does and endeavors nothing toward his preservation as a creature. . . . So I say that man, before he is regenerated into the new creation of the Spirit's kingdom, does and endeavors nothing to prepare himself, and when he is regenerated he does and endeavors nothing toward his preservation in that kingdom. . . .

> . . . I will not tolerate that moderate middle way which Erasmus would, with good intention, I think, recommend to me: to allow a certain little to free will, in order to remove the contradictions of Scripture. . . . The case is not bettered, nor anything gained by this middle way. . . . [W]e must go to extremes, deny free will altogether and ascribe everything to God! (132–33)

In short, Erasmus's efforts to avoid conflict were to no avail. He could not protect either himself or Luther from Luther's vision of God. Operating out of this vision, Luther used against Erasmus the very weapons Erasmus had intentionally rejected employing. It turned into a gladiator match after all.

Gladiator match notwithstanding, the future of the Protestant Reformation, one of the most studied and best known moments of dissent within Christian history, depended in certain profound respects upon Erasmus's somewhat minimalist version of dissent. The written work produced by Erasmus's commitment to seek the truth with relative dispassion exerted serious influence on the Protestant Reformers, most notably upon Luther himself. Neither Erasmus nor Luther originally sought schism within the church. Both were simply doing their jobs,

as they understood them. Ironically, the protest led by Luther that
was to divide the church was dependent in no small part on the work
of Erasmus, who never left the church and whose theology Luther
vehemently rejected.

ANABAPTISTS

The Anabaptist movement represents dissent in the form of intentional
separation from the dominant culture.[17] This sixteenth-century dissident
movement was founded on the premises of adult baptism (the believers'
church) and the separation of religion and state. The Anabaptists
emerged in protest against the Protestant movement, specifically against
the Reformed Church in Switzerland. When the Reformed Church
not only resisted the efforts of the Anabaptists to purify its practices
but also executed, persecuted, or exiled them, the survivors sought,
largely through separation from the surrounding culture, to form new,
voluntary religious communities based solely on biblical principles
as they understood them. Although the term *Anabaptist* means "re-
baptizer," it would be more accurate to call the members of this initially
heterogeneous movement "Baptists," for they rejected the efficacy of
infant baptism altogether.

The movement began in opposition to the Swiss Protestant
Huldrych Zwingli in 1525. Frustrated by the slowness with which
Zwingli executed change within the Reformed Church in Zurich, a
group of his one-time followers, led by Conrad Grebel and Felix Manz,
among others, began baptizing one another, initially by sprinkling, later
by immersion. Meeting for prayer in private homes, the group sought a
revival or spiritual awakening among those in attendance. In addition,
they regularly celebrated the Lord's Supper, stripped almost entirely
of all formality. Thus, these house fellowships established separate
communions outside the governance of both the Reformed Church
and the Zurich magistracy. In 1526 the government responded with the
macabre symbolic action of ordering all of the participants drowned.
The movement nevertheless spread throughout Switzerland, Germany,
the Netherlands, and Moravia. Because of Anabaptist commitment to
separation of religion and state, Catholic and Protestant religious and
political leaders alike considered them, along with spiritualists and anti-
Trinitarians, to be radicals—potentially if not actually seditious and
heretical. The radicals as a whole covered a range of often-conflicting

beliefs, practices, and lifestyles. Some were nonviolent; others were violent. Some were sexual libertines; others lived in traditional families or were celibate. Some communities practiced communism; others were individualistic. Some were Bible-centered literalists, while others appealed to the Holy Spirit as authoritative in and through personal experience. Some groups were apocalyptic; others were not.

Within this range of radical reformers, the Anabaptists themselves were diverse. For example, the Moravians, unlike other communities, were opposed to private property and held all things in common in accordance with their understanding of the biblical book of Acts. By the mid-sixteenth century, unable to sustain heterogeneity, the Anabaptists soon split into three distinct sects—the Swiss and South German Anabaptists, the Mennonites of Holland and North Germany, and the Hutterites in Moravia.

Though Anabaptist attempts to sustain heterogeneity ultimately failed, the movement sought at one point to clarify the range of its theological diversity through a document known as *The Schleitheim Confession of Faith*, which grew out of a meeting held in 1527 at Schleitheim, located on the Swiss-German border. This confession, along with other assorted documents, including a letter from a Dutch Anabaptist martyr, allows us insight into the rationale for separatism as a type of dissent.[18]

The Schleitheim Confession set out the norms of most, if not all, Anabaptist communities at the time.[19] The document begins with words of consolation and assurance to all those across the Anabaptist communities. The point is to clarify the limits of what is acceptable practice and belief. The focus is on communal and personal life as it should be lived in relation to God through Christ. First and foremost the writers dissociate themselves and their movement from the libertine practices of some of its members. The libertines included persons or communities who "have turned aside from the faith in the way they intend to practice and observe the freedom of the Spirit and of Christ . . . [who] think faith and love may do and permit everything. . . ."[20] The writers admonish their members to separate themselves from the "perverted."[21] The document then proceeds to expound, among other things, seven articles on which the writers, representing their communities, agree. These include: adult baptism; the exercise of the ban or excommunication; the restriction of communion to the legitimately baptized; separation of the believers from all who are not members of the community, particularly with respect to religious differences; the proper calling of pastors; rejection of political involvement with the state and with it any use of violence;

and the prohibition against swearing oaths. The practice of baptizing or re-baptizing adults, the prohibition against taking oaths, the exercise of the ban, and the injunctions on religious and political separation are of particular relevance to a discussion of dissent.

The restriction of baptism to consenting adults and the resultant re-baptism of those so persuaded constituted acts that directly challenged religious authority, Catholic and Protestant alike. From the perspective of theological orthodoxy, the restriction to consenting adults put infants and older children at risk of eternal damnation, should they die before reaching adulthood. When such believers rejected the efficacy of their own infant baptisms and confirmations and instead baptized one another and constructed new communities out of such activity, they directly challenged the institutional structures and authority of Catholicism and Protestantism as holders of the keys to salvation. Thus the practice stood in open defiance of both doctrine and polity. Similarly defiant, but in a different arena, refusal to swear oaths challenged, among other things, the legal system and the authority of the state. This refusal further constituted a rejection of loyalty to the state.

The articles addressing the separatism of the communities flow logically from the rejection of normative religious and civil authority and deserve extended attention. The injunction to withdraw from interaction with the dominant culture assumes a dualism of good and evil in which the wider culture, respecting both its religion and its politics, is evil, under the rule of the devil. To the authors, "truly all creatures are in but two classes, good and bad, believing and unbelieving, darkness and light, the world and those who have come out of the world, God's temple and the idols, Christ and Belial; and none can have part with the other."[22] From the believer's perspective the issue is to avoid the contamination of a holy people by a corrupt and sinful world. God has called such a community into existence to live in Christ according to God's rule as revealed in scripture. Whatever is not addressed explicitly in scripture, rather than being a matter of indifference as the Protestants would have it, is in fact expressly forbidden.[23] Thus there should be no compromise; neither should there be contact with those who believe otherwise.

Violence is of central concern in the rejection of the wider culture associated with nonbelievers. In respect to rejecting Catholic and Protestant religious authority, the writers acknowledge that they are, by virtue of their separation, inviting violence, but they instruct their fellow believers not to respond in kind (133). The discussion of the rejection of state authority, referred to metaphorically as the sword, includes a more extensive articulation of why the Anabaptists reject violence as a viable response to oppression, one that is grounded christologically (134–35). The communities are to remain nonviolent, because Christ teaches nonviolence both by example and by explicit statement. Jesus' interaction with the adulterous woman in the account in John 8:2-11 serves as the authority for nonviolence in the face of state persecution. They are to cultivate an attitude of mercy and forgiveness, one that counsels against sin but is otherwise nonjudgmental. This attitude should carry over into ordinary disputes, both external and internal. Resort to civil authority to settle such disputes is eschewed. Indeed, members are instructed to reject official political involvement of any kind. The writers appeal to Christ's rejection of kingship (Matt. 4:1-11; Luke 4:1-13) and to his injunction to the disciples to take up his cross and follow him (Matt. 8:24-26; Luke 9:23-27) as authoritative support against assuming political office.

The cultivation of an attitude of mercy, forgiveness, and warning extends further to self-governance as well. The lapsed or heretical members will receive first private and then public admonishment to repentance and renewal of their faith (Matt. 18:15-20). Should the admonished prove incorrigible, they will be banned, but they may not be treated with violence for their recalcitrance.

Ecclesiastical and political authorities viewed Anabaptist practices of adult baptism and the rejection of oath-taking as well as the separatism of Anabaptist communities as acts of heresy or alternatively as acts of sedition. In Germany, by 1530, Catholic and Protestant princes alike agreed to invoke an ancient Roman law against heresy. Membership in an Anabaptist community was subject to punishment by death, though the evangelical provinces tended to regard membership as seditious and to seek first the deportation of the dissenters before executing them.[24]

Persecution and martyrdom without respect to age, gender, or status subsequently followed Anabaptists wherever they went in Europe. *The Schleitheim Confession* makes clear that the authors knew well what would befall them at the hands of the world. The rationally expounded rejection of materialism, earthly power, and violence as associated with Catholicism and Protestantism alike, as well as with civil government in any form, reflects highly intentional dissent. Echoing Paul, the confessors affirm the cross, along with the suffering and sacrifice it entails, to justify and authorize their dissent, even as the cross provides for them solace in the face of present persecution and focus on the heavenly kingdom to come. A letter by a Dutch woman

named Elizabeth Munstdorp, written as a last will and testament to her
newly born daughter Janneken, further confirms both the deliberation
of Anabaptist commitments and the christology that authorized it.[25]

Facing imminent death, Elizabeth begins the letter with the words
"written to Janneken my own dearest daughter, while I was (unworthily)
confined for the Lord's sake, in prison, at Antwerp, A.D. 1573." The
events leading up to the letter include Elizabeth's marriage to Janneken's
father, their life together for six months, his seizure and execution, her
imprisonment while pregnant, the removal of the child, now a month
old, and her placement with other relatives. Elizabeth interprets all
these events as the will of God and to be expected in light of Jesus'
death on the cross. She writes:

> [W]e may see and read, if we diligently examine and read the
> Scriptures, that much is said concerning the cross of Christ.
> And there are many in this world who are enemies of the cross,
> who seek to be free from it among the world, and to escape it.
> But, my dear child, if we would with Christ seek and inherit
> salvation, we must also bear His cross; and this is the cross He
> would have us bear: to follow His footsteps, and to help bear
> His reproach; for Christ Himself says: "Ye shall be persecuted,
> killed, and dispersed for my name's sake." Yea, He Himself
> went before us in this way of reproach, and left us an example,
> that we should follow His steps; for, for His sake, all must be
> forsaken, father, mother, sister, brother, husband, child, yea,
> one's own life. . . ." (148)

Of herself, Elizabeth goes on to explain, "So I must now pass through
this narrow way which the prophets and martyrs of Christ passed
through, and many thousands who put off mortal clothing, who
died for Christ. . ." (150). She holds out hope, though very little, for
deliverance from death, if it be God's will, but notes:

> If they have persecuted the Lord, they will also persecute us;
> if they have hated him, they will also hate us. . . . For His
> kingdom is not of this world; therefore the world hated Him.
> So it also is now: since our kingdom is not of this world, the
> world will hate us; but it is better for us to be despised here by
> the world, then that we should hereafter have to mourn forever.
> But they that will not taste the bitter here can hereafter not
> expect eternal life; for we know that Paul says that all that will

live godly in Christ Jesus shall be persecuted and be a prey to everyone. . . . [A]nd Christ Himself did not spare himself for us, but delivered Himself up to death for our sakes. . . . (150)

Her concern is to leave her daughter a remembrance of her mother so that Janneken might grow up to fear the Lord and choose the same path. Elizabeth instructs her child regarding the virtues Janneken should practice, among them, to avoid the ways of the world and "look at the little flock of Israelites, who have no freedom anywhere, and must always flee from one land to another, as Abraham did. . . ." (149). She counsels her to honesty, chaste speech, humility, resistance to violence in the face of inevitable persecution, obedience to her caretakers, and frugality.

Elizabeth's primary concern, however, is with the significance of persecution itself. The text reveals a christology of Christ as exemplary suffering servant and martyr who demands nothing less of his followers. Such demands necessitate that the followers will be few in number, a chosen few identified with the Israelites particularly in terms of their suffering as wanderers, enslaved, and in exile. Nevertheless, these are the very people of God, whose holiness will ultimately bring them eternal life with God. The "remembrance" Elizabeth left her daughter ("This do in remembrance of me!") was the legacy of her own dissent, an example for Janneken to follow. Generations of Anabaptists, quite ordinary people by most standards, inherited this legacy and passed it along to those who followed. Thus, a christology of the cross, combined with a concern for communal holiness or purity, produced and continues to produce dissent as non-violent but adamant refusal to conform to worldly authority of any kind, even at pain of death.

CALVIN AND SERVETUS

Historians are unclear as to why the Spaniard Michael Servetus came to Geneva in 1555, where at the hands of French refugee John Calvin he would meet his death as heretic and heresiarch.[26] Earlier, in 1534, he had arranged a meeting with Calvin in Paris, only to fail to appear. In 1545 Servetus began to correspond with Calvin, during which time he expressed serious criticism of Calvin's *Institutes of the Christian Religion*. Later, in 1546, he had sent Calvin a manuscript of his theological ideas, *Christianismi Restitutio*, with a letter requesting once again that they meet. Calvin refused him audience, kept the manuscript to prevent its publication (though it was later published in rewritten form), and told his colleague Guilliame Farel that, should Servetus ever come to Geneva, Calvin would not allow him to leave alive. Both Calvin and Servetus, men about the same age, were trained as humanist scholars. Both had studied law as well as theology. Servetus had also studied medicine and even discovered the circulatory system of the human body. Nevertheless, the theological differences between the two men could not have been clearer or more extreme. Calvin, however much the Protestant Reformer, adhered strictly to doctrinal orthodoxy in regard to the Nicene Creed, which affirmed the Trinity, and the Chalcedonian Formula, which affirmed both Jesus' humanity and divinity. Furthermore, he supported infant baptism. By contrast, Servetus, in *De Trinitas Erroribus* (1531), *Dialogorum de Trinitate* (1532), and *Christianismi Restitutio*, challenged the Nicene doctrine of the Trinity, by implication rejected the two-natured Christ of Chalcedon, and rejected infant baptism. From Calvin's perspective Servetus was not simply a heretic (and on this matter the Roman church agreed entirely by earlier proclaiming him a heretic), but worse still, a teacher of heresy or a heresiarch, thus jeopardizing the souls of others. Not surprisingly, the defenders of the Roman church felt the same way about Calvin!

The case was one of dissident against dissident. That Servetus had come to a Geneva securely under Calvin's control to meet his death is not entirely the case, however. Geneva was far from Calvin's at the time of Servetus's arrival. Calvin's own history with Geneva was contentious. With Farel he had sought to make Geneva a model Christian community. Their efforts elicited resistance from the civil authorities who in 1538 banished them from the city. In 1541, when Calvin's opponents were ousted and replaced by his supporters, he was persuaded, though with great difficulty, to return. Upon his return, he effected many, but not all, of his desired reforms of church and state relations that would eventually produce a representative democracy that would protect and accommodate the church. Chief among them was the formation of the *Consistoire*, a body charged with the ecclesiastical discipline of the Genevans. At this initial point in its existence, however, the *Consistoire* held the power to discipline up to but not including excommunication, a power that, to Calvin's chagrin, was reserved for civil authorities. Meanwhile, Calvin had opened up Geneva to a rapidly growing number of Protestant refugees, largely from France, but also from throughout western Europe. Opposition from within Geneva arose not only to the *Consistoire*'s exercise of discipline, but also to the influx of foreigners, most of whom supported Calvin. Even as Calvin's fame spread internationally, resistance to him grew within Geneva itself. His opponents won the elections of February 1553. Thus, when Servetus arrived incognito in Geneva, and was later recognized and arrested in August 1553, the stage was set for a political battle as well as for a doctrinal one. The stakes were extremely high and the outcome at the time unknown. Whether Geneva would ultimately side with Calvin remained altogether unclear.

In the beginning, both Servetus, along with his supporters, and Calvin, with his, proclaimed their orthodoxy. Both men were outsiders to Geneva, though Calvin certainly had enjoyed an enduring, albeit tumultuous, relationship with the native Genevans. Previous to his arrival, Catholic ecclesiastical authorities in Lyons had condemned Servetus as heretical, based on evidence supplied by Calvin to his friend Guillaume Trié. Condemned to be burned at the stake in Lyons, Servetus escaped to Vienna before proceeding to Geneva. Meanwhile, in Geneva, Calvin had been forced to defend himself against various charges, among them Arianism and error in his doctrine of double predestination. Though he defended himself successfully, he was constantly embattled with his opponents over theological issues. In their mutually exclusive claims to orthodoxy, for both Servetus and Calvin the very criteria for orthodoxy were at stake.

Placing himself in the radical camp, Servetus challenged the standards by which orthodoxy was determined. Indeed, Protestants in general challenged Catholics on a number of beliefs and practices, among them: the relation between faith and works, whether and precisely how Christ was present in the sacrament of the Lord's Supper, the Mass as sacrifice, assorted practices surrounding penance, the total number of sacraments, the requirement of celibacy for clergy, and most importantly the authority of the hierarchy in relation to the place of scripture. Catholics and Protestants alike nevertheless agreed on two crucial standards by which heresy was determined. The first, known as the Nicene Creed, originally developed in 325 C.E. and later modified, articulated in its final form that God was three persons or *hypostases*— Father, Son, and Holy Spirit—united in one essence or substance. It further stated that the Son, the second person, was both co-eternal with the Father and begotten by the Father.[27] The second, formulated at Chalcedon in 451 C.E., proclaimed the two-natured Christ, truly God and truly human, perfect in Godhead and perfect in humanity. Calvin specifically referred to both as standards to which he claimed to hold his own doctrine of God and his own christology. For Servetus, these two creeds in particular exemplified the corruption of the church.

For Servetus, like his Anabaptist peers, the creeds were simply not biblical. Whereas Servetus sought to reconstruct orthodoxy altogether by establishing it prior to the Nicene Creed and the Chalcedonian formula, Calvin sought to defend orthodoxy as defined by the creeds themselves. Like Calvin, Servetus saw scripture as ultimate authority; furthermore, his worldview was highly christocentric. Unlike Calvin, however, he argued that whatever was not found in scripture—namely highly elaborated concepts like the Trinity and the two-natured Christ—was not to be deduced, imputed, or imported, nor made in any way authoritative. Like Calvin, he sought to take the church back to an original purity based on the authority of scripture; in contrast to Calvin, he drew the line chronologically earlier, at the early fourth century. From his perspective, the corruption of the church began with Emperor Constantine's tolerance of Christianity under the Edict of Milan (313 c.e.) and his ongoing intervention into the affairs of the Church. In other words, from Servetus's perspective the fourth-century controversies that produced the supposedly definitive creedal statements entangled church institutional life needlessly in the politics of the state and thereby led to internal theological and institutional corruption, as well as external political abuse, characteristic of the sixteenth century. Like Calvin, Servetus distinguished between civil and ecclesiastical authority; unlike Calvin, who saw a protective role for the state to play in relation to the church, Servetus argued for a very strict separation between the two.

The encounter between Servetus and Calvin provides insight into the difficulties involved in distinguishing dissenters from the establishment. Both Servetus and Calvin sought as dissidents to purify the church by means of their own respective versions of doctrinal orthodoxy. From Servetus's perspective, Reformed Protestantism as represented chiefly by Calvin stood in as much need of purification as Catholicism itself. Regardless of their commonalties, their vastly differing perspectives on what purification required exemplifies the role played by contention over orthodoxy in the initial formation of an established order. Protestantism, though it rejected many Catholic practices and beliefs, also rejected what reformers like Luther and Calvin viewed as the extremism of the Radicals. In the deft hands of Calvin in particular, Protestantism positioned itself by providing a "middle way," in terms of theological doctrine, institutional structure, and relations to the state.

The controversy between Servetus and Calvin further reflects the shift to a separation between religion and state that was to grow in momentum and later dominate the modern period in the West. In his critique of imperial or triumphalist Christianity, Servetus sought to dissociate religion from the state altogether. Calvin, by contrast, argued that the state, whatever form it took, reflected the will of God, unless and until the state intervened in spiritual matters, at which point, and only then, there was just cause for revolt against the government. Though Calvin preferred republican democracy to monarchy, as long as the state protected the church, aided it where needed in the transformation of the world to God's will, and otherwise stayed out of the church's affairs, it mattered little to him what form it took. In short, Servetus took what U.S. constitutional scholars today would designate a strict separationist stand, while Calvin took what they would call an accommodationist perspective of religion-state relations.[28]

Equally importantly, the interaction of Calvin and Servetus indicates how dissident communities, once established, maintain their dominance if insufficient provision is made for future dissent. Their interaction also indicates simultaneously how heretics may foreshadow, at their own peril, what would later become culturally and politically normative. The trial and execution of Servetus in effect assured Calvin's power and place in Geneva, and thereby Calvin's place for the future of Protestantism. Once Servetus was executed, Calvin's supporters swept the elections, and Calvin's policies were pushed through, especially the much sought-after right of the church to perform excommunication. Geneva became Calvin's, the model Christian community for which he and Farel had striven. What began with dissent in Calvin's case ended as established belief and practice, framed as democratic theocracy. By contrast, Servetus, though he had sympathizers, left no immediate disciples as such. A generation later, however, the elder Socinus, Lelio, an Italian lawyer who wrote theological tracts in secret, was to read Servetus's work and be influenced by his challenge to the Trinity. He transmitted this influence in his notes to his son Fausto, who founded the radical Socinian movement in Poland, later to be represented by Unitarianism in the United States, known for its tolerance as well as for its departures from orthodoxy. Thus, Calvin the dissident played a role in the development of republican democracy, even as his theology and organizational genius helped to lay the groundwork for what would become known as the Protestant work ethic, an ethic that in secular form would ultimately achieve global economic dominance. He played this role without conscious intention off the back of Servetus, who ever remained the dissident whose death helped to produce the free expression of religion and, with it, the legal right to dissent.

Popular Religious Traditions, Inquisitorial Practices, and the Theological Skepticism of Cornelius Loos

Conceptually speaking, what constitutes a *popular* religious symbol, belief, or practice is elusive. In regard to religion, "popular" often forms a binary with "elite." Ascribed to religion, "popular" refers to what lay people worship, practice, and believe set in contrast to the educated elites, the powerful, and particularly those who exercise regulatory control within religious institutions. The relationship between "popular" and "elite" is one of power, as skewed by social class, gender, age, and race or ethnicity. Popular traditions are usually very heterogeneous. Their range may include the practice of magic, for good and for ill, possession of a believer by spirits, trance, the transformation of humans into other animals, healing through folk remedies, animal sacrifice, attempts to foretell the future, ancestor worship, and alchemy. They may simply consist in the veneration of mass-produced icons of a dominant tradition, for example, household shrines to the Virgin or pictures of Jesus hung on walls in Protestant households. Such traditions are often transmitted orally and through material images. By comparison, elite traditions tend to be more uniform, text-centered, and analytically elaborated, though elites themselves are often at odds with one another. Furthermore, lay people and elite practitioners may share the same symbols and practices, appropriated in entirely different, sometimes opposing ways. The contrast of popular and elite may be used either to reinforce the superiority of the elites or to romanticize the comparatively less powerful.

What counts as popular may be a tradition that preexists the dominant tradition and has nevertheless survived, continuing to coexist, more or less modified, more or less subverted, more or less sublimated. As with any religion that grows by evangelization, Christianity has historically assimilated, with alterations, some of the symbols, beliefs, and practices of those who convert. So, for example, the Christmas tree, beneath which a crèche or nativity scene often appears in the Christian home, is in origin a northern European symbol celebrating the winter solstice. Likewise, some scholars argue that the reverence accorded to Mary the mother of Jesus, as well as the practices surrounding her veneration, represent an assimilation and sublimation of goddess worship.[29]

A popular tradition may also reflect a deliberate appropriation or syncretistic gesture, as exemplified by what we currently call the New Age movement with its appropriation and integration of Native

American spirituality with Hindu beliefs in reincarnation. Whether this appropriation challenges a dominant culture or extends the dominant culture by assimilation depends largely on the social context, particularly the configuration of race, class, and gender, of those who appropriate and those appropriated. Throughout the history of Christianity, laity and in some cases clergy have intentionally held beliefs and observed practices from heterogeneous sources. These beliefs and practices sometimes migrate from other major coexisting traditions, as when Christians practice Buddhist meditation; they sometimes come from more diffuse, ancient, now marginalized traditions, as when Christians seek charms, offer animal sacrifices, or cast spells in efforts to shape future events. Whether intentional or unintentional, popular religiosity or piety reflects not only spiritual hunger and creativity but may also pose significant challenge to the religious and political authority seeking to regulate or police orthodoxy. Thus the elites of a dominant religion may come to view popular religious traditions, particularly as practiced by adherents to the dominant tradition, as transgressive or heretical and in need of domestication. So, for example, the contemporary Christian Right has appropriated and modified rock music into its services, music it once denounced as sinful in straightforwardly racist terms.

The concept *popular religion* at this point in history thus covers a vast range of phenomena that cannot be abstracted from intricate religious, political, and economic power struggles that form their context. To make things more complicated, symbols, ideas, beliefs, and practices circulate in all directions. What was once popular may become assimilated into elite traditions; conversely, what was once elite may become popularized. In the end, because of the central role played by power, just as the winners of a theological or political controversy define heresy in relation to their self-proclaimed orthodoxy, so they also distinguish, for a variety of reasons, the popular from the elite.[30]

The eleventh and twelfth centuries saw the rise of popular movements like the Cathari and the Albigensians in France that seriously threatened the authority of the church. In response, in 1231 C.E., Pope Gregory IX instituted a tribunal that came to be known as the Inquisition.[31] It existed in a variety of forms and exerted varying degrees of influence at different times and in different geographical locations in western Europe and Latin America until 1908. At that time, under Pius X, it officially became the Holy Office, later to be renamed the Congregation for the Doctrine of the Faith by Paul VI in 1965. The Inquisition began as a judicial process or set of processes for determining and punishing heretics. In their most violent manifestations, these tribunals resorted to torture to produce confessions of guilt. Those condemned to heresy who did not recant and those who, having recanted, relapsed, were turned over to the state for execution. At the time, heresy was a crime against both church and state and, in the latter case, tantamount to treason. In the modern era, what came to be known as the Inquisition ultimately became a comparatively benign means of sustaining order, right practice, and right belief among Catholics.

The fourteenth century saw a widening of the definition of heresy to include something called "witchcraft," in actuality an association of heresy with popular practices and beliefs involving magic.[32] Witchcraft gradually transmuted into diabolism or devil worship, taking all forms of magic with it. Its purging escalated into the witch-hunts that were to haunt Europe and the Americas well into the eighteenth century.[33] Theories vary as to why the witch-hunts arose, gained momentum, and finally ceased. Clearly a number of factors such as the widespread instability of economic, religious, and political institutions, the socio-psychological peculiarities of local intra-communal conflicts, as well as misogyny in combination with ageism, were involved.[34] Though men, women, and children alike were charged with, tortured for, and convicted of witchcraft, those prosecuted were disproportionately women—roughly three out of four people charged—and these women were often older women. The total number of those executed is disputed among scholars; estimates range from 60,000 to ten million.[35]

By the sixteenth century, Catholics and Protestants alike, irrespective of education or social status, shared a belief in the reality of witches as worshipers and instruments of the devil.[36] For centuries it had not been uncommon for men and women to observe the sacraments strictly while also seeking or administering folk cures, manufacturing charms, and practicing fertility rites that pre-dated the entry of Christianity into their culture. By the early sixteenth century, all such practices were suspect. By the end of the sixteenth century, inquisitional testimony clearly evidences the communal construction of diabolical witchcraft as a social practice, internalized by those charged with and tortured for the crime, as well as their accusers. Accuser and confessor alike assumed a highly elaborate conceptual scheme that produced ritualized narratives or accounts of diabolical acts. This scheme or scenario included, among other beliefs: the aerial flight of male and female witches; the "Devil's Sabbath" as a sort of anti-Mass; that devils or demons assume human form; that witches perform human sacrifice, particularly on children; and that witches renounce God and form pacts with the devil, with whom they have sexual intercourse. The grammar and vocabulary of diabolical witchcraft was as taken for granted and was as pervasive as the rhetoric of the human potential movement is today. The ritualized forms of torture and confession served not only to compel the accused to identify themselves as witches, but to get them to give the names of others as well. Anyone who challenged witchcraft, now defined exclusively in terms of devil worship, as a fabrication by church or by secular authorities was vulnerable to charges of heresy as well.[37]

Cornelius Loos provides an excellent case in point. While not the first to challenge the existence of witches as practitioners of Satanism or devil worship or to question the excesses of the tribunal prosecutions, he was one of the few who did so.[38] Though he did not lose his life for his dissent, he was forced to recant in order to save himself. A Dutch theologian at the University of Trier, Loos witnessed firsthand many of the prosecutions that took place in Trier from 1581 through 1593. In response he protested directly to the authorities, though to no avail. He then wrote a manuscript *On True and False Magic*, denouncing the trials and defending the prosecuted, at which point the authorities confiscated his manuscript and imprisoned him. In 1593 he was forced to recant publicly before an assembly of church authorities. Loos's recantation was preserved in full and is of interest in that it reveals by negation elements of the stand he must have taken in his manuscript against the trials on behalf of the prosecuted.

The recantation covers sixteen points.[39] Among them Loos recants his claims that aerial flight is fantasy and superstition, that there are no witches who renounce God and worship the devil, that magic is witchcraft and magicians are witches, that humans can make covenants with the devil, that devils assume human bodies, that the devil has sexual intercourse with human beings, that one can see spirits, that witches can do what devils do with the devils' aid. In short, in his manuscript he had rejected the whole conceptual apparatus of diabolical witchcraft as bogus, as fantasy.

He not only rejected the conceptual framework but also challenged the motivations for the witch trials and the means by which confessions were sought. Regarding motivation, he recants charging the magistracies with tyranny, corruption, and greed ("a new alchemy gold and silver coined from human blood").[40] He also recants his charge that the popes who granted the power to proceed against witches were coerced into doing so out of fear that they too would face accusations of practicing magic. As for means, he takes back the charge that false confessions are extracted through torture and that consequently innocent people are butchered.

Among the sixteen points, the sixth and the fourteenth are explicitly theological. Point six takes back his charge that magic should not be identified with diabolical witchcraft (*maleficium*) nor with those who perform it identified as witches (*malefici*). From point six it is clear that in his manuscript he had disputed the legitimation of diabolical witchcraft by the appeal to Exodus 21:18 ("You shall not suffer a witch to live"). In the manuscript he had argued that the passage was to be understood to refer to those who use "natural poisons to inflict death."[41] From this particular recantation and from the title of his destroyed manuscript, it is clear that he originally argued not only against the existence of diabolical witchcraft but also in favor of a legitimate practice of magic, an argument he makes on theological grounds. Point fourteen reflects a christological undercurrent. In it Loos recants his previous assertion "that the opinion of a superior demon can cast out an inferior demon is erroneous and derogatory to Christ."[42] In other words, Loos must have originally claimed that no demon had power sufficient to challenge that of Christ. In short, he rejected the power granted by his interlocutors to demons and projected by them onto those designated witch and heretic, because such projections diminished what he understood to be the power of Christ. Although his full christology is lost to us, one can draw inferences. At the very least the figure of Christ relativized evil for Loos and served as a caution against attributing the kind of power to the devil, demons, and witches—that is, to evil personified—that the ecclesiastical and civil authorities of Trier sought to attribute.

In regard to Loos's own motivation for recanting, he states in point one that his initial claims "smack of rank heresy . . . partake of sedition, and . . . savor of the crime of treason."[43] In short, he was fighting for his life. He lived to fight another day, only to be charged with relapsing and subsequently imprisoned. Upon his second release he fell under suspicion once again, only to die before he could be tried for a third time. The record of his recantation, a testimony to the nature of his dissent, survives only in a treatise written by Peter Binsfeld, one-time bishop of Trier, to defend the prosecutions.[44]

The case of Cornelius Loos poses a host of troubling issues regarding the social psychology and politics of demonization of the "other," the role of demonization in the social construction of reality, and the overwhelming strength of its resistance to dissent. Loos's own dissent, grounded in a theologically justified skepticism, followed by his recantation, followed by his subsequent imprisonment, also raises the ethical question of self-sacrifice in relation to self-preservation. His case raises the issue of unrecorded dissidence and other forms of resistance as well. Just as we do not have Loos's original manuscript and therefore only a bare idea from his recantation of what form his dissent took, we also have very little access to successfully executed strategies of continuing popular practices and avoiding prosecution.[45]

THE MANY FACES OF DISSENT

These four examples of dissent represent a wide range of intentional and unintentional practices of both individuals and groups. The case of Erasmus and his relationship with Luther indicates how difficult and relative it can be to distinguish the forces that represent dissent from the forces that represent established norms and practices, for Erasmus at the time of the debate represented both. Furthermore, even as Luther and Erasmus conduct their debate, Luther performs this same double representation as simultaneously dissenter in relation to Roman Catholic institutions and representative of the status quo in his relations with the peasants leading up to and during the Peasants' Revolt! The Anabaptist movement manifests the significance of communal dissent practiced as separatism from the dominant culture, in this case Protestantism itself. How does Protestantism become established? The interaction between Calvin and Servetus demonstrates the role of dissent in establishing a new, dominant religious and political order within the old, namely, Geneva, an order that retains the practice of intolerance of differing religious and theological perspectives and practices. Both the Anabaptist and the Calvinist narratives exhibit well the reciprocal role of ideas, values, and religio-ethical practices in relation to the material order as both products of and building blocks for culture and society. All three narratives illuminate the necessity for communities of support to sustain dissent. This necessity remains, regardless of whether the dissenter seeks reform from the inside, as in the case of both Erasmus and initially Luther, or separates from the dominant order, as in the case of the Anabaptist rejection of the world, or claims to reestablish the dominant order, as in the case of Calvin with his view of its transformation. All three narratives represent the turbulence of internal dissent, expressed as critique, dispute, daily practice, or open, violent conflict, in the ongoing struggle for political power and religious regulatory control.

The fourth narrative takes on the issue of external difference, the ostensible non-Christian, as distinguished from the misguided and wrong Christian. The persecution of those who practiced popular traditions reconstructed as diabolical witchcraft, either instead of Christianity or alongside it, occurs, along with the forced conversions of Jews in Europe and of indigenous peoples of the New World, as a series of tragic moments in Christian history. Looking back, such tragedies serve not only as cause for mourning and repentance but also as veritable laboratories that reveal the processes at work in the demonization and fabrication of "others" in the extreme.[46] In the case of the witch-hunts, as with the martyrdom of Anabaptists, Catholicism and Protestantism alike represented the violence of the establishment. Formal dissent, by which I mean open and publicly articulated challenge to the tribunals, was almost nonexistent. Unlike the historical figures of the other three narratives, Cornelius Loos, the rare lone dissident, had no community to support his advocacy on behalf of the victims of persecution. Indeed, one of the most troubling aspects of the whole sorry mess is that the dominant worldview appeared virtually dissent-proof. Dissent evidenced that one was a manifestation of the very "other" whom the established community sought to destroy and thereby vulnerable to torture and execution. What becomes remarkable is that anyone could or would openly dissent at all.[47]

Dissent he did, however. Loos's case raises the issue of the source of his own empowerment in the roles of witness and advocate. He had seen the trials firsthand. He sought to advocate for those who could not defend themselves. From what source did Loos derive the strength initially to agitate, later to write a book, and, even after his recantation, to "relapse"? Though he did recant, he appears to have persisted in his efforts as dissident to witness and to advocate. Any answer to these questions would be sheer speculation. All the same, his religious beliefs, his own possible practice of magic, and his reading of the one other extant text that rejected the existence of diabolical witchcraft—the one by Weyer—surely played their part.

Loos's case also raises by implication the issue of whether there was *popular* resistance to the tribunal practices and what forms it might have taken. If so, given that the populace was unlikely to have left written records, it would be virtually impossible to detect what these strategies would have been, particularly if they were successful. There is some evidence, from the trial documents of those prosecuted, that individuals practiced verbal evasion and feigned cooperation.[48] Historians of earlier periods of the prosecution of heresy in other manifestations have detected forms of individual and social resistance that might be extrapolated to the sixteenth century as well. Such practices as playing one inquisitor against another and the use of underground support systems of kin and fellow-practitioners number among the possibilities.[49] Certainly resistance in the form of violence erupted from peasant groups and some of the so-called heretical sects during this time, though the victims of the witch-hunts appear to be far less clearly organized and, being predominantly women, less likely to have collective violence as an option available to them.

Apart from resorting to violence as a response, the strategies on the whole typify forms of resistance that are less clearly recognizable as such. To practice one's beliefs in secret, to appear publicly as docile and cooperative, to distract by drawing one's interlocutors into debate with one another—these practices and many others reflect differences in control over one's circumstances based on gender, social status, and type of literacy. (I say type of literacy because those who are at the mercy of authorities develop a nontextual literacy; they learn quickly to read gesture, facial expression, tone, posture, and other nonverbal forms of communication in order to survive.) The issue of social location and its relationship to nonconventional forms of dissent arises in the case of Anabaptist Elizabeth Munstdorp as well. Her legacy to her infant daughter, her letter, registers child rearing as itself a form of dissent.[50] Though she presumably did not survive to see her child grow into adulthood, she bequeathed to Janneken her counter-cultural beliefs, values, and practices in the face of her own death—indeed, in spite of the possibility that these values and practices could produce the same destiny for Janneken. Elizabeth Munstdorp's last will and testament implies that, had she survived, she would have reared her child accordingly.

Thus dissent can include individual and communal practices performed in spite of the risk involved, but performed in secret in order to survive.[51] Dissent can further extend to living out and passing on individually or communally held counter-cultural values through familial lines without necessarily drawing attention to them. In either case, dissent becomes covert, though in the latter case, still open for those who have eyes to see. Likewise resistance—more generally in the form of reading and responding to nonverbal signification in ways that allow dispossessed individuals and subjugated communities to survive—may assume the disguise of consent or agreement (in which case its distinction from collusion may become extremely fine). In whatever form dissent takes, the discursive practices of dissent always stand directly within the networks of power they resist, even when the dissenters separate from their immediate cultures, simply because dissent itself depends upon minimal communal support and a past filled with resources to draw on.

Both the conventional and nonconventional expressions of dissent that I have identified so far can in theory be abstracted from their immediate historical contexts and employed in various modified ways as strategies in other specific times and places. One more approach to dissent that is specific to a Christian context remains to be discussed. While all four narratives exhibit a number of distinctive differences from one another, they do share, albeit minimally in the case of Loos, some kind of christological formulation that either grounds or confirms dissent. For Erasmus it was Christ as moral exemplar in contrast to Luther's image of Christ found in the neighbor. For many Anabaptists it was Jesus, the herald of God's kingdom whose cross they were called to share, calling them to found new voluntaristic communities under God's rule on earth—without reference to Trinitarian formulation. Servetus also rejected the Trinity in the face of Calvin's insistence on Jesus the Christ as truly human and truly God, the second person of the Trinity. Loos at the very least represented Christ as the relativizer of demons such that the diabolism fabricated by the tribunals and their defenders constituted a defamation of Christ's power.

Not one of these christologies was new for the sixteenth century. Every one of them, along with many, many more construals of the figure of Jesus, had appeared within the first five hundred years of the history of the traditions. Indeed, of the lot, the Anabaptist focus on Jesus as herald of God's kingdom appeared among the earliest interpretations, while Calvin's "orthodox" version numbered among the latest to be articulated.[52] Furthermore, religious authorities had declared some of them heretical over and over, long before the controversies of the sixteenth century. They nevertheless persisted and continue to persist to this day.

In the last analysis, however, there are patterns of dissent that, in spite of their differences, often produce the tyranny of the next establishment. Dissenters, just like those against whom they dissent, privilege their own individual and communal memories of suffering, their outrage, their own righteousness, their own vision for the future—as did Luther in relation to the peasants and Calvin in relation to Servetus. While such memories, the energy of the outrage they produce, and their vision of an alternative future may be creative and precisely what a particular community needs in order to thrive in ethical ways, privileging the elements of one's dissent and the demonization of the other that accompanies it reproduces the oppression and the violence of the dominant group. Dissent as a force for communal and individual self-criticism and growth, though it needs to be built into communal structures, is not sufficient for its own sake. To avoid contributing to future tyranny, it requires the undergirding of a certain quality or orientation of desire, a generosity born of a wider consent or love.

Fyodor Dostoevsky, cartographer of human desire par excellence, required that he write in a space from which he could view a Russian Orthodox Church. At the flat on Kuznechney Lane (his home at the time of his death), he took the corner room as his study, which looks out onto the Church of the Vladmir Mother of God Icon.

4

DISCIPLINES OF DESIRE

[T]o be a human being among people and to remain one forever,
whatever misfortunes happen, not to fall into despair and perish—this is
what life is, this is the task.
—Letter of Fyodor Dostoevsky to his brother Mikhail[1]

The Dostoevsky family's last flat, now a museum, is located in St.
Petersburg, at 5 Kuznechney Lane, on a street corner. Fyodor Dostoevsky
loved corners—street corners, apartments situated on corners, corners of
rooms.[2] He insisted that he and his family live in such locations. He further
required that he write in a space from which he could view a Russian
Orthodox church. As was his habit, he took as his study the corner room on
Kuznechney Lane, a corner that looks out onto the Church of the Vladmir
Mother of God Icon.
    Perhaps his love for corners grew out of his experience of imprisonment,
first in Peter and Paul Fortress in St. Petersburg and later at Omsk Prison in
Siberia. Arrested, tried, and convicted for publicly reading aloud material
censored by the Czarist government, Dostoevsky spent eight months in
solitary confinement in Peter and Paul, where the church that centered the
prison was likely all Dostoevsky could see from the cramped quarters of his
cell. Who knows what he viewed later, upon returning to his cell at Omsk
at the end of a day's hard labor, day after day for four years, his only reading
material a copy of the New Testament? In any case, between confinements,
he and his cohorts in the Petrachevsky Circle underwent a public mock
execution for their subversive activities. Facing down a firing squad in an
open, public space, only to find that it was a performance of political theater
on the part of the state—that his life was spared—perhaps drove him to
seek manageable, protected space. Certainly, situating oneself in a corner
with a view of the source of one's salvation from despair simultaneously
provides both security and openness. Dostoevsky could look out from a
clearly self-defined, intimate space upon an edifice that symbolized for him

what he desired and cherished most—full humanity. Dostoevsky's last flat, in which he wrote what many view to be his greatest novel, The Brothers Karamazov, *sits at a corner, looking out onto a church.*

Today, standing in the corner of this same room and looking out the window, you can see not only the church but to the right you will see also an "erotic" shop advertised by a pair of large, puffy, red neon lips. Farther down the street a vast indoor fish, poultry, meat, and produce market thrives. In stark contrast to the market's abundance, the street itself is still under repair, somewhat dreary, and populated by a mélange of beggars. Old women who unsuccessfully hawk their vegetables and flowers in competition with the indoor market mill around shabbily dressed middle-aged street people, male and female, who squat on the sidewalks in circles to haggle over cigarettes. This neighborhood is only a few blocks down from the famous Nevsky Street, the Fifth Avenue of St. Petersburg, a street that never seems to sleep, at least not in the early summer when daylight stretches on endlessly and the stars never shine. Provided you can afford it, you can buy virtually anything you want here, including the experience of visiting Dostoevsky's flat. Beggars, hawkers, and hagglers nevertheless attest to the fact that not everyone can afford to pay the required price.

It's all readily available, everything the heart desires: God, Jesus, sex, food, necessary retail goods, and luxury items alike. This abundance is vividly present to all the senses, yet for the beggars, absent in its very presence. Need and desire, their denial, and their transgression converge at 5 Kuznechney Street—a convergence that would not have escaped Fyodor Dostoevsky's notice, one of the nineteenth century's major architects of human desire, a man who for himself desired most simply "to be a human being among people" and to remain so forever.

DOSTOEVSKY AND THE PROBLEM OF DESIRE

Most of us, most of the time, do not imagine, experience, or practice desire as a hunger for a good that we cannot fully know—the good of others, a good they might determine for themselves outside our control. We do not know how to desire the good of others without measure in the midst of material scarcity and existential limit. For all that we want and seek and have, for all that we wish and hope for others, we suffer a severe poverty of desire.

Sappho, Plato, the apostle Paul, the author of the Gospel of John, Augustine of Hippo, Dostoevsky, Sigmund Freud, Emanuel Levinas,

René Girard, Toni Morrison, Michel Foucault—all these activists, mystics, poets, and thinkers have located desire at the center of an ongoing discussion of what it means to be human. Much of this discussion focuses on the human will in conflict with itself over what constitutes ethical ways of desiring, what are the appropriate objects of desire, what mediates desire and how desire is mediated, what can we know about desire and its objects, and how to behave in relation to human desires. Central to this ongoing conversation is love as the highest form of human desire, the most valued and valuing expression of the human will. The continuation of this ongoing conversation on the nature of desire reflects in its modern manifestations a troubling inability to think outside a series of binaries set in mutually exclusive relation to one another, namely, dualisms of materialism versus supernaturalism, self-fulfillment versus self-denial, and individual self-interest versus a common good. The inability to think outside these dualisms has the ironic effect of continually reproducing them and their associated conflicts in daily human life and behavior. We are subtly, often unintentionally, taught to assume these dualisms, just as we assume the operation of the laws of gravity as necessary to staying grounded and upright. These dualisms help produce a culture of false choices that wreak havoc in human life.

Sigmund Freud provides an excellent example. In *Civilization and Its Discontents*, he distinguishes *eros*, which he identifies as sexual desire, from altruistic love, which he understands as the attempt to love all people whether or not they deserve it. From his perspective, altruism reflects an unhealthy inability to discriminate, as well as a failure to exercise good judgment. He pathologizes altruism as deviant and unnatural, like religion in general, at best an illusion and at worst delusional. In other words, what Freud might have construed in a number of different ways—the nature of human desire in terms of the relation between what one wills for oneself to what one wills for others—necessarily becomes a conflict. This conflict conducts itself within individual psychobiological life and is writ large socially within "civilization" itself in ongoing struggles founded on the repression and sublimation of sexual desire. Freud then argues for one "side" (*eros* as he construes it) as opposed to the "other" (altruism as he defines it). He legitimates his argument against altruism by turning altruism into a dysfunctional attitude manifested in problematic behavior. He authorizes his argument for the primacy of *eros* by appealing to biology, to nature. Given his logically prior assumption that conceives a dualism of real nature with a fictional supernature and that dismisses the supernatural as a perversion of desire, Freud, if he is to consider himself a scientist in the context of his times, must opt exclusively for a crude scientific positivism.

The legitimacy of Freud's approach to science having long since been disputed and refuted, the lingering effect is nevertheless that he enacts or performs what he thinks he is merely describing. Freud, with others before him and since, has set the terms for a universe in which it makes no sense to recognize or speak constructively of a desire for the good of others known and unknown that is not measurable in quantifiable and dualistic terms of deserving and undeserving. This universe has no place for a good one desires but cannot fully know, or for a concept of desire that gives up control rather than seeking it. In addition, this dualistic framework, inherited, assumed, authorized by so narrowly defined a conception of nature, and further transmitted to future generations through Freud, masks the socially constructed nature of desire, its mediation, and its objects—in short, the politics of the social construction of reality itself. Self-interest as the primary defining feature of human desire, understood to drive the very survival and possibly the death of both particular human individuals and the whole species, transmutes into a socioeconomic Darwinism that presently fuels economic theory, capitalist practice, and global foreign policy in Western society. Theory, ironically understood as materialist, at once reflects, perhaps quite accurately, selected features of the material order (more broadly defined), organizes the features in relation to each other, and reproduces them as if they were exhaustively the whole. In so doing, theory sustains its own projections as "the way things inevitably are."

Dostoevsky influenced Freud, who read his work and found it profound. The contrast between the two on the issue of self-transcendent desire is striking, however. Throughout his novels Dostoevsky grasped and represented desire ranging from criminality to transcendence with extraordinary depth and few illusions. His characters set out vividly the human desire to be gods, as well as the human desire to kill God, features of the human will that Freud himself grasped profoundly. Dostoevsky also comprehended the full political, economic, and moral terror of both a world with no freedom and a world without rules, the tension between the two later underlying Freud's *Civilization and Its Discontents*. Dostoevsky further portrayed the world of his own habitation without flinching in regard both to its relentless suffering and evil and to its banality, the world to which Freud so stoically responded throughout his work. Unlike many theorists of desire like

Freud with dualist assumptions, however, Dostoevsky understood the desire for self-transcendence, the desire to love without measure, yet with great joy, what may well be utterly foreign, possibly even repulsive to the ego and its self-perceived interests.

In many respects (though not entirely) Dostoevsky wrote his fiction outside the dualisms of nature and supernature, self-fulfillment and self-denial, individual self-interest and a common good, even as he engaged these conflicts through his unforgettable, anarchic characters. Through his novels, as with those of Toni Morrison a century later, Dostoevsky revealed that we are what we want and how we want. He illuminated in minutest detail that we are taught, disciplined, formally and informally by our circumstances *to* want, *how* to want, and *what* to want. And within that world of wanting, beyond criminality and hideous suffering, we may be taught, may receive the gift of wanting a good that, while it includes our own good, far and away exceeds any good that we can imagine. We can further want this good beyond full knowing for all creaturely life, known and unknown, past, present, and future. We may give ourselves over to this wanting and to its disciplines without knowing the full magnitude of such desire and therefore without seeking to control it. We can glimpse this desire, live however briefly and sporadically out of it, live for this wanting, await this teaching. When we do, it can turn the world upside down.

Desire is a central issue throughout Dostoevksy's work. In *The Brothers Karamazov* Dostoevsky explores human desire in relation to deity through his development of the relation of two of the brothers, Ivan and Alyosha Karamazov. Within this framework Dostoevsky presents us with a number of alternatives. Like Ivan, we may seek ultimately to be gods or successfully to kill God at the peril of our own madness; like Alyosha, we can remain fully human in solidarity with all humans. We make God, something both Ivan and Alyosha knew, partly through longing for solidarity with all humanity itself, something only Alyosha knew. Thus, we may, as finite humans, even in our despair, love what God loves as God loves it, ironic in that God is a god of our making. Human finitude and its harrowing circumstances notwithstanding, by grace we can love beyond measure the stranger, the destitute, the criminal, and the helpless—those humans with whom we come joyously to stand together. For Dostoevsky the figure of Jesus, which he understood quite clearly also to be an artifact of human imagining, served as a disruptive, anarchic force that healed and freed humans from living death—a force that mediated and disciplined this desire.

How this Jesus-formed desire operates in human life today is the subject of my final chapter. For the moment, I want to focus on what happens in U.S. society or culture as it is marked by the absence of this desire.

My thesis is simple. Modern secularism by virtue of its assumptions about human nature and the dualisms that form their context cannot by definition acknowledge a place for a love beyond measure. Whereas *secular* simply refers to this world or this age, *secularism* refers to elaborate processes of state-building. Secularism, understood as a worldview, represents and produces ways of being secular, or "this-worldy," that do not exhaust fully what actually goes on in this world.

By *modern secularism* I mean a loosely organized cultural system that orders political, economic, and religious life in relation to a nation-state, territorially mapped, that claims for itself religious neutrality and the authority of some version of scientific knowledge. Its polity may vary, but in a contemporary context will construct human identity in relation to some form of nation-state, including one with empire-building intentions. Secularism's economy in the West will be capitalist and global in scope, therefore, dependent on measuring human worth, insofar as humanity enters into the calculus of the market, in relation to productivity, consumption, credit, and debt, as well as in regard to success and failure, where success depends on eliminating the competition. As a system that orders political, economic, and religious life in relation to the nation-state, modern secularism depends upon an economy of scarcity.

By *discipline* I mean everything from the informal cues or lessons in life that we continually receive from the circumstances within which we find ourselves, to the distinctive symbols, the central narratives, the formal teachings, and the ritual and ethical practices of our political, economic, and religious traditions. *Discipline* refers to how these various, often conflicting, events and forces configure to establish the habits of daily life that make us who we are as ever-changing beings. Discipline produces desire. Grounded in an economy of scarcity, the disciplines of modern secularism produce narrowly defined desires that align self-interest with the interests of the state.

Modern secularism cannot formally recognize desire or love beyond measure or sustain the disciplines that support it, though this is not to say that such a love cannot make itself felt in the world (the focus of the next chapter). Such a love is in fact very this-worldly, though it exceeds the boundaries of any given present, in part by continually pointing to the dimly known past and the faintly hoped for future. At the same time, however, because secularism in the West grew out of and depends on Christian traditions, it draws upon these traditions to perform, produce, and sustain human desires commensurate with the desires of the nation-state. In short, I am arguing that U.S. secularism extends itself in the interest of the state through the figure of Jesus, implicitly if not always explicitly, to discipline the desires that produce individual and corporate identity as American.

Though the possibility for recognizing and sustaining love beyond measure materially exists within Christian life and practice and makes its presence known in the world in startling and disturbing ways, Christian traditions as historically transmitted likewise never ultimately escape the impoverishment of secularist desire. If cognizant of their own history and disciplines, these traditions live caught between the economies of desire in the face of scarcity and desire without limit, just as they live caught between sin and grace. In the present context, no matter how critical of U.S. secularism they may be, most white Christian movements for reform or revolution wittingly and unwittingly assimilate into their reform efforts secularism's narrow conceptions of desire and the practices that discipline this desire to want so meagerly. Whether conservative, liberal, or radical, these movements often fail to sustain this highly agnostic and disturbingly disruptive love as central to their visions of hope for the future.

Nowhere is this failure more blatantly obvious in the present than with regard to politically conservative, fundamentalist, evangelical Christianity. By *fundamentalist*, I mean those Christians who designate themselves as such, who understand this to mean, among other things, that they take the Christian Bible literally as infallible truth. By *evangelical* I mean those Christians who claim an individual experience of personal salvation through encounter with Jesus the Christ. Not all evangelicals are fundamentalists, nor are all fundamentalists evangelical. Nor are all fundamentalist evangelicals politically conservative. As I hope to demonstrate, politically conservative fundamentalist evangelical Christians have lost sight of the love they are called to by the scriptures they presume to take literally. They are, in this respect, no less entangled in secularism than those Christians whom they regard as apostate, heterodox, or otherwise not genuinely Christian.

Before proceeding further with this analysis, however, a word of caution is in order. What follows is my analysis and critique of what I regard to be dominant trends in U.S. society. I focus on white, relatively affluent Christianity. I do not presume to cover all current dissenting movements, nor do I think that any given movement is uniform and unvarying in its assumptions and practices. I do not directly address the "old line" established churches, which I assume that the reader already realizes to be largely secularized in profound ways. Furthermore, I make my critique as a secularized Christian; it is self-critique as well. My point is not that secularism is a great evil or that it is somehow escapable or that dissent is useless and ineffective. Rather, my point is that secularism and the practices of dissent it historically has sought to protect emerge out of a religious context and remain in many formal respects religious, albeit often in disguised ways. My concern is that we do not critically recognize the full implications of secularism's pervasiveness in our lives as it regulates our desire for the good by narrowing it ever further. Most importantly, I suggest that we do not think sufficiently outside secularism to grasp the full magnitude of its limitations. To me, what is most problematic about modern secularism is its assumption of an economy of scarcity as the governing principle of human desire, an assumption that results in a nationalism that severely endangers future global life. Secularism as taught and practiced assumes that scarce material resources and finitude by definition prevent the possibility for a boundless love that generates deep, wide generosity and care in response to the specificity of all creaturely life. White dissident movements in particular, on both the Left and the Right, have assimilated this assumption into their own activism; and they have done so in the name of Jesus. Because the Christian Right is presently in ascendance, I will focus particularly on its relationship to secularism, though critique of the Left will be obvious throughout what follows.

SECULARISM IN THE UNITED STATES: A HYMN TO BATTLE

The root meaning of the word *secular* is simply "temporal" or "this-worldly." Secularism has taken many different forms throughout Western history. For much of Western history, the secular or worldly order did not, strictly speaking, exclude the spiritual or eternal realm; rather, as divine creation it was upheld by, saturated with, and—even when distinguished from—related to what moderns would call grace, the spiritual, or the supernatural. Until roughly the sixteenth century, the meaning of secular did not, on the whole, so much exclude religious life and practice as it intertwined with them, even when distinguished from them. "Secular" simply referred broadly to common or ordinary people and the ordering of human life that fell to those institutions and rulers not directly responsible for the governance of the church; defined more narrowly it referred to monastics not ordained to "regular" or "religious" orders. Since almost everybody in western Europe was, by virtue of baptism, Christian, to be among the laity or to govern their earthly affairs did not mean to be religiously neutral, any more than being Christian meant to be nonpolitical.

Modern secularism, distinguished as religiously neutral, is itself a product of a number of dissenting forces that emerged in the sixteenth century, including Renaissance humanism and Anabaptism, along with later Protestant and philosophical dissidence that challenged seventeenth-century religious tyranny perpetrated by Protestants and Catholics alike. Secular*ism*, as we know it today, constitutes a human-generated system of thought, institutions, and practices that produce and sustain national identity for the nation-state. The aim, not always articulated and often masked, is to produce and regulate among its citizenry, who are themselves its own makers, desires that secure and extend the state's interests both within and beyond its own boundaries. This aim may or may not be consciously held, deliberately intended, or explicitly articulated by those who govern from on high. Rather, the state most effectively enacts itself through informal as well as formal negotiations of individual and communal desires and interests "on the ground," so to speak, and becomes what it becomes moment by moment, most often as a convergence of unforeseen consequences resulting from unintended causes.

Secularism, as practiced specifically in the West, fuses European Enlightenment political philosophy with capitalist economics through a distinctively Protestant work ethic. Western secularism thus contrasts in its economic beliefs and practices with modern Eastern forms of secularism, historically grounded in socialism (though socialism, like modern capitalism, emerges historically out of western Europe as well). How political, economic, and religious forces interact to produce secularism will also vary across Western nation-states. For example, French secularism, *laïcité*, differs markedly from secularism as formulated and practiced in the United States, particularly on the issue of free exercise of religion; in contrast to U.S. secularism, French legal practice has regulated free exercise far more stringently than the American courts. Nevertheless, in both cases, secularism operates as a network of political, economic, and educational systems that can vary culturally and geographically even within a single nation-state.

A central feature that distinguishes modern Western secularism in general from other cultural and sociopolitical systems is secularism's performance of para-religious or meta-religious functions under the guise of religious neutrality. To cultivate and discipline human desire appropriate to national interest, secularism, ostensibly neutral, performs some of the work that Christian traditions and institutions once did, and still do where there is little or no separation of religion and state—the formation of individual and national identity, as territorially mapped.[3]

U.S. secularism in particular emerges out of European colonialism as characterized by Christian evangelism and Christian dissent. It is in its historical origins largely the project of white male landowners, influenced heavily by ancient Greek and modern British philosophy, as well as by Protestant Christian teaching, practice, ethos, and institutional structure. The result of a successful violent insurrection against the British government, the United States represents a highly intentional, rationalized nation-state, formed by a series of documents, most notably the Declaration of Independence and the U.S. Constitution.

These documents, among other founding documents, reflect multiple philosophical and theological influences, manifested as a series of compromises that register internal, interrelated conflicts that continue into the present. These conflicts include at the very least philosophical, economic, political, and religious contentions. In regard to philosophy, conflicts have periodically erupted over who counts as a person in the legal and moral sense and the related issue of how to relate the good of individual persons to a common good. Historical and ongoing debates over whether to hold slaves, how to count slaves, who gets to vote, and whose rights have priority during pregnancy illustrate the struggle to extend personhood beyond its initial conceptualization. Closely related to the concept of how to define "person" are the economic conflicts over slaveholding as it frames the present debate over making reparations for slavery. In regard to political power, establishing relations between individual states and the federal government, as well as proper relations between individual citizens and government in general, plays out in the courts to this day. Last but not least, religious tensions erupt regularly in the arenas of public education and medical institutions over the free exercise of religion, freedom not to practice religion at all, and the prohibition against state (federal or otherwise) establishment of religion.

The founding documents and the subsequent conflicts at whose center they stand map an uneasy interaction in the early relations between church and state that give a highly distinctive character to U.S. secular life as manifested particularly in the First Amendment religion clauses on free exercise and anti-establishment. These clauses, taken with the rest of the First Amendment, protect religious and political dissent, albeit in ambiguous ways. They register at one and the same time the divisions between religion and state, along with their highly fluid, multifaceted interactions. Whatever the intentions of the founders, and however diverse these intentions were at the time, the First Amendment lies at the heart of the secular-religious distinction. In short, what we now call secularism and what we now recognize as Christianity have interacted historically to produce each other over the last two centuries in distinctive ways on U.S. soil.

As many other scholars have noted, chief among them Robert Bellah, secularism as practiced in the United States, far from religiously neutral, reflects specifically Reformed Protestant virtues, practices, and desires, though often stripped of their specific theological content so that their religious functions remain masked. U.S. polity is structured as a representative, bicameral democracy, influenced in part by the Presbyterian *Book of Order*. U.S. economics grew in part out of a Calvinist ascetic work ethic necessary to accumulating and investing capital. U.S. political ideologies of individualism and manifest destiny echo, albeit faintly, the solitary nature of human-divine relations and the communal sense of the people of God that are trademarks of a Calvinist doctrine of election. Stripped to some extent of explicitly theological content and stretched to accommodate other forms of monotheism such as Deism, Anabaptist traditions, Lutheranism, Methodism, and Anglicanism, U.S. secularism eventually absorbed Judaism and Catholicism as well, insofar as Jews and Catholics assimilated to secular, implicitly Protestant practices. When the absorption of non-Protestant traditions is taken into consideration, U.S. secularism stands directly in symbiotic, albeit sometimes morally ambiguous, relationship with what were once the mainline Protestant churches. While to some extent tolerant of extremely diverse religious traditions, secularism has for the most part reflected privileged white mainline Protestant attitudes, values, and practices both politically and economically.

Since the mid-twentieth century, marked by the end of World War II, the United States has successfully extended and sustained itself as a globally dominant power. Economic interests shared by those in political power with wealthy businesspeople have defined current domestic and foreign policy. Not for the first time in U.S. history, these interests find justification through mass-media technology through a discourse that focuses heavily on securing the country from subversion and terrorism within its boundaries, on the one hand, and spreading democracy and freedom abroad, on the other. U.S. culture is likewise increasingly market driven, as witnessed by reference to entertainment, the arts, and more recently to the sciences as industries. Because research and education assume a materialist worldview, the epistemology of which demands skepticism and self-criticism as necessary to the pursuit of knowledge, these institutions, especially as public entities, have increasingly drawn fire from conservative Christians. The place of religion in relation to the state is also under contention, even as the historical religious traditions suffer volatile internal division over social, moral, doctrinal, and cultural issues. In other words, the form U.S. secularism takes at present is one in which economic practices significantly determine political policy, and the influence and authority of religion, particularly that of evangelical, fundamentalist Christianity, is in ascendance. We are now witnessing a major renovation of secularism and the nation-state, if not their demise altogether. Such a moment compels a careful look at the desires secularism cultivates and the disciplines of secularism through which the state enacts its power and authority to shape individual and national identity. The figure of Jesus, its significance a major point of contention, plays a central role in the production of the secular citizen.

SECULARISM AND DESIRE

Under secularism, the state becomes an entity to which social and political theorists attribute interests, aims, and intentions. To attribute desire to the state so personified requires no great conceptual leap. The state desires to sustain and extend itself, the United States of America no less so than any other state, particularly one that understands itself as a—if not the—global leader. Domestic political practices of the United States, particularly at election time, reflect a series of conflicting desires of state that produce multiple identities as secular, among them a desire for progress in human knowledge, material well-being, and moral development; desires for economic, social, and legal justice, however variously defined; a desire for religious and political tolerance among the people; a desire for internal security to protect the people from subversive and terrorist threats; a desire for control over natural resources to meet and vastly exceed fundamental human needs for shelter, food, education, work, health, and well being; a desire for wealth; and a desire for acknowledged, respected leadership abroad. An underlying desire to control the global environment at once constructs, orders, and realizes all other desires.

That the desire to control the total environment orders all other desires mirrors a materialist view of desire as primarily, if not exclusively, defined by individual ego understood as a universal human condition, now writ large as national, economically driven political interest. Scientific views of human nature often tend to reduce human desire ultimately to some form of sociobiological self-interest, that is, to want or scarcity quantified in terms of more and less. Under this definition its exercise requires total control in the midst of limited resources, for which there can never be "enough." The individual person or its corporate reflection, the state, must always seek "more." Naturalized by biology, politicized as individual economic and political self-interest, magnified as national interest, desire justifies lust, greed, corruption, and violence as "just the way things are." Christian theology, where needed, reinforces this view through highly articulated doctrines of sin: The human being, by virtue of Adam's fall into sin, is depraved. Human responsibility for producing desire as a result of socioeconomic and political practices is masked as a scientific discovery, sometimes theologically sanctified, of what is necessary. Human construction of this "necessary" condition through our practices, through how we regulate limited goods and human behavior in the face of this limitation, is unthinkable. That we might construe human desire itself differently, once the purview of religious discipline, draws the charge of social engineering, even as we socially engineer violence under the banners of democracy, individual freedom, and overall happiness.

As I noted above, a fundamental desire for global control presupposes what the state, in this case the United States, regards to be a realistic recognition of human nature and material scarcity—indeed, a scarcity of goods in every sense of the word "good." If goods were not limited, there would be less need or desire to control as much of the environment as possible. If control were not threatened, these concomitant desires would fade or be redefined. As I noted in the introduction to this book, fear is desire at risk, a product of threatened or actual loss of control or power to accomplish desire. U.S. secularism organizes and manages this fundamental desire to control in the face of scarcity through the production of associated desires. These associated desires, often registered as fears, determine secular identity among the people during times of historical upheaval, as is the case now, in light of the events of September 11, 2001.

I note parenthetically that the mainline, white churches have reciprocally shaped and assimilated these assumptions and deployments of U.S. secularism into their own communities, even as they have on occasion produced dissent against them. More to the point of this discussion, dissenting Christian movements on the religious and political Right and Left have selectively internalized and re-deployed an economy of scarcity and the specifically secular desires, including fears, that it produces as well, though in vastly different ways.

What kind of citizen does the United States require to enact control over the national destiny? The short answer is one who wants individually what the state wants as a whole—control in the face of scarcity. In the United States, in particular, desire for control plays out through the political desire for a minimal common good sufficient to support maximum individual freedom and happiness. This common good depends on formalized legal constraints as well as other formal and informal social mechanisms for cultivating tolerance of differences sufficient to keep a relative peace. In regard to the economic aspects of the goods sought, the Protestant work ethic, grounded in theologies and practices of self-denial among laity and secularized in nineteenth-century America, has uneasily wed the individual pursuit of the good life, articulated in the Declaration of Independence as a right to pursue happiness, with national self-interest. A good citizen, for example, desires self-control sufficient to responsible participation in self-government and to productive work. A good citizen also desires material goods at least commensurate with goods available or potentially available through the market. A good citizen may in theory have initially come from somewhere else and may believe whatever she believes, so long as she assimilates secular desires through secular disciplines. Good citizens desire that others become good citizens as well; this requires their education in what constitutes the good, as well as other forms of persuasion or, failing persuasion, coercion. Good citizens will identify their desires with the national interest and, if necessary, give their lives and the lives of their children to secure the state's desires. What they understand to be the best interests of the state will determine whether they march for war or march for peace.

At this point a conflict of desires erupts, especially when desire is extended beyond the national borders. The betterment of self and other, an "other" recreated in the image of the self, has historically presupposed some notion of progress in this country—technological, scientific, material, moral progress—a notion still current, albeit tempered by the constraints of nature and the events of history itself.

While this notion of progress initially presupposed limitless natural resources, it did not and does not presuppose limitless generosity. Rather, progress, as initially and subsequently construed, depends upon assimilation of the other to the desires of the dominant group projected as universal. Ideally, if everyone, including those who live beyond the territorial borders, cooperates and accordingly assimilates, humanity will evolve toward perfectibility, conceived across a range of possibilities that stretches from understanding the state as an all-inclusive network of care to understanding it as solely the enforcer of mature adult individual autonomy. This view of progress has historically dominated much of American thought, practice, and life until well into the twentieth century. It still appears in secular discourse, though now tempered by and interactive with a less sanguine view of the human future, its associated desires scaled back to address scarce resources and ongoing domestic and foreign political resistance to modern notions of progress.

In a postmodern world, one aware of the failures of the modern project as characterized by progress, the desire for economic and military security has come to dominate, where security may be measured in terms of labored, ongoing expenditures of energy and resources to protect property and other forms of wealth, geographical boundaries, and "our way of life." Not so long ago the United States in alliance with western Europe framed this desire for security as an economic and military competition, a Cold War, with the former Soviet Union and the Republic of China, likewise engaged in economic exploitation in their own national interests. More recently, U.S. attempts to export secularism to exert global economic and political control, whether alone or in coalition with western Europe, have produced new forms of violent resistance in response, a religiously justified extremism that seriously threatens the desired control that underpins all other national and concomitant personal, communal desires deployed by U.S. secularism to sustain and preserve the state. In other words, evangelizing progress as a means to realize the often-exploitative desires of national interest has elicited violence on the part of those who do not share these desires. This resistance has fueled repressive measures at home as well as abroad. Within domestic polity, from the Cold War to the "war on terrorism," the desire for national security at all costs is taking a severe toll on the right to dissent. The disciplines or practices that produce the desire for progress have accordingly modulated in relation to the disciplines that produce the desire for security.

DISCIPLINES OF SECULARISM

Secularism's extraordinary effectiveness as the enforcer of statism is due in part to the success of its disciplines to mask its statist agenda. These disciplines require entanglement with the dominant religious traditions with which the state engages even as they mask secularism's own political and philosophical particularism. These disciplines must be disguised in order to validate the state's economic exploitation of its own workers as well as foreign workers in the interest of multinational corporations. Secularism's disciplines must hide overt and covert forms of violence exercised upon others both at home and abroad to secure the state's control of its environment, perceived as global.

The most elegant way to enforce the state's control through the disciplines of secularism, however, is to universalize finite, self-interested desire—either by appeal to the authority of God or by laying claim to the laws of nature. Whether we understand self-interest to be God-given or natural, we project it as universally shared. As theologians we may attribute it negatively to a sinful nature. As scientists we may neutrally ascribe self-interest to a sociobiological nature that is selfish and competitive (traits that are actually positively valued as long as they are restricted to straight white males). Or as policy makers we may positively construe self-interest as in the best interest of all humanity in ways that obligate us to extend them beyond ourselves. In any case, both God and nature authorize the projection that all humanity wants freedom, understood as individual self-determination, grounded in self-interest, best accomplished by Western democracy and free-market capitalism. Nature, if not always God, ordains that self-determination take the form of active, competitive participation as a worker-consumer in free-market capitalism, naturalized as "market forces" or "the Market." In the case of economic desire, socially constructed desires for highly specific goods transmute into a universal human nature, grounded in the so-called science or discipline of economics (currently practiced in U.S. institutions of higher education as the theology of capitalism). Individualism, freedom, and competition become naturalized as "the way things are." Religion, now redefined largely in terms of belief and privatized as a matter of individual choice, relocates as a commodity to the marketplace of ideas.

Let me emphasize that these social processes, like all other society- and culture-building processes, including those that we call religious, are neither arbitrarily fabricated nor the product of some kind of conspiracy. As I have noted earlier, they occur neither by the hindsight of necessity nor the foresight of chance. Nor are they immutable. These systems or networks of power operate like electricity, produced through human effort in conjunction with dammed water. The resulting electric power courses through nodes, transported by webs of wiring to numerous destinations, simultaneously fueling all kinds of related and unrelated human activity, and dependent on rain from the heavens. Human beings working as individuals and groups produce and are produced by these systems through their reciprocal relations as participants in the daily work of social and individual life. They may be conscious of power or oblivious to it; they may seek it or eschew it; their motives may be good or evil, their actions ethical or unethical, masked to themselves or transparent. In other words, we make the disciplines that in turn produce the desires that define us.

In regard to secularism, these disciplines abound. They may appear more or less transparently religious. They register multiple forms of patriotism that play to different audiences and shape multiple, sometimes deeply conflicting national identities. They reflect and produce different aesthetic tastes and practices. You can track the differences through the different desires they instantiate. One community sings "This Land Is Your Land" while another prefers "God Bless the USA." One community dances to the strains of "War, What Is It Good for? Absolutely Nothin'" and "Born in the USA" while another listens raptly to the narrative of "The Green Beret." Differences notwithstanding, God is, one way or another, as Bob Dylan chanted, on "our" side.

The children from these diverse communities, unless they are Jehovah's Witnesses, will stand together daily in their public or private classrooms and repeat the pledge of allegiance to the United States of America, understood however tenuously as "one nation under God, indivisible. . . ." With their families or perhaps as students, sponsored by their schools, they may make pilgrimage to various historical sites and monuments located throughout the country to pay homage to their historical forebears, irrespective of which side these ancestors represent in whatever historical conflict might be commemorated. These pilgrims can witness their elected officials take their oaths of office by swearing to serve their country on the Christian Bible (though in rare cases, a Hebrew Bible may be substituted). These officials, if elected to a legislature, will likely begin each session of their work with a prayer to a monotheistic God, sometimes authorized expressly in the name of Jesus. From daily practice to the holy days of secularism that attempt to narrate U.S. history—Columbus Day, Thanksgiving Day, Independence Day, Emancipation Day, Veteran's Day, Memorial Day, Labor Day, VE Day, VJ Day, Presidents' Day, Martin Luther King Jr. Day—we are taught and disciplined to love the country, to want what is good for it, to seek its good in terms of our own, and to seek our own good in terms of its good. In effect, the state, albeit an abstraction, assumes the role of God.

Indeed, children and adults alike transact their material desires by the use of coins—economic artifacts—that are distinctly marked by reference to God and connected directly to national heroes, especially the presidents of the past. Through money, the God in whom we are to trust conjoins directly with the national trust and financial trusts to integrate religious, political, and economic desires into a single national identity as American.

The symbols of American identity are not restricted to the explicitly religious, though they nevertheless perform recognizably religious functions to discipline desire to a national good or goods. In a more benign context, children and adults alike will learn through educational systems and other media the defining narratives of the United States told from various, sometimes conflicting perspectives, but most often told in terms of winners and losers or insiders and outsiders as a drama portrayed as destiny, marked by progress, aimed toward a glorious end, a drama for which God is the unnamed playwright. By some accounts, in this drama the losers will eventually become winners and outsiders will be taken in, if governed by the right desires defined by the right ends. These historical narratives serve in their telling to orient desire, in order to produce specific virtues, to regulate certain practices. From the simplicity of never telling a lie, to tolerating differences, to lifting oneself up by one's own bootstraps, to dying for honor of God and country as a soldier, these virtues and their associated practices register deep desires to seek good over evil and to do the right thing. Secularist disciplines of ritual, pilgrimage, economic practice, legal practice, and narrative, sometimes but not always saturated with explicit religious and theological valence, teach desire, molding it interactively in accordance with the desires of the state, regardless of whether one is docile or resistant.

When the more benign disciplines fail to produce a cooperative and complicit citizenry, the state often resorts directly to violence through domestic military occupation, foreign wars, and the legal system. For example, the removal of visible religious symbols notwithstanding and regardless of the distinction between legality and morality, the legal system provides theaters where morality plays dramatize successful and failed attempts to socialize desire, arenas of confession and penance, systems of judgment that may bestow or withhold redemption. Failed attempts merit further schooling through imprisonment where, particularly if the punishment is execution, theatre becomes the performance of a lifetime, summed up by an injection ritually administered, to be witnessed through the communications media as further instruction, a warning to be heeded by the public.

Resistance to the state's desires and its disciplinary attempts is itself built into secularist disciplines through the social practices of dissent, one of our most cherished and most often threatened secular rights. The practices associated with dissent, also religious in origin and often in manifestation, do not fall outside the systems of injustice they confront. Rather, practices of dissent may rest on claims to the same divine authorization or appeals to the same natural law that ostensibly governs secularism itself. These practices select from and draw on the diverse forms of power and the various exertions available to it through the systems or networks within which practitioners participate and from which they receive and reshape their communal and individual identities. Thus dissent against the practices of the state arises out of conflicting disciplines of desire within secularism. They are secularly regulated regardless of whether they are religiously defined as outside secular authority, simply because the state, through secularism, has authority over what constitutes religion. These desires wage internal warfare in the face of material conditions that simply do not mesh with the disciplines deployed. In plain English, desires produced by internal conflicts within secularism, unattended or unmet, generate resistance to the systems that produce them. These systems may be religious, political, or economic; they may be identified with secularism or in opposition to it. Regardless of the systemic source of the conflict, insofar as an economy of scarcity determines desire, the desires that govern dissent are defined by and entangled in secularism.

As I noted in the previous chapter on the complexity of dissent, resistance may or may not be acknowledged as dissent. The legal and political systems of secularism recognize, for example, the nonviolent protest march legally scheduled through the issuing of a parade permit, the death-watch vigil held outside a prison or a state capitol at the time of a state execution, the protest against abortion held at a legally regulated distance outside an abortion clinic, and, at least up to now, the legislative filibuster. Note that the first three examples are often defined by and saturated with a religious ethos and symbolism.

Recall, however, that dissent is more complex than its legally recognized forms would indicate. Graffiti on a public wall is vandalism, not the exercise of free speech. Civil disobedience, albeit nonviolent, represents an intentional transgression of a law regarded as morally unjust. The legal practices surrounding the prosecution of graffiti and civil disobedience exemplify the criminalization of dissent. Dissent may also be medicalized as well as criminalized, as in the case of homosexual practices, once regarded by social institutions of law and medicine as illegal and pathological and often popularly still so regarded. Certainly religious dissent that challenges social norms and secular law, whatever form this dissent takes—from Jonestown to Mount Carmel to parents' refusing medical treatment for children— falls outside dominant interpretations of First Amendment rights, according to the courts.

Thus the state regulates the practices of dissent so as to align desires registered as dissatisfactions with the state in keeping with the state's own projects. The state's tolerance for dissent may accordingly shrink in scope as its interests and security come under threat from dissenters, as witnessed by repeated attempts to pass an amendment to the Constitution prohibiting the burning of the American flag and the rush to pass the Patriot Act after 9/11. In times of shrinkage, the First Amendment and the discourse that celebrates it often rhetorically reinforce the illusion that we are more accepting of self-criticism than we actually are in our daily responses to whistle-blowers or to those whose patriotism takes a different form from that of the dominant political culture.

Modern Western secularism—as a sociocultural system of human interaction that produces and enacts the state by ordering political, economic, and religious practices in accordance with the desires of the state—is of the people, by the people, and for the people insofar as the people reciprocally assimilate the identities required to establish and sustain the state. They take on these identities to the extent that they assimilate the state's desires as their own. The practices of secularism, themselves human made, discipline these desires, that is, they teach the people to want, what to want, and how to want it. By virtue of being secular, desire itself remains impoverished; within the confines of what counts as knowledge of human nature, whether authorized by nature or God, there lies no room for a love that even in the midst of scarcity and threat knows no bounds. For all the criticism from the Christian Right leveled against U.S. secularism as godless humanism, the figure of Jesus has loomed large as the mediator of U.S. secular desire.

JESUS AND U.S. SECULARISM

The "Battle Hymn of the Republic," both its text and its performance, captures well how the figure of Jesus mediates, or disciplines, desire in the production of secular American identity. The hymn is quite literally about how the glory of Christ transfigures "you and me" into proper Americans, an identity folded into Christian freedom fighters who execute the divine wrath as punishment for the sin of slavery. As such, it reflects the values of a progressive Christianity in the service of a secular, national identity and a cosmic destiny. The hymn's origin and the later contexts for its performance are particularly interesting because over time they track a migration that is still in process across the political spectrum, geographical boundaries, and the supposed secularism-religion divide. Written by white abolitionist and suffragist Julia Ward Howe in 1861 in the immediate aftermath of her visit to an encampment of Union troops, the hymn was sung during the Civil War to rally Union forces in opposition to the Confederates, only to be performed over a century later at the funerals of such philosophically and religiously diverse political leaders as Winston Churchill, Robert Kennedy, and Ronald Reagan. Once loathed by southern Americans as a painful reminder of defeat, it has since become a standard-bearer for the country as a whole, regardless of religious persuasion or lack thereof. Its text merits sustained attention as an example of how Jesus figures into American identity, particularly secular, white identity. The text follows in full:

> Mine eyes have seen the glory of the coming of the Lord;
> He is trampling out the vintage where the grapes of wrath are
>   stored;
> He hath loosed the fateful lightning of His terrible swift sword;
> His truth is marching on.
> Glory! glory! Hallelujah! Glory! glory! Hallelujah!
> Glory! glory! Hallelujah! His truth is marching on.
>
> I have seen Him in the watchfires of a hundred circling camps
> They have builded Him an altar in the evening dews and damps;
> I can read His righteous sentence by the dim and flaring lamps;
> His day is marching on.
> Glory! glory! Hallelujah! Glory! glory! Hallelujah!
> Glory! glory! Hallelujah! His day is marching on.

I have read a fiery Gospel writ in burnished rows of steel;
"As ye deal with My contemners, so with you My grace shall
    deal";
Let the Hero, born of woman, crush the serpent with His heel,
Since God is marching on.
Glory! glory! Hallelujah! Glory! glory! Hallelujah!
Glory! glory! Hallelujah! Since God is marching on.

He has sounded forth the trumpet that shall never call retreat;
He is sifting out the hearts of men before His judgment seat;
Oh, be swift, my soul, to answer Him! be jubilant, my feet;
Our God is marching on.
Glory! glory! Hallelujah! Glory! glory! Hallelujah!
Glory! glory! Hallelujah! Our God is marching on.

In the beauty of the lilies Christ was born across the sea,
With a glory in His bosom that transfigures you and me;
As He died to make men holy, let us live to make men free;
[originally: "let us *die* to make men free"]
While God is marching on.
Glory! glory! Hallelujah! Glory! glory! Hallelujah!
Glory! glory! Hallelujah! While God is marching on.

He is coming like the glory of the morning on the wave,
He is wisdom to the mighty, He is honor to the brave;
So the world shall be His footstool, and the soul of wrong His
    slave,
Our God is marching on.
Glory! glory! Hallelujah! Glory! glory! Hallelujah!
Glory! glory! Hallelujah! Our God is marching on.

Howe's poetry joins biblical prophecy and gospel with the theme
of freedom, a theme that crosses the secular-religious divide in a
manner at once apocalyptic and nationalistic. American identity
and God's will become indivisible at Howe's hands. Howe clearly
connects the Union mission to preserve American identity explicitly
to the figure of Jesus, "our Lord," "God"—no less clearly than the
southern clergy who argued for the legitimacy of slavery on biblical
grounds. Her christology is ferociously triumphalist. She has seen
the transfiguring glory of Christ in the campfires. Jesus' role is that of
militant prophet, one who tramples grapes of wrath, while bearing a

sword, presumably a reference to Revelation 14:17-20 and 19:15, 16, as well as to Jeremiah 25:30. The camp becomes the site of an altar marked for human sacrifice. The figure of Jesus metes out judgment according to a fiery gospel written across the steel of cannon and rifles. The opponents, presumably the Confederate troops, clearly line up with those who condemned Jesus and executed him and will be dealt with accordingly by those who are authorized by the very grace of Christ. The Union army and the nation it seeks to save are identified as the righteous, who crush the head of the serpent of evil, an allusion to Genesis 3:15, identified with enslavement of human beings. God marches through the very souls and feet of those who defend the Union in the name of Christ. It is Christ's glory that transfigures *us*, his death that makes *us* holy, "you and me." *We* are to make the same sacrifice for the freedom of others—either through our deaths or through our lives, depending on which lyrics one sings. "Our" God, the Lord, Christ, is coming to rule the earth through the soldiers' marching, bringing victory, marching with us and through us, for ultimately all of us become Christ's soldiers. He extends his wisdom to the mighty and his honor to the brave, presumably the mighty on the Union side and the brave Union soldiers who follow the orders of the mighty. Christ will conquer and enslave evil, making the whole world his footstool. Christ is with the Union and for the Union.

These lyrics reflect and, in their performance, reproduce a clear-cut understanding of American polity as an extension of the will of Christ understood as God. God's will, exercised in this context as wrath, a wrath that is ushering in the very end of time, is marked by an economy of scarcity, an impoverishment of desire.[4] It is a will that, while it desires an end to slavery, leaves no room for moral ambiguity, mercy, or generosity; instead, it counts out act for act, meting out grace according to an absolutist view of righteousness. Furthermore, the righteous ones, the soon-to-be victorious, know the content and inner workings of this divine will with unwavering certainty. There will be no retreat, no changing of the mind. They are, we are, the ambassadors of God's providence.

The white opponents to dissolving the Union, even within the context of *the* American national tragedy, the Civil War, were hardly unambiguously good, notwithstanding their representation to the contrary in the lyrics. As Abraham Lincoln himself knew well, the Civil War was troubled by its own moral failures, political corruption, and economic greed on both sides.

Transferred to a modern context, this national discourse of freedom and slavery, authorized as divine destiny, masks political corruption and economic greed of global proportions. Today, performance of this hymn of righteous winners and evil losers, and the marchers that it militantly portrays as the evangelists of freedom, accompanies virtually every formal, national event, is played during many different forms of political protest, and is sung in church services throughout the country. Though rarely sung in its entirety and sometimes sung with vigor by opposing sides on the same issue, its text, rehearsed over and over, schools our deepest desires to bear freedom to the world—by force where necessary—in the secure knowledge that God in the form of Jesus the Christ is on our side, extending his holiness to us and to our causes, marching with us and through us toward fulfillment of our national destiny. This discipline to a national identity that connects individual desire to the desires of the state travels back and forth across not only the so-called secular-religious divide, but also the spectrum of its white Christian manifestations. When sung with fervor by white progressives in particular, the singing reveals the severe limits of their own desires for the alien.

SECULARISM AND THE RELIGIOUS RIGHT: FROM BATTLE HYMN TO CHARGE TO KEEP

The shift from Julia Ward Howe and white Christian progressivism as it continues to bear her imprint today to President George W. Bush and the contemporary evangelical Christian Right does not require as great a leap of imagination as one would, on the face of it, expect. On the one hand, the contrast between someone like Howe and someone like Bush is obvious in regard to the content of their politics. As an abolitionist and later suffragist from Boston's most privileged intellectual and social classes, Julia Ward Howe was a dissident who challenged the attitudes of both her church and her government. She penned "Battle Hymn" in the midst of a violent political conflict, the outcome of which had yet to be determined; indeed, at the time of her visit to the Union encampment there was every reason to fear that the Union troops would lose and that the Confederate States of America would determine the shape of the future. Her song inspired courage at a time when northern soldiers and civilians alike stood in need of it. Once the war ended, she spent the rest of her life working for women's suffrage at home and for peace throughout the world. In 1871 she served as the first president of the American branch of the Women's International Peace Association.[5] She defined her life through her commitment to progressive causes and her leadership within progressive movements. She lived her life as a progressive and, in the broadest sense of the word, an evangelical Christian, devoted to her country and to internationalism, as well as to her God.

By contrast, George W. Bush represents the interests of the Christian Right, itself a loose coalition of various groups, Catholic as well as Protestant, often defined by themselves and by the media in terms of their reactions against progressive politics and secular scientific and political principles and assumptions. Conservative Christian critics and activists reject religious neutrality and point out, rightly I think, that there is little that is neutral about U.S. secularism in regard to its moral and political values, as well as its legal regulation of religious identity and practice. President Bush, representing conservative religious attitudes toward a scientific worldview, has actively challenged the authority of science in regard to global warming, has heavily constrained scientific research in regard to stem-cell research, has tacitly supported introducing the teaching of intelligent design as science in the public schools, and has fought making sex education and the full range of birth control products readily available both in regard to U.S. domestic policy and in regard to financial support for the United Nations.

At the same time, politically conservative fundamentalist and evangelical Christians, like their more progressive, philosophically secularized counterparts, lay claim to their own history of dissent. From the founding of Christian fundamentalism in reaction against secularized approaches to scripture to its opposition to teaching biological evolution in the schools to current opposition to *Roe v. Wade*, sex education, and homosexuality, politically conservative, fundamentalist Christians have resisted the established authority of both the government and liberal Christianity. Likewise, they, not unlike their progressive counterparts, have understood their dissent in highly nationalist terms, in which Christian symbolism and practice play a central role. Though initially isolationist, populist, and nativist in their politics, they have increasingly wed the interests of Christian evangelism and biblical apocalypticism to an imperial, global foreign policy. The election to the presidency of George W. Bush as their representative symbolizes not only their ascent to political power but also the success of the upward socioeconomic mobility of their leadership. In other words, fundamentalist Christians share with progressives the formal characteristic of protest against established power and, like their counterparts on the Left, once they become established, they mold secularism as well as the state it serves to fit their agendas, just as they are molded by secularism, in spite of their critiques of it.

The features of secularism to which conservative Christians object clearly distinguish them from progressive Christians. Progressives are likely to challenge the economics of secularism, from slavery to labor laws, to property rights for women, to minimum wages, to the treatment of the environment. Conservatives, as noted, will likely challenge the political values and practices and the scientific assumptions that underlie secularism. Conversely progressives are more comfortable with the values of religious tolerance and pluralism and will engage intellectually with secular philosophy and science, just as politicized conservative Christians are comfortable with the values and practices surrounding the market. So, for example, while progressive Christians engage in interfaith dialogue focused on a critique of global capitalism shared with representatives from the progressive wings of Buddhism and Judaism, Jerry Falwell and other leaders of the Christian Right self-avowedly run their megachurches like businesses.[6]

When we consider the differences between these selective critiques, however, it is precisely at the point of being critical of established authority that a connection to secularism shared by both groups becomes transparent, even though it is almost always overlooked by scholars and theologians. Regardless of their resistance to secularism, both movements tend to assimilate secularist assumptions about human desire, what it is, and how it operates. That is, both movements uncritically assume an economy of scarcity with respect not only to a scarcity of material goods, but also in regard to the limitations of human finitude. This economy of scarcity precludes a human capacity to desire without limiting the good of others. Operating out of this assumption, both movements, often in their most generous expressions, presume to know the good and the other or others for whom they desire it based on their limited self-knowledge projected as universal. Both movements find it intolerable to live out of a desire beyond their immediate control for a good they cannot fully know for others quite different from them in relation to their own self-knowledge. (Nowhere does this play out more clearly than in the venomous polemic that the leaders of the Christian Right direct at other Christians.) The respective disciplines of desire characteristic of these initially dissident movements evolve accordingly. We have seen how desire plays out in relation to discipline in the case of progressive Christian practices. I turn now to the desires of conservative Christian movements loosely referred to as the Christian Right and the disciplines these movements deploy.

THE CHRISTIAN RIGHT AND DESIRE

While the Christian Right has on the whole rejected secular philosophical liberalism with its associated scientifically authorized, materialist worldviews, it has wholeheartedly embraced the economic practices and imperial aspirations to sustain world power that characterize U.S. secularism. So, for example, Robert H. Schuller's ministry and the Crystal Cathedral in Garden Grove, California, epitomize the identification of election to grace with material success. This embrace of capitalism, theologically and biblically authorized through the weekly sermon and the daily devotional, distinguishes the Christian Right not only from progressive Christian movements on the political Left, but also from other evangelical, fundamentalist, and Pentecostal movements as well. One need only compare the economic values and practices of evangelical Jim Wallis with those of fundamentalist Jerry Falwell to appreciate the extent to which the Christian Right has thoroughly assimilated, often with deliberate calculation, the secular economics of a desire grounded in scarcity and impoverished in its generosity. On the one hand, Jim Wallis, with other evangelicals, sometimes allied with progressives across religious and political traditions, leads a movement to end material poverty in the United States. On the other hand, political conservative Jerry Falwell, known for his entrepreneurialism, has played a central role in the intentional founding and sustaining of a middle-class conservative Christian material culture, modeled explicitly on laissez-faire capitalist business practices. This fluid yet distinctive culture deploys disciplines suited to the production of a Christian identity that is at once individualist in its theology and aggressively evangelistic in its exclusivist, patriarchal communal self-definition. The exclusivism characteristic of the culture of the Christian Right extends to its patriotism, itself often grounded in fear. Its evangelism likewise authorizes its imperialist understanding of the place of the United States in a global order.

The economically driven culture-building of the Christian Right takes many quite conventional forms, for which there are comparable examples across the spectrum of Christian material cultures, both Protestant and Catholic—from founding its own educational institutions and think-tanks to shaping a popular music industry to founding its own version of an entertainment industry. This marriage of capitalism with politically conservative religious evangelism appears most crassly and most blatantly, however, in the marketing of individual, "other-worldly" religious experiences through the popular media that apocalyptically connect male authority with divine authority, as it in turn interacts with a national identity, centered by a global destiny that is decidedly "this-worldly" in its exercise of power. In other words, economic, political, and spiritual power travel up and down a line of desires for which the fixed nodes in ascending order are male-centered, heterosexual, and white—namely, the male head of household, the boss at work, the military commander, the leaders of the country, and the God of our Fathers incarnate in the Christ, agent of our individual personal experience of saving grace. One need only visit a megachurch worship service and listen attentively to the sermon on just about any given Sunday. Conversion, marketed and consumed as the defining moment of individual identity, reflects a theology directed toward making the convert feel good about himself in light of a divine love that is conditionally determined by the exclusion of those who disagree with the teachings and public practices of the leadership, explicitly identified in nationalist as well as religious polemic. This transaction of power gets negotiated most clearly through the follow-up call to the altar. Firmly located in an apocalyptic worldview, now commercialized and marshaled in behalf of a distinctively American identity, desire for the good is contingent on accepting the authority of human leaders to define absolutely what is good for you.

THE DISCIPLINES OF THE CHRISTIAN RIGHT

The transformation of the evangelical conversion experience into a commodity, the desires such a transformation addresses and effects, and the disciplines that distinguish its marketing from other ways of evangelizing require lengthy consideration. They need, among other things, to be located in the wider context of how aesthetic and religious experiences get produced, marketed, and consumed today and what this reflects about advanced capitalism in a global market in general. At this point I will discuss more selectively how the individual experience of conversion to faith in Jesus Christ, as currently marketed, assumes and disciplines an impoverished desire that helps structure American identity through the popular media technologies of the paperback and the movies by looking at one particular narrative.

One need only read the *Left Behind* series, view the movie, surf the related web pages, and check out the sales figures in order to grasp the interconnection of marketing genius with religiously politicized outreach, directed particularly at pre-adolescents and adolescents. The content of text, movie, and website practices surrounding both vividly reveal the paltriness of desire, even as the series, taken as a sustained teaching to advocate for conversion, produces it. I focus here on the text.

The rapture has taken place. Those who have accepted Jesus as their personal Savior and Lord have been lifted into the heavens; those who have not are left behind to find their place in an ongoing millennial struggle of good with evil, mapped as Christian freedom fighters, all U.S. citizens, mostly white, in opposition to the United Nations. The struggle is essentially one that pits a vicious, atheistic, power-hungry, totalitarian world order, allied with its progressive, do-gooder dupes and pawns against those with the potential to convert to the true faith, a potential that, if actualized, will ultimately enable them to rejoin their raptured loved ones. The drama, as in the case of "Battle Hymn of the Republic," is one of biblical proportions in which the divine will itself shows a remarkable lack of desire for the good or the redemption of most of its own creation. While the forces for good are much more individualized, solitary, and scattered than the Union army and its supporters, they are no less certain in their knowledge of the divine will, whether exercised in behalf of particular individuals or realizing its cosmic destiny. The cosmic struggle of good and evil reflects and refracts the inner struggle of the individual souls standing judged before Christ, those not yet entirely lost who battle the forces of evil. The function of the nation, the United States, is that of conduit for a divine order.

The usually solitary reader is invited to identify as a potential convert at every point. The reader additionally often identifies enough to purchase and read all twelve volumes, while the authors, Tim LaHaye and Jerry B. Jenkins, rake in vast profits. Readers may ultimately seek community through websites and chat rooms as well. How seriously readers take the narrative is not entirely clear. There is some indication that readers range far and wide not only in their commitments to apocalyptic views of history, but also, insofar as they are apocalyptic in worldview, in their interpretations of the time-line itself.[7] The story line and its highly successful marketing nevertheless effectively combine commercial profit with evangelical outreach and nationalist impulses, well-honed disciplines that structure the desires of both evangelizer and evangelized. The figure of Jesus stands at the center of it all.

JESUS AND THE CHRISTIAN RIGHT

Conversion to faith in Jesus the Christ marks a definitive point in an identity that, in some contexts on the Christian Right, is at the very least morally and spiritually problematic in the desires it produces. Conversion in traditional evangelical experience in general registers only the beginning, however, of an extended process of identity formation that is marked equally importantly by finding one's calling in the service of Christ as Lord. For all Christians, unless one is called to celibate religious orders or to culturally separatist lay religious communities, one's calling directs one's life as entangled within a highly pluralistic world beset by conflicts that interact with the internal struggles of the one who is called. Nothing less than one's eternal life depends on executing this calling with disciplined success. The call, placed in the context of the apocalypticism and the political aspirations of the Christian Right, constitutes a calling to join with the forces of good in the battle against evil at a level that identifies the interest of national security with cosmic destiny.

The 2004 election of George W. Bush to the presidency by a narrow margin represents the greatest accomplishment of the Christian Right to date. Bush's political autobiography, *A Charge to Keep*, as well his response to the events of September 11—at that time and in subsequent speeches—exemplify well how his image of Jesus shapes his self-understanding and his exercise of national and international leadership. I find Bush's grandiosity and narcissism dangerous. At bottom, his conversion and his call to serve as President in a time of crisis rest on an identification of his will with the will of God, mediated through the figure of Jesus, thoroughly and exclusively divinized. A brief analysis of the role of the metaphor of "charge" in the title of his autobiography reveals both the self-deception and the astonishing grandiosity of this identification.

The title of Bush's autobiography, written with Karen Hughes as Bush entered his first campaign for the presidency, refers to the Methodist hymn, "A Charge to Keep I Have," the lyrics of which were written by Charles Wesley. Familiar to most Protestants, its lyrics reflect a humble desire to fulfill one's calling to do God's will. In contrast to "Battle Hymn of the Republic," the figure of Jesus hovers implicitly in the background rather than at the forefront:

> A charge to keep I have,
>   A God to glorify,

A never-dying soul to save,
And fit it for the sky.

To serve the present age,
  My calling to fulfill;
O may it all my powers engage
To do my Master's will!

Arm me with jealous care,
  As in thy sight to live,
And O, thy servant, Lord, prepare
A strict account to give!

Help me to watch and pray,
  And on thyself rely,
Assured, if I my trust betray,
I shall forever die.

Compare President Bush's appropriation of Charles Wesley's "A Charge to Keep" with Howe's lyrics. The Wesley hymn constitutes a call to serve with diligence the present age, the secular order, to the glory of God. This service is to take place in strict subordination to the divine will; recalling Pauline concerns though not explicitly in a Pauline context, the relationship is one of human servant or slave to divine master. In his autobiography, Bush's interpretation of the hymn, in light of his conversion to Christ, authorizes his claim as a disciplined responsible husband, father, businessman, and, at the time, governor of Texas, to run for the office of President of the United States. To do less is to reject God's will revealed to him through his personal relationship with Christ in the daily and weekly disciplines of biblical study and prayer; to do less is to place his soul at risk of eternal death.

Bush's claim to a personal experience of a saving relationship with Jesus has subsequently further clarified this leadership as a sitting president, providentially, especially in the face of the national catastrophe of September 11, 2001. Bush is reported, for example, to have confided to associates that God, in God's providence, called him to the presidency precisely to serve in the face of this specific catastrophe.[8] Later, in a speech that marked the one-year anniversary of the U.S. delivery of political power to an Iraqi interim government, Bush linked his calling as President to that of the military to protect the

American people from terrorism, a shared calling that demanded self-sacrifice on the part of the military as well as the civilian population. (The President's own sacrifice continues to remain unaddressed.) Five times he referred to 9/11, for him the beginning of a war for which the invasion of Iraq constitutes only a chapter. The fact that, prior to the U.S. invasion of Iraq, no connection was ever established between Al-Quaida and Iraq has, in regard to public appearance, simply never registered for Bush. We have invaded a country in the name of a divinely ordained war on evil, led by a divinely ordained President and Commander-in-Chief for the purpose of protecting ourselves so as to continue our divinely ordained national destiny of evangelizing freedom in our own, divinely ordained image. An extraordinary feat of theological narcissism, Bush's own immortality, now conjoined with national security, is at stake in a terrorism of his own making! In the last analysis the divine will, the national destiny, and Bush's salvation become so entangled with each other as to blur all distinctions. Bush does not so much serve the divine will as enact it and represent it in his own willing and doing. Bush's desire, stubbornly self-deceived in his ignorance taken as certain knowledge, commingles and merges with God's. They become one.

Consider once again the lyrics of "Battle Hymn of the Republic" and the scarcity of goods they assume. Recall the hymn's apocalyptic condemnation of its opponents, its presumed restriction of righteousness and holiness to its own community, its projection of its own finite view of freedom as a universally shared desire. The lyrics of both hymns, performed in contemporary contexts of fear-inspired patriotism, assume narrow desires authorized by God in Christ, their narrowness lying in their very presumption to know fully what is good, to know it is good for everyone, to know everyone for whom it is good, and to impose this good by manipulation of its media representations and, failing that, by military force if necessary.

At the beginning of the twentieth century, Mark Twain wrote a parody of the "Battle Hymn of the Republic" to denounce the Spanish-American War. It captures well the nationalism of its time, under an ostensibly progressive government. It foreshadows just as well the nationalism of our time under a conservative Christian regime. The lyrics speak for themselves:

> Mine eyes have seen the orgy of the launching of the Sword;
> He is searching out the hoardings where the stranger's wealth is
>   stored;

He hath loosed his fateful lightnings, and with woe and death has
    scored;
His lust is marching on.

I have seen him in the watch-fires of a hundred circling camps;
They have builded him an altar in the Eastern dews and damps;
I have read his doomful mission by the dim and flaring lamps—
His night is marching on.

I have read his bandit gospel writ in burnished rows of steel:
"As ye deal with my pretensions, so with you my wrath shall deal;
Let the faithless son of Freedom crush the patriot with his heel;
Lo, Greed is marching on!"

We have legalized the strumpet and are guarding her retreat;
Greed is seeking out commercial souls before his judgement seat;
O, be swift, ye clods, to answer him! be jubilant my feet!
Our god is marching on!

In a sordid slime harmonious Greed was born in yonder ditch,
With a longing in his bosom—and for others' goods an itch.
As Christ died to make men holy, let men die to make us rich—
Our god is marching on.

THE FIGURE OF JESUS AS THE CENTER
OF CONFLICT OVER NATIONAL IDENTITY

The political triumph of the Christian Right epitomized by the
presidency of George W. Bush has itself recently come under fire from
Christian evangelicals in alliance with a wide range of other Christians.
New, Christian-identified progressive movements that protest the
economics and the religious nationalism of the Christian Right on
theological grounds are emerging with their own apocalyptic urgency.
On June 22, 2005, the Christian Alliance for Progress, founded by
Jacksonville businessman Patrick Mrotek, officially launched itself by
holding a national press conference in Washington, D.C. The Alliance
framed its identity in direct opposition to the Christian Right in no
uncertain terms. One of its chief spokespersons, Presbyterian Timothy
F. Simpson, announced to his adversaries on the Right: "We will hold a
press conference [the next day] outside of the First Baptist Church [in

Jacksonville, Florida] to say while we recognize you [Southern Baptists] as brothers and sisters in Christ, we see things very differently in terms of what the Bible is calling us to do in the public sphere, and we believe that you all—through your affiliation with the Southern Baptist Convention, which has become almost a wholly owned subsidiary of the Republican Party—have abandoned the values of our founder, Jesus Christ." The group specifically picked the First Baptist Church to hold its next press conference because its minister, Jerry Vines, had made headlines in 2002 for calling Mohammed a "demon possessed pedophile." According to Simpson, the membership of the Christian Alliance for Progress, strongly opposed to religious bigotry, is comprised of rank and file Christians from all over the country. As Simpson put it, "I'm a minister. We go to church. We are fully plugged into the life of our community. We are the Sunday-school teachers. We take up the offering. We watch the nursery. We fix the church suppers. That is our life, too, but we understand that the Gospel is calling us to do very different things than just hobnob with the wealthy and lay down moral cover fire for the invasion of Iraq." The Alliance further distinguishes itself from the Christian Right in its strong support for separation of religion and state.[9]

The proclamation of the group's identity formulated as the "Jacksonville Declaration" and posted on its newly established website reflects the historical tensions and the entanglements of Christian progressivism as it challenges the narrowness of the desires of the Christian Right, while seeking to sustain wider and deeper desires for the good, mediated by its grasp of the figure of Jesus.[10] At the same time its hostility toward the Right and its self-definition in righteous indignation against the Right run perilously close to reproducing the apocalyptic dualisms that are part of a Christian legacy that all too often threatens successfully to force reform into newly established structures of authoritarianism. The impulse to fight against this devolution to a new tyranny is present in Simpson's recognition that with their opponents the members of the Alliance are, after all, brothers and sisters of the same family. Whether they realize the full implications of this kinship in practice remains to be seen.

The apostle Paul, no stranger to contention himself, beleaguered by his opponents, framed his own reaction to opposition as a counsel to the Corinthians to widen their hearts to him as he has widened his to them (2 Cor. 6:11-13). In a polemic every bit as dualistic and demonizing as that of some of Paul's current successors on both the Right and the Left, a later interpolator immediately followed up with a charge to avoid contact with unbelievers in a language that pits belief against unbelief as light against darkness (2 Cor. 6:14—7:1). Christian history could be written in the contradiction of desires reflected in these two contiguous passages. What could "widen" possibly mean? What role might widening the heart play in the world of modern secularism outside our conventional views of an apocalyptic context? What role might Jesus play in the disciplines of widening? The vulnerability of christologically authorized and politically practiced dissent to the economy of an impoverished desire should now be clear. What is the alternative?

The other-shaped face of Jesus can be found today in any number of places, though we, driven by an economy of scarcity, have tried mightily and with success to render it invisible. In this instance, George Lawrence and Valarie Fobbs, who were rescued from an attic near their home, walk to the New Orleans Convention Center on August 31, 2005, while looking for shelter. They were going to the Superdome but floodwaters caused them to change their plans. Image © Michael Ainsworth/Dallas Morning News/Corbis.

5

THE OTHER-SHAPED FACE OF JESUS

Then he poured water into a basin and began to wash the disciples'
feet and to wipe them with a towel that was tied around him. He came
to Simon Peter, who said to him, "Lord, are you going to wash my feet?"
Jesus answered, "You do not know now what I am doing, but later you
will understand."
—John 13:5-7

Hovering over the depths as the winds of creation, God's very breath or
spirit, ruah *in Hebrew, preceded even God's spoken word (Gen. 1:1), so*
the narrative begins. According to Hebrew and Christian scriptures, from
the winds of creation to the great winds of Pentecost, the breath of God has
enlivened, sustained, rejuvenated, and transfigured all life—never more
so than when God breathed directly into the nostrils of the first human
creature, till then a lifeless clump of clay (Gen. 2:7). This breath, wind,
spirit of God, a kiss of sorts, has continued to fire human imagination, has
given it voice throughout the ages to come, to paraphrase the prophet Joel, as
sons and daughters prophesy, the old dream, the young see visions, and the
slaves are empowered (Joel 2:28-29). Centuries later, at Pentecost, according
to the writer of the Acts of the Apostles, the winds of God conjured up flames
that produced a new community that transcended but did not destroy the
many different languages spoken there (Acts 2:1-4). For Christians Pentecost
reconfigured human longing, however briefly, beyond its normal puniness,
its fears, its narrow self-interest, driving the early Jesus community into the
streets in ecstasy.

The apostle Paul defined this spirit first and most deeply as God's love
and saw participation in it as the chief mark of the community, ultimately
the very body of Christ (1 Corinthians 13). For Paul, this love drove Jesus to
take on the humblest of human forms in preference to deity, an act Paul saw
as worthy of human response on "bended knee" (Phil. 2:5-11). The author of

the Gospel according to John took this humility one step further in the image of a kneeling Jesus, washing the feet of his lovers. In John this love mystically unites God to the world, God to Jesus, and Jesus and the members of the early community with one another. Like others before me, I see this love as a divine contagion, God's generosity, an exercise of God's desire—a desire that works from the inside out and the bottom up, a desire that captures human desire and makes it God's own, no matter how dimly felt or feebly practiced, the mark of a new beginning. This desire drives us to our knees in awe before one another, acknowledging the very face of God in every human face, especially the faces of the "least of these" (Matt. 25:40).

In the late eighties I glimpsed this desire at work at a conference sponsored by the Church of God in Christ and held at Trinity University in San Antonio, where I taught at the time. Valerie Bridgeman Davis, an African American student and religion major, put the conference together specifically for Pentecostal women. She asked me if I would give a lecture on the history of women within Christianity. I spoke before a gathering of more than five hundred Black women and a smattering of Black men. I was one of two white women present.

After I spoke, the session that was to have lasted for two hours went on for another four, culminating in a footwashing. I had never participated in this kind of an event, though having grown up in the South, I knew footwashing was common among small Pentecostal churches. I was not sure what to do, whether to participate. It was not my practice.

We divided up into many small circles of women. I sat between two Black women I had never met. The one on my right knelt before me, looked directly into my eyes, and washed my white feet as if they were treasures, caressing them tenderly, drying them gently with a soft towel. Given a nasty history of white racism, particularly in the relations between African American women and white women, the moment was fraught with ambiguity for me. But it was also so clearly not about me per se; it was about something much wider. I felt guilty and loved at the same time. Then I turned and knelt before the woman on my left, looked into her eyes and washed her feet as tenderly as I knew how. I watched as each woman participated in the ritual—from woman to woman, first as recipient, then as giver—a great outpouring among people, many of whom were strangers to one another, each of whom was honored by and humbled before one another. It was a great cherishing, this ritualized performance of values among strangers, a cherishing to be taken into the streets and practiced in a racist world.

As I have noted in the previous chapter, modern secularism rests on the assumption that the characteristics, values, and social structures of people of western European descent represent a universalized human nature that identifies individual interest with national interest—racially white, politically self-determined, economically self-interested, and religiously Christian. We have claimed the center of a universal humanity, authorized by the figure of Jesus appropriated in apocalyptic, triumphal terms. Jesus as Lord of the nation's destiny is the God whose truth is marching on through every step we take, the God who charges us, now made holy, to liberate those others to our way of life. At the same time we have also seen that from the apostle Paul to Fyodor Dostoevsky to the present the figure of Jesus reveals a somewhat humbler version of humanity, one that stands in dissident relation to the narrow desires of self and state, offered through the gift of an unbounded love. In contrast to the economy of scarcity that underlies nationalist grandiosity, a different economy emerges through history, along with and sometimes entangled in an economy of scarcity—an economy of grace. This economy begins among humans with the morally compelling unknowablilty of an other, one that refracts back to welcome the otherness in us. The others—"they"—are not who we thought they were, from criminals, street people, and the working poor, produced by and rendered invisible in the name of "compassionate conservatism," to the refugees and the terrorists that our foreign policy has helped to create, their blood-stained images and those of their victims flitting across our television screens daily. Nor are "we," the universally human selves, who we thought we were, namely, normative for all humanity and in bondage to the poverty, fearfulness, and greediness of our desires. How does this transfiguration of self and other take place? What promise does it hold and deliver? It is finally to this economy of grace, mediated by the other-shaped face of Jesus, that I now turn.

AN UNKNOWN GOD AND AN UNKNOWN GOOD

As the early members of Jesus' community involved themselves in the long, still ongoing process of making Christian traditions, they shared, whether gnostic or universalistic in their view of reality and Jesus' role within it, the faith that evil was not necessary, that reality could be different, better, a reality in which humans might participate fully. For them that repair or restoration of the reality in which they lived began on this planet, through the incarnation of a transempirical, unbounded love, regardless of the negative value many of them attached to material existence and irrespective of their otherworldliness. They saw this love revealed in the figure of Jesus, in his relations with his earliest companions, and in his ministry to others.

Those later branded as heretics, often referred to today as gnostics, imagined that reality in the metaphysical sense unfolds at its origin as a plurality within a divine unity, that it does not exclude but bears within it the source of disruption, that it suffers its own disruptions as they materialize. God, as they understood God, thus differentiated out from within to form what we regard as the material order. Most importantly, this God is unknown, yet dwells within humanity, accessible and made real through various conventional and unconventional disciplines organized around the figure of Jesus. Those who made it into the canon as orthodox imagined that the God who restores and repairs reality also creates it and that human participation in divine creativity extends, augments, expands the divine goodness, through practice. They shared with their Jewish brothers and sisters the resistance to graven images, even as they otherwise claimed that Jesus was the very image of God, now made flesh. They knew that new life is available here, now, and in the future. They also knew from experience that sin arises in part from corrupted and disoriented desire and that the sources of corruption and disorientation exceed individual choice, manageability, and therefore culpability. Subsequent Christians have drawn on these resources as well as contributing their own imaginings over two millennia.

Today, the doctrine of the Incarnation is understood in its best light as a confession that for those in community with him, Jesus reveals this love and makes it available to them and through them to others. Indeed, some of these traditions have identified God as love itself. One might say that Jesus is the manifestation of God's desire, a desire in which others are invited to participate. Within these traditions, devotees have painstakingly explored in detail the nature of such a God and such a love, discriminating minutely the different aesthetic and moral features of love, their ethical implications, their spiritual ramifications, their shaping power on human life and history. Within these traditions, devotees have abandoned families, created new families, left the culture for the desert or the cloister, or, taking whole communities with them, sought to create the kingdom of God on earth. These devotees have cultivated disciplines ranging from stringent practices of self-denial to ritualized libertine frenzies, in order to give their lives over to such love.

That God and love become identified in human thought and practice indirectly manifests human reflection on the activity of valuing itself. The activity surrounding this process of identification constitutes ongoing human participation in making up and making real the act of valuing itself. In other words, we make and bestow value by valuing; we value valuing; we love love. We seek to understand love. We practice it that we might experience it and expand it all the more, that it might compound, transforming the world (making it) into a veritable love fest. Such a world, as represented in the thought and practice of both ordinary and elite Christians in groups and as individuals, sporadically throughout two millennia, rests on an economy that stands in striking contrast to the economy of scarcity assumed and reproduced over and over by secularism. It is an economy of grace mediated by the ever-elusive figure of Jesus.[1] It rests on the paradox of an unknown God bestowing a dimly recognized good to be found clearly and immediately revealed in the human face of the other.

THE FULL HUMANITY OF JESUS

In the first three chapters I explored how both canonical and noncanonical texts, augmented throughout the history of Christian traditions by theologians and mystics, provide an extraordinary diversity of the images of Jesus, often in tension, even in conflict with one another. Though not the focus of this discussion, other image-makers—preachers, liturgists, and artists of all media—have made their contributions as well. These images remain politically volatile, insofar as adherents of Christian faith and practice have repeatedly appropriated them to challenge oppressive religious and political authority, as well as to establish it. Once established, ecclesiastical authorities and other elites have likewise repeatedly managed future challenges in a number of different ways. These strategies include, among others, the proclamation of ecclesiastical authority as absolute, the canonization of texts as the exclusive, revealed word of God, and the development of creedal statements that set out the parameters of right teaching, most notably the Apostles' Creed, the Nicene Creed, and the Chalcedonian Formula.

Viewed in the best light, all institutions must develop recognizable structures of self-governance and transmission in order for traditions to survive. In this context, distinguishing between canonical and noncanonical texts and developing theological teachings and creeds (which are often ritually confessed on a regular basis) may serve positively as guidelines for thinking through the individual and communal life of the faithful and transmitting these traditions to future generations. They may evoke the realities they confess, thus reflecting a sacramental nature. Indeed they may function as acts of prayer and supplication.

At the same time, however, both the canon and the teachings have served as means to establish and sustain exclusivist and absolutist networks of human power in ways that have promoted injustice, suffering, and other forms of violence. Authorities across Christian institutions, as well as academic ones, have sought to restrict or otherwise regulate the interpretation of scripture to ensure their status as authorities. They have likewise sought to police human imagination through the formulation of creeds, catechisms, and other theological genres—to manage dissent against Christian traditions and the state— by establishing orthodoxy with respect to the person and teachings of Jesus. We have already seen how creeds, themselves subject to multiple interpretations, were not sufficient to sustain institutional unity, and on occasion even validated dissent. We also know from the vast number of Christian denominations and sects that have flourished since the sixteenth century that such attempts at regulation often succeeded only in generating further fragmentation, as well as further tyranny.

Subordinating practice to belief by absolutizing "right" belief lies at the heart of the problem. The insistence that the elites of an institution alone, whether hierarchically determined or democratically elected, possess absolute authority in determining and enforcing orthodoxy has had disastrous historical consequences, from the early councils to present church encyclicals on women. Protestant insistence on the canon alone as final authority, particularly when interpreted literally, has likewise been disastrous. Since the nineteenth century what is essentially bibliolatry (worshiping the canonized text) has produced a fundamentalism that in its most extreme right-wing forms is inimical to Jesus' own anti-authoritarianism and dangerous to a religiously plural democracy that protects the fundamentalist's own right to free religious expression. The creeds, including the more modern ones, when viewed as authoritative for all times, are likewise problematic, because they, for the most part, do not recognize plurality, fail to incorporate dissent even in limited forms, and do not explicitly validate any challenge to political and economic values and practices. (There are exceptions, exemplified by early prohibitions against usury and the more recent Barmen Declaration within the Reformed Protestant Church.)[2] Far too often throughout Western history, institutional authority, canonized scripture, and the creeds, viewed as absolute in their authority, have produced dogmatism and tyranny through explicit teaching and ritual practice.

Today secularism has diluted or subdued cruder ecclesiastical attempts to exercise regulative religious authority, and the secular state at its worst has taken over many of these oppressive functions, stripped and not-so-stripped of their religious content. Today religious authority depends on subtler methods, also developed over the past, in order to sustain itself. In order to construe Jesus' relation to dissent today, we need to analyze these dynamics of regulation at work in Christian life and practice. Most relevant to this discussion, a number of specifically christological strategies work against appropriating the dissidence characteristic of many of the earlier images of Jesus. These anti-dissident strategies find their effectiveness in how believers internalize them and employ them as interpretive mechanisms through which to view the overall reality of their lives. These strategies are legion and minimally include spiritualization, exclusivism, triumphalism, anti-Judaism, anthropocentrism, and commercialism.

In Christian traditions, spiritualization takes place through the deification of Jesus, that is, through absolutizing Jesus' status as God. Reminiscent of earlier gnostic teaching, though employed for different ends, spiritualization often equates Jesus with God, as if Jesus only appeared to be human and went through the motions of living and dying as a role enacted in a great divine drama, the ending of which was known in advance as least by God and, as God, by Jesus.[3] Spiritualization occurs when the significance of Jesus' humanity gets minimized or lost altogether, either due to the content of an image or due to the function it performs. Reducing or eliding the humanity of Jesus effectively removes him from the politics and the sheer human messiness that characterize the multiple narratives at the heart of Christian identity. The material reality of human life on earth, as well as nonhuman life, becomes trivialized. De-politicization of Jesus likewise renders faith quietistic, that is, a private, psychological, internal matter that does not relate to daily ethical, political, and economic practices. In my opinion, the strategy of spiritualization enables the other strategies by underlying them and reinforcing them. Exclusivism, triumphalism, anti-Judaism, anthropocentrism, and commercialism proceed from spiritualization in a number of ways.

If Jesus is God, the God of Abraham and Sarah, Isaac and Rebecca, Jacob, Leah, and Rachel, and other witnesses before Jesus' time, then those monotheists who do not acknowledge Jesus (notably Jews, Muslims, and others) do not participate in full relationship with God (exclusivism). Furthermore, if God reveals Godself through the person of Jesus, viewed as uniquely God to the exclusion of all else, and if God is the creator, sustainer, and redeemer of the universe, then the faith of those who confess Jesus as God, grounded in the authority of God's self-revelation, is superior to all other traditions of life and practice, both religious and nonreligious (triumphalism).

As we know, this triumphalism, in its more aggressive evangelizing modes and in its ties to state interests in geographical, political, and economic expansionism, has a generally nasty history around the globe. Triumphalism has played a central role in Holy Wars against Muslims, witch burnings in Europe, forced conversions of indigenous people in the New World, and Christian justifications for enslaving Africans as forced labor to Westernize the New World. It plays a role in U.S. foreign policy today. Jews have likewise paid a high price as the specific, exotic other to Christians, by virtue of their history as God's chosen people who nevertheless refuse to acknowledge Jesus as Messiah (Christ, now also God). From the Christian side, the historical peculiarities of Jewish-Christian relations have fostered both anti-Semitism and a romantic fascination with Judaism and Jews as potential converts on the part of Christians. A legacy of early Jewish-Christian anti-Judaism has lent itself easily to appropriation of Christian symbols in defense of Aryan supremacy and rendered dissent against anti-Semitism, as it periodically erupts, difficult for Christians to imagine, never mind practice. At the same time, Christian fascination with Jews as potential converts on the Christian right has played its own role in the consistently uncritical and relentlessly pro-Israel, anti-Palestinian stance of U.S. foreign policy in the Middle East.

In addition to exclusivism, triumphalism, and anti-Judaism, identifying Jesus as God reinforces anthropocentrism by narrowing the focus on human life to the human soul and its status as saved or damned for eternity in a supernatural world that supersedes the material order. One need only peruse the *Left Behind* series to determine that, from this perspective, nature is at best a way station and not of primary concern. Christian devaluation of the natural order has taken a mighty toll on the environment itself. The Christian right, for whom creation becomes theologically a disposable way-station on route to the rapture, has played no small role in its support of anti-environmental legislation and its opposition to the environmental movement.[4]

Finally the equation of Jesus with God is manufactured, sold, and consumed in a number of images. The problem is not that religious artifacts are made, sold, and consumed as such, for religious images are subject to a variety of interpretations and can play a number of positive roles in human religious life. Nor is it the problem that they are popular. The problem arises when the images undergo dematerialization, sanitizing, and romanticizing at the hands of the manufacturers, marketers, or consumers. In Jesus' time the cross was, for example, a weapon of death, reserved for those found guilty of treason or blasphemy—a weapon that turned one's own human body into an instrument of self-torture and murder. Today, worn as jewelry around the neck, the cross may exemplify commercialization as a form of spiritualization, if it is abstracted from its historical context as a form of capital punishment. Not to recognize this context trivializes the crucifixion, and with it human life altogether.[5] But if Jesus is only God, only divine, then the crucifixion is merely an unpleasant but necessary bridge to the resurrection, viewed as a resuscitation available to all who likewise wish to skip or at least gloss over death.

In the last analysis, belief that identifies Jesus as God in any way that denies his full humanity, whether by excluding it or subordinating it to deity, trumps ethical political behavior. Spiritualization in all its forms essentially subordinates practice (both ritual and ethical practice) to belief, though belief depends upon practice for its internalization. The creeds, the proclamations of right belief taught to and confessed by Christians around the world, serve as major instruments for transmitting belief. Learned, along with the history and theologies of the particular Christian tradition, by neophytes during confirmation class, and ritually confessed by the whole community during church services, the creeds make real the Christian story as "one" story in the lives and practices of the confessors. Among the many creeds formulated over the history of Christian traditions, the most frequently confessed creeds across denominations are the Apostles' Creed and the Nicene Creed. The Apostles' Creed briefly summarizes Jesus' life in terms of a unique supernatural relation and status (God's only son); his birth of a virgin, his suffering under Pontius Pilate; his crucifixion, burial, and descent into hell; his resurrection and his ascension; and his assumption of the role of divine judge. The Nicene Creed (451 C.E.) additionally proclaims Jesus as the second person of a triune God. Both of these creeds attest to Jesus' humanity, though it is clearly a unique human nature, by its association with and subordination to deity, and it is thereby removed from the rest of humanity. There is a whole theological apparatus in place that has justified attributing perfection to Jesus as human as a means to overcome human sin, so that humans who participate in the life of Christ might participate fully in his perfected humanity and in full relation to God. The restoration of human nature depends on variously developed doctrines of sin and grace, centered by the claim that Jesus' death atones for human sin, making eternal life available to all who repent and confess Jesus as Lord.[6]

Reference to Jesus' life and ministry as teacher and healer is noticeably missing from these two most popular creeds and much of the theology that they assume and communicate in abbreviated form. His ethical teachings, his concern for justice, and his care for the well-being of others, including other creatures, undergo elision in them. Furthermore, the confessional purpose of the creeds emphasizes concern for the plight of the sinner, without reference to the effects of sin on the victim. Recited without knowledge of their original context, these creeds all too easily abstract Jesus from the concerns of the material order. Jesus' own victimization becomes sacralized and mystified. Incarnation becomes hierarchical activity that occurs from the top down, rather than from the inside out or the bottom up. These omissions can have and historically have had devastating effects by legitimating suffering rather than challenging its perpetuation.

White racism sustained by selective appropriation of christological imagery serves as one example of this legacy of omission. As womanist theologian Dolores Williams has pointed out in her critique of the doctrine of the atonement, the sacralizing of Jesus' crucifixion reinforces justification of white racism on Christian theological grounds.[7] Atonement is all to easily read as a justification for someone else standing in my place, serving as my surrogate—whether as my redeemer, or as mammy for my children, or as my sexual substitute. Following Williams's lead, Kelly Brown Douglas has argued that white Christians, whether as slaveholders from the past or as people who engage in racially discriminatory practices today, practice a white Christianity, one that reinforces their self-deceptions regarding their own racism and the practices that issue from it. Douglas argues that whites turn all too quickly to highly selective misappropriations of Paul's writings on grace, interpreted as the gift of mercy bestowed by a supernatural Christ, in order to justify or otherwise efface responsibility for racist attitudes and actions.[8] This selectivity lies at the heart of white Christianity. Whether in regard to the atonement or with respect to grace, at bottom, it is the elision of Jesus' ministry from theological discourse and the subordination of the remnants of his humanity to his deity that produce a distinctively white Christian identity.

This deification of Jesus, the subordination of his humanity to his deity, and the elision of it altogether, developed as forms of spiritualization early in Christian history, though subsequent to the beginnings of the movement. Jesus' crucifixion sent the movement into disarray. Was he not then the Messiah, the anointed one? The narratives of the empty tomb and his later appearances reflect the conviction that the significance of Jesus' ministry far transcended his death. From what scholars now know of the earliest extant canonical texts, until the Gospel according to John, the latest of the canonical Gospels, written long after Paul's letters, Jesus' followers regarded him simply as human, albeit a highly elevated humanity surrounded by and invested with supernatural meaning. It is the writer of John who identified Jesus as the Word of God, indeed as God in some binitarian sense. This identification later turned into trinitarian orthodoxy. Even so, as later theologians of the earliest centuries struggled to articulate Jesus' deity, in the last analysis even these authorities determined that his divinity could not exclude humanity.

In 451 C.E. ecclesiastical authority officially declared Jesus to possess two natures—divine and human—truly God, truly human—perfect in his humanity. Whether and how this formulation may or may not make sense in a contemporary context, the point is that to deny Jesus' full humanity remains heresy to this day. However one may construe Jesus' attributed divinity and the perfection of his humanity (and there are many different ways) Jesus was born human, practiced a human ministry, died a human death, and remains human within an orthodox framework.

Insistence on the life and ministry of Jesus as essential to what Christians confess is insufficient, however, if his humanity is reduced to his maleness or is abstracted from his communal relations and their survival beyond his death or is divested of his relations to nonhuman life. As others have pointed out for some time now, according to the various narrative accounts, Jesus becomes the center of a wider cast of characters with whom he interacts in egalitarian ways on a daily basis.[9] He establishes relations with strangers and entire crowds of people by speaking in metaphors and telling parables that draw on natural and agrarian imagery, metaphors and parables that express an attribution of worth to nonhuman life and a concern for it beyond its beauty and usefulness to human beings.[10]

His friends, fellow travelers, and followers continue to interact among themselves as they go on to form new relationships in geographically disparate locations. At the same time, competing renewal groups, detractors, and opponents continue their resistance to the Jesus movement, although some joined the Jesus movement, the best known being Saul of Tarsus, who became the apostle Paul. The communities identified with Jesus that emerge early on not only engage in conflict with those who resist them, but also undergo conflict among themselves over issues of gender difference, the distribution of money and material goods, the significance of slavery, and the communities' relations with the Roman government. In short, Jesus and Jesus' world was not a world of lone individuals who single-mindedly and in lock-step did it their way—certainly not an exclusively male world, not an exclusively Jewish world, and not, until much later, the status quo. To represent Jesus' humanity, including his ministry, as male-centered, individualistic, and without reference to images of him as connected to nonhuman life is as problematic as eliding his ministry altogether. From Paul to Fyodor Dostoevsky, what often captured imaginations and hearts most was Jesus' solidarity with humanity, not his distance or distinction from it. For Paul, Jesus relinquished any claim to deity and clung to what Paul considered the depths of human misery— slavery and crucifixion (Phil. 2:5-11). For Dostoevsky Jesus' solidarity extended to standing with and for the worst of criminals, as well as the innocent, suffering child.

THE OTHER-SHAPED FACE OF JESUS

How then might we communicate through the figure of Jesus a multiplicity of images that emphasize the fullness of Jesus' humanity and connect it to wider life, both human and nonhuman? Obviously, there is no single way to do this, no single image, verbal or visual, that performs all these functions for all time and places. If the imagery depends on context and is plural to begin with, then the point would be to sustain multiple images in critical relation to one another in response to specific contexts, as I have tried to do throughout this book. For a christology of the early twenty-first century, one that seeks to sustain past traditions of dissent without appropriating their tendency to reproduce tyranny, one that seeks to challenge economies of scarcity and the narrow desires they produce, two question arise: where to start and how to preserve a necessarily agnostic quality of faith. The answer to the second lies in response to the first. I propose that one starting point for contemporary, relatively affluent, white Christians begins with the recognition that Jesus' own face is, metaphorically speaking, "other shaped." According to early strains of the tradition, Jesus saw himself reflected especially in the faces of the devalued, suffering, and despoiled other.

Recognizing the other, indeed a multiplicity of others, in Jesus' face and Jesus' face in others is hardly a novel suggestion. It finds its roots in Matthew 25:31-46, Jesus' telling of the great Day of Judgment, when the sheep will be separated from the goats. The text is difficult because of its potential for a reading that is triumphalist, exclusivist, dualist, and spiritualized, as exemplified in Augustine's refutation of the Manichaeans. Such a reading further fits with the so-called Great Commission at the end of the Gospel to make disciples of all nations.[11] For example, the initial image of Jesus is one of kingship, glory, and moral discrimination in that "[a]ll the nations will be gathered before him. And he will separate people one from another as the shepherd separates the sheep from the goats" (v. 32). Furthermore it contains a curse as well as blessing. Within this apocalyptic context one could interpret Jesus' identification with the least of these as a concern restricted to those within his community of followers. Nevertheless, to my mind, such readings are undermined by the ultimate Matthean focus of Jesus' ministry and identity.[12]

I suggest alternatively an interpretation of the passage in the context of earlier Matthean passages that support not only love for the neighbor, but also love for the enemy. There are additional passages occurring in the gospel that identify the "least" with children as well.[13] This shift in context allows for one to read the text against itself. The central theme of the passage lies in Jesus' surprising claim, appearing in none of the other canonical gospels, that he is to be found in "the least of these, my brothers and sisters" (v. 40), enumerated specifically as the hungry, the thirsty, the stranger, the naked, the sick, and the prisoner.[14] Moreover, though his sense of kinship with the least is clear, he does not seem to require that "the least" identify formally with him in any way. As the specific enumeration indicates, Jesus is clearly not identifying with wealth and power.

Certainly this kinship defines his kingship in ways that explode normal assumptions about power and what constitutes powerful rulers. The surprise of his interlocutors evidences a seismic disturbance to their own preconceptions of power. Jesus distinguishes those who will inherit the kingdom of God from those who will not by their ministry to Jesus as he resides in the "least of these." Christological thinking tends on the whole to identify the true followers of Jesus in terms of whether and how well they emulate Jesus. By contrast, this passage distinguishes them in terms of whether they minister to him by ministering to powerless others. Jesus as king and judge of this new kingdom furthermore stands in authority over against "the nations," the non-Jewish groups. Translated into a contemporary context, this designation translates easily in reference to the networks of earthly power and governance, conventionally conceived, sustained, and experienced in terms of the accumulation of wealth and status through cronyism, coercion, and exploitation.

Jesus' identification of kinship *with* the dispossessed, rather than as one who ministers *to* them, represents an important shift in focus for what constitutes the significance of ethical acts for Christians today. Note the reversal. Jesus is like them, the outcasts. The outcasts are not to be made like us, not to be domesticated and rendered universal white humans. We are rather to cast our lots with them. It is an especially important shift for those who would identify their actions on the basis of presuming to emulate Jesus. In this passage, to emulate Jesus would be to identify oneself as needy, in need of ministering. Jesus makes clear here that the significance of what we do as ethical agents is at bottom not about us and the identifications of our own loyalties, affiliations, and egos. Ethical agency is about the other, in fact a multiplicity of others, with whom we engage. Ironically, those who inherit the kingdom seek and find the figure or face of Jesus in the faces of the otherwise effaced. Those who inherit the kingdom respond to the specific situations in which needy others find themselves, not the seekers' own abstracted moral calculus, including the need to accrue moral merit. The least of these, the kin of Jesus, need not in any way identify themselves with Jesus or the seekers and their loyalties. Rather, the hungry, the thirsty, the stranger, the naked, the sick, and the prisoner may be religiously affiliated in any one of a number of possible ways, Christian or non-Christian, or they may be nonreligious or antireligious altogether. They may indeed be despicable. In short, inheriting the kingdom depends on finding Jesus in the other as the other is, in her or his specificity, without requiring reciprocity or accommodation.

Taken as a starting place for a contemporary christology and only a starting place, recognizing and accepting the otherness of Jesus, seeing Jesus in the faces of others and responding to their need, addresses a number of contemporary concerns. The narrative not only focuses ethics first and foremost on the situation of the other rather than the intentions of the self, but it also preserves what lies at the heart of Jesus' own human ministry, the centrality of the plight of those in need. In addition, the reference to multiple others also embraces human difference and plurality and permits extension to include whoever and whatever qualifies as "least" in today's hierarchical evaluations of worth, including nonhuman life as well. Most importantly, the figure of Jesus found in the faces of the least of these, his brothers and sisters, his kin, by virtue of its rejection of moral pretension and sanctimony, mediates vividly the desire to love what God loves as God loves it. It means willing an incomprehensible good for strangers, no matter how different or loathsome.

The other-shaped face of Jesus can be found today in any number of places, though we, as we are driven by scarcity, have tried mightily and with success to render it invisible. Some of the best contemporary examples of the other-shaped face of Jesus come from images of the displaced of hurricane Katrina, stranded and otherwise abandoned for far too long or left to die in attics, on rooftops, in hospitals, in inadequate shelters, and along the interstates, the survivors only to be shipped to destinations unknown to them to futures of unimaginable struggle and suffering—the detritus of more than a century of U.S. racism, economic neglect, environmental devastation, and political corruption. There you find it: faces mostly black, predominantly poor, the aged, righteously angry mothers and fathers with sobbing children, newborn infants among them, sick people, the dying, people portrayed as looters for stealing water and groceries, people who simply stole useless "goods," people held at gunpoint by their own police and military, themselves ordered to shoot to kill, people pointing guns at one another, people in shock, people in grief, exhausted rescuers and caretakers, themselves hungry and sleepless. To look at such faces without responding both collectively and individually is to commit voyeurism, an act of pornography; to look away is surely an act of a mortal sin.

The other-shaped face of Jesus transfigures desire in relation to a different order, realm, or kingdom, one I have identified as an economy of grace, an order without closure, one that challenges every finite presumption to know and to establish permanence on the basis of a presumption to knowledge. This desire, insofar as its bearer, by grace, struggles to live out of it, necessarily places one and one's communities so governed in a relationship of dissent to established authority of an economy of scarcity, precisely because established authority presumes to know and assert scarcity as absolute.

An Economy of Grace

What Christians today name as grace possesses a venerable history that has roots in both Hebrew and Greek traditions, predating Christianity by centuries. In the Greek, grace connoted aesthetic qualities of charm and delight, favor granted by rulers to subjects, and ultimately the power of love (*philia* and *eros*). In Hebrew scripture grace developed over history as the conflation of two concepts governing two different relations, a relation of mercy between God and the oppressed and relations of kindness among humans. Throughout the Psalms in particular, grace has also meant God's steadfast creative love that fills the earth. As in the Greek, grace in a Hebrew context has united aesthetic qualities such as gracefulness and attractiveness with ethical qualities such as worth. Here grace also takes on personlike status (as do wisdom, word, and divine presence). In the prophets, most notably Hosea, grace comes to mean a free spontaneous love for God, as well as a divine love that takes on the power to save a people. For Hosea, God initiates a covenant of grace as love, a covenant that establishes loving relations both between God and God's people and among God's people. In later antiquity, these various usages of grace pervade the writings at Qumran as well. At the time of Jesus, grace, mentioned only briefly in the Gospels according to John and Luke and in the noncanonical materials, finds its fullest expression in the Pauline epistles. Later Christian theologians over two millennia draw upon all of these resources, often conflating grace and love.

Even in its earliest usage grace brought together what people commonly view to be conceptual opposites. Grace is the only word I know that captures both the commonness and the specialness of life. It unites nature with supernature. It conjoins order with disruption. It challenges both worldviews defined exclusively by necessity or fate and worldviews that attribute everything to chance. Grace establishes simultaneously an absolute difference between God and humans and the grounds for relationship between the two, while equalizing human beings in their worth as persons created by God and in relation to one another before God. Within this order, grace distinguishes individual human beings from one another according to different gifts bestowed to them, to be exercised in the service of God. Reflecting particularly Hebrew roots, grace saturates the material order, such that, considered in the context of God's creative, sustaining, and redeeming love, all that is, is a gift of God, bearing a sacramental quality. As one tradition would have it, from initial creation, through the restoration of life in the face of sin, to the new life promised for all reality, divine creativity is at work, continually creating out of nothing save the love of God. Put simply, grace is the ongoing, boundless self-giving love of God that makes things be what they are in their goodness.

Various Christian theological traditions have differed over how grace, understood as God's redeeming love, transforms human life. Theologians have debated the relationship between faith and grace, the relation of grace to God's law established at Sinai, and the effects of grace on human ethical activity. These differences have historically produced deep divisions within and across Christian institutions and served both to cause violence and to justify it after the fact. At this point in history, Catholic teaching agrees with much mainstream Protestant teaching that Christians are saved by faith through grace, a salvation that will, by grace, produce good works in the life of the saved. Whether those who are saved are predestined to number among the elect (those called to salvation by God) or whether all are invited remains a subject of dispute across some Christian confessions; within some traditions election is a subject of embarrassment to be studiously avoided.

What makes grace relevant to this discussion is that it bespeaks an order or economy strikingly different from the one in which we live, that is, under various forms of secularism grounded in an economy of scarcity. Simply put, "grace" means "gift." An economy of grace rests on giving without measure. Within such an economy the most precious gift is the gift that produces bounty, generosity itself, namely, a certain type of love.[15] Because this love is the gift of generosity itself without measure, there is always more than any human being or all of us taken together can ever imagine; no one can hoard it; no one can own it or steal it; no one can have more than someone else. It operates outside scarcity, greed, and insatiable lust.

This love is to an economy of grace what blood is to a circulatory system, the difference being that this love, unlike blood, is not bounded. An economy of grace thrives on change, transformation, surprise, the disruption of established ways of human thinking and acting, even as it bears witness to steadfastness, harmony and beauty. An economy of grace challenges hierarchy within the human realm, as well as anthropocentrism in regard to planetary life beyond the human species. One who lives within this economy participates simultaneously as lover and beloved. Available to anyone, in its specifically Christian theological formulations not everyone will find it compelling or necessarily even come to recognize it. For many Christian theologians and mystics those who do participate in grace are called to nothing less than to love what God loves as God loves it.[16] They are to desire what God desires. To those whom it attracts, this realm of grace is irresistible, contagious, self-perpetuating, expansive, and generous without recompense. The beloved cannot repay the lover as if love bestowed were a debt accrued;

she can only pass on the love, keep it in motion. In this respect, an economy of grace works from the inside out and the bottom up rather than from the top down.

Though it may be obvious, a cautionary word is in order here. Not all love is by definition necessarily good. One may love others selfishly, partially, and poorly; one may also love in ways that devalue oneself.[17] The love of which I speak wills the good for others for their own sakes. It is a love for persons as ends in their own right rather than simply as means to a lover's satisfaction. It is a love that loves individual others in their specificity within a love that wills the good for all others, known and unknown. In the thought of many mystics, desire is a function of the will. Within an economy of grace, willing the good for all determines all other particular desires.[18] One may thus distinguish good love from bad in terms of whether the lover seeks the good of the beloved as informed by a wider desire for the good of all. This general principle extends to self-love as well.[19] Thus love for particular human beings and love for the self do not stand in opposition with love for all; rather, they inform each another.

Much of past philosophical and theological discussion addressed to ethical love, identified by theologians with love for God and neighbor, takes place as if the ethical agent, the lover, stood outside the rule of love.[20] This discussion usually assumes that to will the good for all stands in opposition to particular desires. It further presupposes that the lover can presume with certainty to know what this good would be. I am proposing as an alternative that the lover loves as one beloved, as other to other selves, from within the rule of love. As a beloved lover she is subject not only to its obligations but also its benefits. As the context for particular love, willing the good for all provides a context for other kinds of love in response to the attractions of particular others. Willing the good for all works against using and abusing both others and oneself, since both are included in the community of all. At the same time, precisely because persons are ends in themselves, however constituted by their relations they may be, one cannot presume to know with certainty precisely what their good is, individually or collectively—past, present, or future. In this respect, humankind's ultimate ignorance of the fullness of the good functions in the same way as the unknowability of God. Indeed, it identifies goodness with God as limiting and exceeding human imagination.

Love grasped as willing the good for all, the immeasurability of this love within an economy of grace, and its lack of recompense between the gift of love and the beloved who embrace it stand in startling contrast to individualist self-interest identified with nationalist self-interest, an economy of scarcity, and the fear and greed they inevitably produce. Grace constitutes the gift of a future, not its theft. An economy of grace generates and sustains a future for planetary life. This gift of the future stands in critical relation to the present social order. In contrast to the secularist economies of scarcity defined in terms of profit and loss, credit and debt, work and consumption, an economy of grace can be measured only by the depth of the grief that comes when love is lost, pain suffered, and life violated. Economies of scarcity rest on an ostensible meritocracy that masks networks of cronyism and privilege. By contrast, an economy of grace is egalitarian in regard to human worth and nurture and acknowledges the place and value of all life, beyond simply its usefulness for humans. Within this widest possible context, an economy of grace registers special concern for the detritus of economies grounded in scarcity, namely, the poor, the outcast, the children, the elderly, the stranger, the powerless, the uneducated, the victim, the criminal, the sick, the dying—in short, those who are unproductive or are not in a position to consume.

An economy of grace, understood as the perpetual circulation of self-giving love, disrupts the lives of those possessed by such love. Grace turns individual lives upside down, inside out, and backwards when it shatters the possibility of accepting the present dominant social order. The antithesis of sentimentality and complacence, such a love is a fierce love as well as a tender one, consuming as well as empowering, challenging as well as comforting, demanding as well as fulfilling. Such love does not mean a conflict-free life. Rather it requires engaging in conflict differently, that is, focused with hope on a partially known good in the making without presuming to know the outcome in advance. It demands inescapably self-interested people learning to work for a good that transcends their self-interest, even as it includes the good of everyone involved. An economy of grace does not preclude disagreement. Embracing the pluralism from which disagreement emerges, grace reorders disagreement as an opportunity, often experienced painfully, for communities and individuals to grow beyond their internal and external oppositions. Such love does not mean the avoidance of tragedy. On the contrary, one by such love possessed faces tragic decisions with courage and grief; she recognizes the moral ambiguity of her place in the midst of conflict and loss. Because the norms of the politics and economics of an economy of scarcity do not define the authority of an economy of grace, living possessed by such a love places communities and individuals at serious risk in relation to dominant social and cultural authorities. In this respect, living within and from an economy of grace makes one vulnerable to misunderstanding and violence. It is a risky love.

Like an economy of scarcity, an economy of grace is present here, now, not somewhere else. Found here and now in both the beauty and the violence of this material order, grace is neither uniformly safe nor in a conventional sense moral, particularly in its demand to love what is otherwise regarded as despicable. Like an economy of scarcity, an economy of grace works, among other ways, from the inside out, through the structuring of human desire. In the context of Christian life and practice, this desire, defined by an economy of grace, is mediated by the other-shaped face of Jesus.

DESIRE TRANSFIGURED

Living out of an economy of grace represents a grand experiment in human living that emerges variously and changes over time throughout the monotheistic traditions. Within a specifically Christian context, disciplines that cultivate the transfiguration of desire have existed as long as religiously affiliated people have practiced asceticism and mysticism, both as single individuals and in community with one another. Orthodox and heretic alike number among these practitioners, as do Catholic monastic orders and radical sectarian communities of Mennonites, Hutterites, Quakers, and Shakers. Their range extends from intellectual elites to illiterates. The disciplines and practices to which they have submitted have been more and less codified, varying according to circumstance. Variance in practice and circumstance has produced a plurality of human experiences.

Differences in circumstances, practices, and experiences, as well as commonalties in function, have captivated theologians and scholars of religion from Jonathan Edwards and William James to Dorothee Soelle. Scholars of religious and theological studies, however, with few exceptions have tended to focus particularly on individuals and communities that officially separate in some sense from their dominant or normative culture. Whether sectarian, priest, nun, or monk, they have entered a time-space carefully regulated from sunrise to sunrise, week to week, month to month, to structure a desire to live from God's desire. If sectarian, they live apart from the dominant culture in ways that allow them to rear their children according to their alternative culture's values. If they belong to religious orders, they have chosen to give up ties to immediate family and work in a social order unstructured by capitalism. Establishing alternative communities in clear separation from the dominant culture and its practices and values requires courage and commitment. Life so designed also allows for a valuable critical distance in relation to the world, one that is not available to those who remain in the world. What of ordinary people who nevertheless wish to live intentionally according to a different economy? How they live out of an economy of grace yet do not withdraw from scarcity-driven dominant cultures is, sadly, often lost to history and for the most part remains obscure. Yet, if we attend with care to the lives of those around us, it becomes clear that people do live *in* but not *of* this world precisely because they are undergoing a transfiguration that relocates them, however partially, within an economy of grace. How does this transfiguration happen? What does it look like in ordinary human life in the midst of economies that produce fear, acquisitiveness, greed, and misery?

However circumstances may differ from time to time and person to person, living out of an economy of grace reflects a paradigm shift that may begin suddenly or gradually, but in either case, once begun, continues over time. This shift marks the transfiguration of human desire to conform to God's desire, namely, the goodness of all creation. But, assuming that "God" is a fitting word to declare the limits and the transcendence of human imagination, I have posited a largely unknown and unknowable God. At the same time, we know more than we realize as the beneficiaries of all past human making, for better and for worse. From ancient texts to subsequent history to present life, there are clues everywhere that may draw us into the processes of making up and making real a realm, the dimensions and effects of which reciprocate beyond our reckoning. And we do this as participants in the realm, not mere observers outside it.

Christians used to talk about this paradigm shift as conversion or as "justification" and "sanctification," and many still use such terminology. These conceptions bear a noble, if not always untroubled past. I nevertheless find them unsatisfactory for this discussion because they distract attention from what I think constitutes the proper object of desire, namely, the good of all creation found first in the faces of the helpless and most vulnerable.

It is no doubt the case that entering an economy of grace requires turning around or away from the economies of waste, excessive consumption, corruption, and coercion. Christian tradition has held that this turning around or away is itself a gift, though diverse Christian communities have differed over the human role, if any, in the bestowing of this gift. Does the human will cooperate (or choose not to) in receiving the gift or is the will utterly passive in the face of an irresistible gift that includes even the power to receive it? This same question plagues the issue of justification, construed as that moment before God, variously represented as occurring inside or outside time, when one, upon receiving forgiveness, receives faith. Forgiven and confident in a new order, one is now counted as pure or righteous in spite of past sin. Conversion, like justification, has traditionally marked the beginning of processes of human transformation that continue throughout human life as sanctification, a process of making the convert holy.

Across traditions, the ultimate focus is God—often represented as God's sovereignty and God's glory—as this extends to include the well-being of all life. Christians are to love God and to love their neighbors as themselves. Nevertheless, conversion, and with it justification and sanctification, focuses the energy on the making of the Christian subject or agent. This sustained, often all-consuming focus on the agent, albeit often a moral one, makes it all too easy to lose sight once again of the radical orientation to others of Christian life and ethics. This focus on the other, apprehended in Jesus' identification as the other in need, should collect and sustain the desire to will the good for all creation. Making people pure through the forgiveness of sins and holy through their subsequent actions is in this respect a by-product, a means to a further end, and at best a secondary concern. When concern for one's purity and holiness becomes the central force driving human life and action, however, it subordinates God's will for the good of all, and the faces of those others who mediate God's will to the desires of one's ego. This subordination constitutes a form of religious or spiritual narcissism.

There is at the same time a wisdom underlying a moral concern with the character of the faithful. People who desire to love what God loves as God loves it are usually made, not born. Furthermore, they are made out of people whose desires have been mediated through coercion and misdirected away from what is good for all life. Their lives are often damaged and damaging to others. In this respect the line between the needy and those who minister to them blurs. The transfiguration of desire as a process that reorients them must address these circumstances and their effects, ranging from lack of self-worth, shame, and guilt of those who have suffered abuse to arrogance and abusiveness toward others, all of which all too often reside in the same person. Historically speaking, different disciplines or practices have addressed these varying circumstances in a number of ways.

At the center of God's desire, however, lies the willing of the good of *all* creation. An unconditional love, this includes love for the damaged and damaging who inherit the task of God's desire, whose desires undergo transfiguration. In this respect they too number among the others who, bearing the face of Jesus in their circumstances regardless of their affiliations, mediate this love. The human lover is thus beloved as well. The lover lives out of a realm in which she, like the other to whom she ministers, is no longer measured by debt and credit, success and failure. She too shares in the benefits of the divine good will, the pleasure of the divine good pleasure. As a participant in divine love, she begins to love both the neighbor and herself, apart from egocentrism, without measuring either self or other by false standards of worth. Within the economy of grace, both ministering and ministered alike bear the face of Jesus as recipients of God's love.

For ordinary people to undergo this transfiguration in the midst of things, rather than in seclusion from them, all other differences notwithstanding, this much can be said: Living out of an economy of grace requires commitment, takes practice, and entails experimenting; experimentation involves risking failure and requires a certain skill of recognition, craftiness. At the same time, the transfiguration of desire lies in cultivating the virtues of paying attention (listening), patience (especially with oneself), humor, wonder, and courage (heart, resilience, the ability to face the ambiguity and messiness of human life—one's own and that of others). One possible side effect for the participant who lives from an economy of grace is a self-sustaining, peculiar kind of joy.

We may become possessed by the face of the other, ecstatic with divine love, or lured in spite of skepticism by the hint of a promise of a different, better life for all. In either case, we begin the process of transfiguration with a resolve, an intentionality, a commitment to transformation, however tentative it may be. Transformation means the never-ending process of practice, a practice that produces a second nature out of initially alien habits and values, albeit one that will likely never be free of struggle. Like the dancer, the musician, and the athlete, we learn our gifts and practice them. In the economy of grace we learn where we fit in the fullness of life at any given moment. In other words, we practice responsiveness to the ever-changing circumstances we encounter. One ethicist describes this practice as the fitting response, another as contextual ethics, and a third as practiced spontaneity.[21] We practice over and over for the rest of our lifetimes how to act out of a reality that wills the good for all life without the actor knowing the fullness of what that might be. We practice responding within the immediacy of specific circumstances, for the well-being of another in hope for the well-being of all life, in spite of our own finitude and partial knowledge, as well as a certain agnosticism with respect to how things are going to turn out. In short, we will the good of another without knowing fully or with certainty what form that good will take.

Given such high variability as well as human limitation, practice of this kind necessarily involves a willingness to experiment that presupposes by definition the risk of failure. Such failures should not be regarded as trivial. Nor should the prospect of failure be automatically and consistently avoided out of fear. While a relative fear is a realistic, indeed possibly a fitting response to some situations, for fear of any kind to govern one's life displaces and distorts love. To live fearfully results in loving badly. It is antithetical to an economy of grace.

The practice of the fitting response, the sense for context, the disciplined spontaneity that transfigures desire, relocating one as a participant in the economy of grace, requires and fosters certain strengths or virtues. Rather than pre-conditions for practice, these virtues develop reciprocally in relation to practice, as well as to each other. Paying attention, patience, humor, wonder, and courage number among them. The ability to respond in the midst of ever-changing circumstances for the good of another depends on focus, alertness, awareness—elements of paying attention. Paying attention is a learned skill that requires patience, especially patience with oneself. Patience, especially patience with oneself, requires a sense of humor (perhaps a taste for the ironic), coupled with wonder, wonder about the world inhabited by others. If ethical responsibility is first and foremost about the other, then learning how to pay attention with patience, humor, and wonder cannot become yet one more exertion toward promoting self-achievement.

To stay in the fray, as attentive as possible to others with patience, good humor, and wonder, to deflect from the need to turn everything into achievement, most of all takes courage.[22] By courage I mean heart, stamina, energy, the ability to recognize our fear and yet move through it and beyond it in the face of risk or threat. It takes courage to practice day after day in the face of our own personal defeats, flaws, and limitations, not to mention courage to keep confronting the immediate, local manifestations of the tragedy and suffering that characterize much of planetary life. Unless and until it becomes second nature, such courage usually comes from outside resources, as well as practices of ongoing regeneration. These resources may include formal and informal communities manifesting partially, if not fully, an economy of grace through liturgy, sacrament, and fellowship. Disciplines of meditation, contemplation, prayer, physical exertion, and good nutrition number among possible regenerative practices. Likewise, we should never underestimate the power of beauty to sustain the heart and, when needed, to restore it.

Transfiguring desire to conform it to an economy of grace reorients identity and value over time. Grace weans our identity from a life defined by work, inside or outside the home, whether chosen or imposed, loved or hated, by nurturing it with better food. Conformation to an economy of grace redefines what we consider enough materially, away from consumerism and waste toward a boundless generosity. Transfiguration consists of letting go of the desire to secure the political and economic future for oneself and one's family at any cost to discover a wider family of mutual care, the love of which is far more steadying and much more trustworthy than the futures market. The resources and disciplines of grace detach one from emotional involvement in and dependence on a system of profit and loss, credit and debt as the measure of our worth, to new life without the need to measure the self at all.

It happens, though there are no guarantees, that life transformed and transforming—life lived out of the love of God—makes available to beloved lovers a peculiar kind of joy that sustains the circulation of love through them in the midst of the world they challenge.[23] I say a peculiar kind of joy because it is a complex feeling or affection. It is haunted. Any mature person with imagination who experiences the joy of the love of God finds it tinged by sorrow in the face of misery. Just as Jesus' ministry should not be elided, neither should Jesus' suffering and death be circumvented. Such circumventions undermine the suffering and need of the others with whom he identified. His promise of new life does not compensate for their suffering as if by some mathematical equation or as if the suffering has never happened. Suffering cannot be undone; at best, it can only be survived, healed, and moved beyond to new life. Joy that erases the hideousness of the suffering that goes on around the world without ceasing is the joy of spiritual and moral amnesia.

At the same time, it is equally a spiritual and moral failure to reduce this world to its violence. It is, after all, a world likewise possessed by goodness and beauty. It is a world created by God as good, the arena for the economy of grace as well as economy of scarcity. Not to acknowledge its goodness and beauty—first and foremost in the "least of these"—is as problematic as ignoring or forgetting its suffering. Thus theologians of old referred to God's "good pleasure" to emphasize God's own delight in creating life, sustaining it, healing it, and renewing it. God could be said to take pleasure not only in creativity but in the creatures God makes as well. To participate in the love of God (an economy of grace), a participation that begins with recognition of the other as other-shaped face of Jesus found in the least of these, is to participate in the divine good pleasure itself. There is joy to be shared and felt here, new life promised for others and for oneself. While not a motive, joy is a realization of the economy of grace that, by its contagion, compounds and expands divine love itself.

DISSENT AS A WAY OF LIFE

We come into the world in the middle of things to which we are indebted, things not of our own making, for whose repair we nevertheless become responsible. We die in the middle of things, leaving the legacy of our shared yet unique presence, including the effects of our mistakes, to strangers we will never know. In the last analysis the transfiguration of desire means receiving every moment as an opportunity, however small and seemingly inconsequential, to live out of an economy of grace. Transfiguration becomes a way of life, a perpetual revolution, and, as such, a gift to the future. Many ordinary people live this way, however falteringly they may do so. Ordinary people go about anonymously doing extraordinary things as if it were normal all the time.

Some of them are quite intentional; that is, some people mean to live lives of dissent against dominant social systems and cultural norms. I have a colleague whose life epitomizes that of the leftist political dissident. He teaches the history of labor from a self-consciously leftist perspective; he consults with unions; he helps organize rallies and marches; he supports and is heavily involved in radical and experimental theater. Albeit a white man, the local African Americans with whom he works trust him as one of their own; college students across all lines of difference turn to him when they are in trouble. He does not duck the tough issues, the messiness and ambiguity of human activity; when called for, he finds the right lawyers, puts up the bail money on his own nickel, stands on the picket line.

I teach students who turn in their papers early every year to catch a bus to Columbus, Georgia, to march against what was once known as the School of the Americas, a U.S. government-funded training institution for right-wing Latin American paramilitary and military forces.[24] I teach students who participate in anarchist movements on a global scale. Every year a substantial number of graduating seniors make a pledge to live their lives dedicated to the environmental health of the planet. One of our alumni has established a center for victims of political torture; another works as a paralegal for a law firm dedicated exclusively to defending legal and illegal immigrants; another has entered nursing school with the goal of starting women's health collectives in impoverished minority neighborhoods. Having taught substantial numbers of both liberal and conservative students for over two decades in higher education, I could go on and on with examples of students from across the political spectrum who have intentionally challenged established social systems and cultural norms as a way of life. They come from many different ethnic, national, and socioeconomic backgrounds; they cross virtually all religious and nonreligious affiliations; and they represent both genders and various sexual orientations. One of them monitors violations of human rights in war-torn countries, while another takes a feminist stand in Baptist Bible Study and her local Republican Party precinct. These are stories that will likely never make the news. Yet, that I encounter such people in the classroom every day, year after year, is not the slightest bit unusual; anyone who teaches for any length of time can tell many such stories.

As we found in the sixteenth century, however, dissent does not always take such recognizable, intentional forms. Like the Dutch Anabaptist Elizabeth Munstdorp and many of the men and women accused of practicing witchcraft, people may dissent against their culture in the way they do their jobs, how they rear their children, when they, without considering the possible consequences, hesitantly speak out against prevailing unjust practices. Sometimes people wake up to the discovery that, due to no fault of their own, they are, like Erasmus and Loos, taking on social systems with whose values they identify and to which they are loyal. Circumstances intervene that drive them to do things they would never have intentionally set out to do in advance. Two slightly extended, contemporary examples will suffice, one global and one local.

The history of the small Asian country designated Burma by British colonialists and Myanmar by the present oppressive military dictatorship is a brutal one. From the ancient Chinese to the present United

States-led multinational corporations, outsiders have invaded and sacked the country for its wealth. The country is rich in natural resources, particularly minerals, ranging from natural gas to rare gems. It is the only country in the world whose soil yields imperial jade, the deep-green stone possessing what appears as an internal flame, the hoarding of which preoccupied Chinese rulers for centuries. Its soil is also perfect for growing poppies, the source of opium, now a means by which arms may be purchased by both the Myanmar government—so oppressive that almost every major country, including the United States and excepting China, has placed it under embargo—and the local tribespeople who resist the government. More recently, American-European multinationals have formed consortia to pipe the country's natural gas to heat Western nations' industries and homes in the winter.

The Myanmar government, in an effort to improve relations with the outside world, particularly with multinational corporations, agreed to build the roads to process and ultimately to pipe the gas. They have used forced labor to do so. (This practice is not new; the government has a long, violent history of employing forced slave labor on behalf of foreign nations and business interests.) When Burmese citizens refuse to cooperate, the Myanmar military destroys whole villages; troops torture the men who refuse to work; they rape the townswomen and female children; they murder the elderly and the very young. Any survivors flee, often across the borders to Thailand. Whole villages pick up and leave when they hear that the military is coming. Recently, however, the Thai government has reestablished positive relations with Myanmar; not only are the Thais now refusing to accept new refugees but they are returning those who fled before relations thawed, thus placing them in double jeopardy. Some of the victims, with the support of human rights groups, churches, and legal defense organizations, have taken the multinationals, particularly Unocal, to court under the anti-piracy act of 1789 for violations of human rights. The courts have consistently decided in favor of the victims through the appeals process. In response, the U.S. Congress is considering repealing the anti-piracy legislation in the name of national security. More recently Unocal has stood at the center of a bidding war conducted between the Chinese and the United States. China withdrew from consideration due to U.S. domestic protest, leaving the field open solely to United States-owned Chevron. Once Chevron takes possession of Unocal, it is unclear whether human rights abuses will end; it is also unclear what impact the change in ownership will have on the court cases. Throughout these processes of forcing labor, suing, selling, and buying, thousands of Burmese lowlanders and hill people have been displaced, not only those who flee beyond the borders but also those who flee by relocating within the borders.

Rick, the son of missionary parents for one of the Reformed Church denominations, grew up in northern Thailand.[25] He is white.[26] When he went to college in the United States, he joined the Army R.O.T.C. Upon graduation he entered the military, training as a member of the Special Forces. Although at the time he thought he would serve in the Army as a career officer, once he attained the rank of major, Rick grew restless. Taking leave from active duty, he returned to school at Fuller Theological Seminary. Upon graduation he was commissioned as a missionary and returned to Thailand to continue the work of his parents within the tradition of his childhood. College graduate and army officer turned missionary, Rick was the poster boy for clean-cut American masculinity.

Not long after his return to Thailand, however, he began to slip over the Thai border to Burma to help refugees. With others, he would relocate small but entire villages of tribespeople as they fled the Myanmar rulers who sought to make them slave laborers and who tortured and killed them when they resisted. Rick's task was to help them, according to their wishes, find safety within the jungles of the Burmese hill country. He brought medical supplies, food, and Bibles, and he trained tribespeople to work with him in like fashion throughout the region. (There is a longstanding history of established, morally ambiguous working relationships between some of the tribes and Reformed Protestant missionaries. At the invitation of the British, American Baptists, Disciples of Christ, and Presbyterians entered the region and succeeded in converting whole tribes, disrupting longstanding traditions of animism, while further exacerbating already existing enmities with the dominant lowland Buddhists.)

As the violence perpetrated by the Myanmar military increased in intensity and frequency, Rick found himself more and more often faced with the dilemma of whether to take up arms in defense of the tribespeople he sought to aid. He was honest with his mission board about his dilemma. The board members questioned the use of violence, even in defense of others, and feared, among other things, an international incident. On very defensible grounds they forbade him to take up arms. On equally defensible grounds Rick resigned. In his thirties and with a family to support, he agonized over what to do next. As an evangelical Christian, he saw his dilemma in terms of trying to discover God's next call for him. The call came when his sister arranged a meeting between him and the legally elected Buddhist leader and

Nobel Peace Prize winner Aung Saung Su Kyi. They met. He gave her his Bible from his seminary days. They agreed to continue working together to build interreligious and political solidarity among the tribes with the Burmese who resist the Myanmar government. This is no small task. Longstanding enmity, analogous to the historic relations between Americans of European descent and indigenous Americans, exists between the Burmese and the tribes. The tribes not only stand in conflict with the lowlanders, but also have long histories of violence with one another. These internal conflicts have kept the military junta in power. Since his meeting with Aung Sung Su Kyi, Rick has devoted much of his time to building relations among the tribes and between tribes and lowlanders in spite of this bad history and deep religious differences. Rick also continues his rescue and support work, using it as a further opportunity to develop structures to bring the disparate, opposing groups together in the face of their common Myanmar oppressors. As far as I know, he still takes up arms in defense of the refugees he relocates.

More recently his work has attracted the attention of the Myanmar military. Rick's friends in the Thai government have warned him that the Myanmar government has ordered his death. Rick continues his work anyway because, to his mind, this is what God, through Jesus, requires of him. His self-identification and his language are christocentric, his politics conservative in a traditional sense, quite intentionally articulated. He articulates his critique of the U.S. government, to which he is highly loyal, in a traditional theological language that rejects as idolatry any identification of religion with nationalism. He sees the United States as threatened by growing corruption and deterioration as exemplified by the Patriot Act and its infringement on constitutionally guaranteed rights.

I personally do not agree with the fundamentals of Rick's conservative politics, though, for different reasons, we both abhor current U.S. foreign and domestic policy. I do not share Rick's evangelical piety or the literalness of his beliefs. As for his taking up arms in defense of others, may I never face his dilemma. At the same time, I see a pattern of grace at work, a radical ethics in response to the other. A man of warmth, he confronts danger with disciplined alertness and composure, skills he developed from his early days as a child of missionaries, through his career in the military, on into the present. At great risk to his own life that, moreover, entails the threat of significant loss to his wife and two children, he ministers to the forgotten, violated, and despised of the Burmese mountains. His daily existence challenges unjust religious, political, and economic institutions at every point—in Burma, Thailand, and the United States.

In a very different vein, immigrants cross daily into the United States from many countries and for a wide range of reasons. While many immigrants flee overt political oppression and torture, many flee the violence of poverty and seek new opportunities for better lives for their children. If they cross into this country illegally, they by definition live as criminals in fear of being caught and deported. Those who seek to help them are also technically breaking the law.

Ellen and I knew each other mainly over lunch and afternoon coffee at the faculty club at the university where I used to work.[27] Ellen is a Unitarian. Like Rick, she is also white. She and I have most often talked about our children. At the time she and I were drinking coffee on a regular basis, Ellen was a single parent of two sons, one of whom, like my own son, excelled at Latin. Our boys competed with each other locally and then stood together on the same team at state, regional, and national meets. At the local level their respective high school clubs see-sawed back and forth as the top two clubs in the city. Her son's club was headed by a young Taiwanese boy, a year older than our son, who excelled without peer not only in Latin but also in every other academic subject. Sam, his younger brother, and Judy, his little sister, lived with their uncle and aunt and, outside Latin club events, kept pretty much to themselves. Our boys were casual but real friends to them.

One day Ellen and I discovered that Sam, his brother, his sister, and his mother lived as illegal aliens, their green cards having expired years earlier. They lived in a run-down motel operated by his absentee father (from Taiwan) in a rough part of town. The motel catered to prostitutes and drug users and served as a money-laundering operation. The kids stayed with an aunt and an uncle during the week so that they might "legally" attend what was one of the best high schools in town. We learned all of this because the INS (Immigration and Naturalization Service) was on their trail. As we scurried to figure out how to deal with this situation, the INS raided the motel and seized the family, except for Sam, who happened to be away from home at the time. The mother was locked up in jail and the children went to juvenile detention as they all awaited deportation. Sam had escaped, but had nowhere to go. If he returned to his aunt and uncle (who were legal), the INS would find him. He called me from a phone booth, and I got him to our house, where he stayed for about three weeks while Ellen and I, with others, figured out what to do next.

Ellen is a genius at solving problems. She connived with the Registrar of the school where we taught to get Sam admitted to the university. After three weeks at my house in August, he began life as a first-year student in the dorm, still illegal. At this point we had no idea where the money to pay for this would come from or how to make Sam legal. We ultimately found an immigration lawyer who took on the case for the whole family pro bono. Meanwhile the president of the university got wind of the situation and was initially furious at us. He later came around and persuaded a trustee to finance Sam's education. The registrar traveled with Sam to Canada to get a new green card so that Sam could legally enter the United States and remain here as a student. The lawyer, who habitually takes on such cases, managed to work out a deal, with the consent of Sam's mother, that he and his brother would be allowed to remain in the country under the sponsorship and legal guardianship of Ellen. The mother and, at the mother's insistence, her daughter Judy, would be deported to Taiwan and reunited with Sam's father. In spite of Ellen's efforts, we failed to convince the mother that Judy should stay with her brothers so that she, too, might get a good education and a shot at a better life.

It took Ellen some time to work through taking on such a tremendous responsibility, one that I knew right then our family could not possibly have assumed. After some thought, however, she agreed. She essentially redefined her family by committing herself and her two biological sons to two more sons. (This commitment would have included a daughter as well, had things turned out differently.) She has since seen all four boys grow into young adulthood. She got them through college. Her oldest biological son, Sam, and Sam's brother proceeded on to postgraduate degrees in medicine and engineering; her younger son went on to a career in the military. She has witnessed all of their marriages as well. Sam and his brother maintained their relationships with their family of origin but have managed, in no small part thanks to Ellen, to escape entanglement in their father's criminality. Instead of deportation, they got a second chance at an altogether different life. Ellen treated them like her other two sons. They had to get jobs, find scholarships, and learn to be resourceful.

I do not know where Ellen found the emotional and financial resources at the time, but find them she did. What was initially and temporarily a clandestine team effort, fraught with legal and moral ambiguity, became for her a full-time responsibility for some years that has turned into a lifetime commitment. She took a stand against several different systems and norms—the immigration system, the legal system, the prevailing academic system, and most importantly the norm that family is first and foremost defined by biology. As a single mother, she put her own biologically defined family at no small risk, at first briefly because of the illegality in which we were all involved, then on a much longer term basis because of the financial and emotional commitment she personally took on.

There is no single recipe for the disciplines that transfigure desire, nor a one-size-fits-all form for the dissent it produces. Both Rick and Ellen are ordinary people, trained to certain virtues and habits by their traditions, who simply responded and continue to respond to the circumstances that befall them with an amazing generosity and a clear focus on the needs of others. Their responses have placed them repeatedly at odds with the prevailing culture. They did not initially desire that their lives turn out the way they did; rather, they began with different intentions, hopes, and dreams and ended up winging it, so to speak, in an oddly disciplined way—Rick with his calm in the face of danger and Ellen with her genius for problem solving. While it has hardly been easy for either of them, it has hardly been drudgery either. They appear borne by a peculiar inner joy.

A PECULIAR KIND OF JOY

In the last analysis, if you look squarely into the face of the other and see that dissident Palestinian Jew, then changes happen to you. The poor, the homeless, the stranger, the prisoner, the ill, though they may be with us always, cease to be just part of the shadowy landscape of our lives. They no longer lurk about the edges, making us vaguely uncomfortable in ill-defined ways. Rather, they reveal themselves as persons, ends in themselves, who face us back, their need dissonant, challenging even the most hectic and inattentive circumstances of our existence. Their insistence on recognition constructs a different shared humanity. Their refusal to be reduced by our pity and distantiation shatters the possibility that we deceive ourselves any further that ethical action and morality are about us—about the puniness of our vision of ourselves as universal humans. To desire as God desires and to act accordingly is to labor with these others—to eat, drink, and share clothing with them, to build houses with them, visit with them, and stand by them as they seek to fulfill their own ends.

What if we, all of us, could and would desire what God desires? What might it look like? If it happened with any magnitude, it would be an outpouring of love of cosmic proportions, generous beyond comprehension, saturating all life, many forms of which we cannot even imagine. This love would seize us, overtake us, making us vibrate with goodness, richness, depth, and expansiveness, such that we would all be delirious, rejoicing with a never-ending joy—sated, warmed, befriended, freed, whole, and in love without measure with one another. Permit me just one glimpse.

Somalis fleeing their chaotic homeland arrive daily in the Twin Cities. Though a few are secular or Christian, they are by and large Muslim. The Dean of International Studies at Macalester College organized a conference to bring Somalis together to preserve and to celebrate their culture, as well as to address their problems as exiles and immigrants to the United States. Though most of the participants came from the Twin Cities metropolitan area, where there is a heavy concentration of refugees, many also came from all over the country for the occasion. Both academics and community leaders spoke of the particular problems Somalis confront. For example, as Muslims, they must devise ways to negotiate an economy of credit and debt in order to purchase cars, houses, and the things many U.S. citizens simply charge on their credit cards. The Qur'an's prohibition against participation in an interest-based economy makes housing, employment, transportation, and properly educating their children difficult. Even renting is a problem, since most landlords want to run a credit check on potential renters. In addition to the difficulties produced by living in a capitalist economy, there are medical issues for women associated with Muslim practices of modesty and chaperonage as well. Moreover, as with immigrants and refugees from other countries, child-rearing practices are affected. For many Somalis, parent-child roles undergo reversal, as the children, who have learned English, may become the primary means for negotiating the system for their non-English-speaking parents. Their traditional authority undermined, parents thus come to depend on their children for survival in a new, strange, and in some cases offensive culture.

These difficulties notwithstanding, Somalis are particularly well known for their poetry and their music. The dean devoted the first and last nights of the conference to concerts. My husband, Phil, and I attended the opener with other faculty and colleagues, almost all of whom were white. The audience was, of course, predominantly Somali. Some of the Somali women were covered; others were not. Of the covered women, some wore Middle Eastern garb, while others wore more Indian-looking clothing. Most of the men wore Western clothing.

Instrumentalists and singers cast spells upon us with their performances of traditional and contemporary Somali music. Irrespective of dress or gender, the Somalis knew all the words by heart. With almost no exception we whites knew no Somali. Two of the performers, one male and one female, sang songs to each other—ancient poetry, so we were informed, recast as lyrics to a contemporary sound. Even in our ignorance of the language the subject was clear: They sang love songs to each other and to us. The music was filled with yearning and at the same time with taunting and enticement. The audience moaned, roared with laughter, hooted, and sighed with the performers as they enacted an eroticism that required no translation whatsoever. In deep, haunting, sensuous, yet humorous and mocking tones, performers and audience alike approached ecstasy.

After each number, the crowd went wild. The Somali women ululated full force. Those seated in the row behind us would apologize for getting carried away and being too loud. My female colleague seated next to me and I would protest, no, no, we wish we could make that sound; teach us how. And they did. Louder, louder, they would say, as we tried to move our tongues and make noise at the same time. The concert ended with dancing—on the stage and in the aisles. My friend and I left knowing that we would need a lifetime of practice to express such joy in such a way.

To give oneself over to the generosity of another, stranger or friend; to humble yourself before another, stranger or friend; to bear witness to suffering beyond your own; to ache with a yearning for another that transports one beyond the limits of her social experience to a new intimacy and to pay this transformation proper tribute—it takes at least a lifetime to learn and to exercise such desires. They are gifts beyond measure—in their expansiveness, suggestions of a participation in God's own creative and rejuvenating desire.

We pray, if we pray at all, to a largely unknown God, made up and made real through centuries of conflicting traditions of liturgical, sacramental, ethical, theological, and textual practices. Held captive by the possibility of an unlimited generosity we call divine love, mediated by a multitude of different faces taken on by the figure of Jesus, we undergo a transfiguration that puts us at odds with the very world we might like to call home. Life lived in this world but not of it is difficult to sustain, messy, and ambiguous. There is no conclusion to an economy of grace, no end to the transfiguration of desire. Love is always in the making, the figure of Jesus confronting us in the most surprising circumstances, teaching us, disciplining us to a new desire until this desire becomes the breath within us upon which our lives depend.

NOTES

CHAPTER 1

1. Emma Goldman, *Living My Life* (New York: Knopf, 1934), 56.

2. I originally presented these remarks as part of a keynote lecture for an international conference on "Corporeality, Gender, and Religion," sponsored by the University of Groningen and held at Nieuen Schwans, the Netherlands, on December 17–19, 1998. *Crosscurrents* later published them in extended form in *Crosscurrents* 48:2 (Summer 1998) 185–97.

3. Prior to the sixties my mother would not have been allowed into the black schools. She went to work for the YWCA in the early sixties in order to stabilize her income. While at the "Y" she instituted a program for dancing in the local black schools. Later, her classes at the "Y" became a primary means of attracting African Americans into racially integrated programs.

4. My mother's only criticism of this essay was to wish that I had spent more time talking about the ecstasy produced by performance.

5. As my colleague Diane Neal pointed out, baton twirling and, in some contexts, tap-dancing are associated with nationalism in this country.

6. For example, Billy Graham's son Franklin once characterized Islam as "evil and wicked" (quoted by Harvey Cox, "Religion and the War against Evil," *The Nation* [24 December 2001]; http://www.thenation.com/doc/20011224/cox).

7. To be sure, these movements, especially the more recent ones, were not exclusively Christian or necessarily religious. Furthermore, all of them met with great resistance from religious communities, particularly the Christian churches.

8. John 14:6 has from time to time become a shibboleth in Christian relations to other traditions. The General Assembly of the Presbyterian Church (U.S.A), arguably one of its more liberal bodies of government, voted almost unanimously to reaffirm that Jesus the Christ was indeed the *only* way to God ("No one comes to the Father but by me"). I shall return to this issue in Chapter 5. See *The Catechism of the Council of Trent*, trans. John A. McHugh and Charles J. Callan (Rockford, Ill.: Tan Books & Publishers, 1982), 11–13, and John Calvin, *Institutes of the Christian Religion*, ed. John T. McNeill, trans. Ford Lewis Battles;

Library of Christian Classics, 20 and 21 (Philadelphia: Westminster Press, 1960), 2.16.5; 4.1.2; 4.1.20.

9. See Robert Wilken, *The Myth of Christian Beginnings: History's Impact on Belief* (Garden City, N.Y.: Doubleday, 1971), and James M. Robinson and Helmut Koester, *Trajectories through Early Christianity* (Philadelphia: Fortress Press, 1971).

10. See Ernst Troeltsch, *The Social Teachings of the Christian Churches and Sects* (New York: Macmillan, 1931).

11. The topic of greed and its relation to consumerism is a vast one about which much has been written and said. Greed has certainly occupied the minds of religious practitioners and theologians within Judaism and later Christianity for millennia, and the subject of consumerism has troubled ethicists, theologians, social scientists, and social critics for more than a century. For a recently published history of the consumerism viewed through the lens of its deployment to effect political change, see Lizabeth Cohen, *A Consumer's Republic: The Politics of Mass Consumption in Postwar America* (New York: Knopf, 2003).

12. Augustine, *The Confessions*, ed. and trans. Philip Burton (New York: Knopf, 2001); Immanuel Kant, *Critique of Practical Reason*, trans. Werner S. Pluhar (Indianapolis: Hackett, 2002).

13. Whether capitalism leads inevitably to piracy is unclear, particularly given that capitalism is not monolithic. Nevertheless, capitalism unregulated does produce piracy. Capitalism unregulated is greed unregulated. As Max Weber, Robert Bellah (with others), and Cornel West have pointed out, capitalism depends on values that are not indigenous to it in order not to become socially (and I would add environmentally) devastating. For examples, see Max Weber, *The Protestant Ethic and the Spirit of Capitalism*, trans. Talcott Parsons (New York: Routledge, 2001); Robert N. Bellah et al., *Habits of the Heart: Individualism and Commitment in American Life* (Berkeley: University of California Press, 1996); Cornel West, *Race Matters* (New York: Vintage Books, 1994).

14. The following account is drawn from a composite of news stories in the (Minneapolis/Saint Paul) *Star Tribune* and the *New York Times*, running from July 29, 2003, through August 3, 2003.

15. See, for example, Daniel Altman, "Economics Can't Solve Everything, Can It?" *New York Times*, August 3, 2003, Business section, p. 4.

16. Romans 12:2 and John 17:11-16, NRSV.

17. Matthew 25:40, NRSV; see also Dorothee Soelle, *The Silent Cry: Mysticism and Resistance*, trans. Barbara and Martin Rumscheidt (Minneapolis: Fortress Press, 2001).

18. I use the term *Jewish* advisedly. As evidenced by the work of contemporary Jewish scholars of Late Antiquity, what we now think of as religiously Jewish, namely, Talmudic Judaism, does not become the dominant form of what we now call Judaism until the fifth century C.E. During Jesus' time, a number of groups, whose members' lives are centered by the practice of *Torah* and whose ethnicity is loosely Jewish, contend with one another over what it means to be the people of God. These include at the very least the Temple cult (the culturally dominant group at the time), the Essenes, the followers of John the Baptizer, the Pharisees, and Jesus' own highly diverse compatriots. I use the term *Jewish*, unless otherwise specified, to include all these groups. By contrast, some scholars of late antiquity, most notably, Daniel Boyarin, prefer *Israelite* as the comprehensive term. Assuming that most of my readers are not scholars of late antiquity and that they associate *Israelite* with the Exodus story, I use the term *Jewish* instead. Among other things, it clarifies that Jesus was not a gentile, something occasionally forgotten by many Christians. See Daniel Boyarin, "The *Ioudaioi* in John and the Prehistory of 'Judaism,'" in *Pauline Conversations in Context: Essays in Honor of Calvin J. Roetzel*, ed. Janice Capel Anderson, Philip Sellew, and Claudia Setzer (London: Sheffield Academic Press, 2002), 224–50.

19. *Dissent* as we understand it today is also heavily informed by a Platonic or Socratic view that later combines with Christian theological views, particularly during the sixteenth-century Renaissance. See Richard A. Horsley and Neil Asher Silberman, *The Message and the Kingdom: How Jesus and Paul Ignited a Revolution and Transformed the Ancient World* (New York: Grossett/Putnam, 1997); and Richard A. Horsley and John S. Hanson, *Bandits, Prophets, and Messiahs: Popular Movements in the Time of Jesus* (San Francisco: Harper & Row, 1988).

20. Philippe du Plessis-Mornay, "Vindiciae contra tyrannos," in *Constitutionalism and Resistance in the Sixteenth Century: Three Treatises by Hotman, Beza, and Mornay*, trans. and ed. Julian H. Franklin (New York: Pegasus, 1969).

21. See Pierre Bourdieu with Jean-Claude Passeron, *Reproduction in Education, Society and Culture*, trans. Richard Nice (Beverly Hills, California: Sage, 1977); Ludwig Feuerbach, *The Essence of Christianity*, trans. George Eliot (Buffalo, N.Y.: Prometheus Books, 1989); Gordon Kaufman, *The Theological Imagination* (Philadelphia: Westminster Press, 1981); and Elaine Scarry, *The Body in Pain: Making and Unmaking the World* (New York: Oxford University Press, 1985).

22. See, for a contemporary example, John Dominic Crossan, *Jesus: A Revolutionary Biography* (San Francisco: HarperSanFrancisco, 1995).

23. Arthur Miller, *Resurrection Blues* (New York: Penguin, forthcoming 2006).

24. For my understanding of the making of culture in general and the making of religious traditions in particular, I am indebted to Ludwig Feuerbach, *The Essence of Christianity*; Gordon Kaufman, *The Theological Imagination*; and Elaine Scarry, *The Body in Pain*; among others.

25. I address this issue at more length in subsequent chapters. I am aware that in what follows, I am engaging in my own act of christological imagining. See Geza Vermes, "Jesus the Jew," in *Jesus' Jewishness: Exploring the Place of Jesus within Early Judaism*, ed. James H. Charlesworth (New York: Crossroad, 1991); Alan F. Segal, "Jesus, the Revolutionary," in ibid.; Horsley and Silberman, *The Message and the Kingdom*; and Horsley and Hanson, *Bandits, Prophets, and Messiahs*.

26. All references to scripture and quotations from scripture come from *The New Oxford Annotated Bible with the Apocryphal/ Deuterocanonical Books, NRSV*, ed. Bruce M. Metzger and Roland E. Murphy (New York: Oxford University Press, 1989).

27. In *The Nag Hammadi Library in English*, ed. James M. Robinson (San Francisco: HarperSan Francisco, 1990), 220–43.

28. *Acts of John* 94, in *New Testament Apocrypha*, ed. Wilhelm Schneemelcher, trans. R. McL. Wilson (Louisville: Westminster/John Knox, 1992), 2:181–84.

29. The metaphor of the kaleidoscope evokes a rich history of visual images of Jesus. Were I better trained in understanding the historical conditions that produced both elite and popular visual images—for example, the patronage systems of the sixteenth century and the significance of the industrial revolution for the mass production of popular images in the nineteenth century—I would have included attention to visual images as well. That, however, is worthy of a book in its own right. Instead, I have restricted myself to focusing exclusively on written texts— documents from the first five centuries, theological texts across time, in one instance a letter, in another a statement of recanting, the lyrics of a famous hymn, and modern, intentional works of fiction such as short stories, novels, and drama. I have selected these texts in some cases because of their familiarity and in other cases precisely because of their unfamiliarity. In either case, while others might have chosen differently, the texts exemplified for me some aspect important to an understanding of making up and making real the figure of Jesus the Christ.

30. See Gregory Riley, *One Jesus, Many Christs: How Jesus Inspired Not One True Christianity, but Many* (San Francisco: HarperSanFrancisco,

1997), and his *The River of God: A New History of Christian Origins* (New York: HarperSanFrancisco, 2001).

31. R. Laurence Moore, *Selling God: American Religion in the Marketplace of Culture* (New York: Oxford University Press, 1994).

32. See Shane Phelan, *Getting Specific: Postmodern Lesbian Politics* (Minneapolis: University of Minnesota Press, 1994).

33. For my understanding of the distinctive tasks of academic theology, see Cooey, "Immigration, Exodus, and Exile: Academic Theology and Higher Education," *Journal for Teaching Theology and Religion* 3.3 (October 2000): 25–32.

CHAPTER 2

1. For a classic discussion that remains unsurpassed, see Hans Jonas, *The Gnostic Religion: The Message of the Alien God and the Beginnings of Christianity* (Boston: Beacon Press, 1963).

2. See Daniel Boyarin, "The *Ioudaiaoi* in John and the Prehistory of 'Judaism,'" in *Pauline Conversations in Context: Essays in Honor of Calvin J. Roetzel*, ed. Janice Capel Anderson, Phillip Sellew, and Claudia Setzer (London and New York: Sheffield Academic Press, 2002), 233.

3. See *Jesus' Jewishness: Exploring the Place of Jesus in Early Judaism*, ed. James H. Charlesworth (New York: Crossroad, 1996).

4. Daniel Boyarin, *Dying for God: Martyrdom and the Making of Christianity and Judaism* (Stanford: Stanford University Press, 1999); Rosemary Radford Ruether, *Faith and Fratricide: The Theological Roots of Anti-Semitism* (New York: Seabury, 1974).

5. Boyarin, *Dying for God*, 14.

6. Quoted by Boyarin, 14. See also Sozomen, *Ecclesiastical History* 2.4, in Sozomen, *The Ecclesiastical History of Sozomen, Comprising a History of the Church, from A.D. 324 to A.D. 440*, trans. Edward Walford (London: Henry G. Bohn, 1855), and Aryeh Kofsky, "Mamre: A Case of a Regional Cult?" in *Sharing the Sacred: Religious Contacts and Conflicts in the Holy Land First Centuries C.E.*, ed. Guy G. Stroumsa and Aryeh Kofsky (Jerusalem: Yad Ben Zvi, 1998), 19–30.

7. Hans Jonas, *The Gnostic Religion*.

8. For an example of a Jewish gnostic text, see the Sethian texts such as *The Paraphrase of Sehem* and *The Three Steles of Seth*. For a pagan example, see the *Poimandres* of Hermes Trismegistus. There are texts that are not Christian, but may be either Jewish or pagan as well. See, for example, *Asclepius*, in *The Nag Hammadi Library*, ed. James M. Robinson (San Francisco: HarperSanFrancisco, 1998).

9. Robinson, *The Nag Hammadi Library*.

10. Ludwig Wittgenstein, *Philosophical Investigations: The German Text, with Revised English Translations*, ed. G.E.M. Anscombe (Oxford: Blackwell, 2001). The notion of family resemblances arises in Wittgenstein's later philosophy as developed throughout this text.

11. See Calvin J. Roetzel, *Paul: The Man and the Myth* (Columbia: University of South Carolina Press, 1998).

12. See Richard Rubenstein, *My Brother Paul* (New York: Harper & Row, 1972); Daniel Boyarin, *A Radical Jew: Paul and the Politics of Identity* (Berkeley: University of California Press, 1997); Calvin Roetzel, *The Letters of Paul: Conversations in Context*, 4th ed. (Louisville: Westminster John Knox, 1998), and *Paul: The Man and the Myth*.

13. Boyarin, *A Radical Jew*.

14. Roetzel, *Paul: The Man and the Myth*, 120–34.

15. Ibid., 106.

16. Robin Scroggs, "Paul, Myth Remaker: The Refashioning of Early Ecclesial Traditions," in Anderson, Sellew, and Setzer, *Pauline Conversations*, 100.

17. See Romans 13.

18. For an analysis of the use of parable as a discursive practice, see Sallie MacFague, *Metaphorical Theology: Models of God in Religious Language* (Philadelphia: Fortress Press, 1982); for a feminist analysis of the significance of miracle stories, see Rita Nakashima Brock, *Journey by Heart: A Christology of Erotic Power* (New York: Crossroad, 1980).

19. Boyarin, "The *Ioudaioi* in John," and "The Gospel of the Memra: Jewish Binitarianism and the Prologue to John," *Harvard Theological Review* 94:3 (July 2001): 243–84.

20. Elaine Pagels, "Issues of Authority," House of Hope Didier Seminar, House of Hope Presbyterian Church, St. Paul, February 9, 2003, and *Beyond Belief: The Secret Gospel of Thomas* (New York: Random House, 2003).

21. See Walter Bauer, *Orthodoxy and Heresy in Earliest Christianity* (Mifflintown: Sigler Press, 1971); James M. Robinson and Helmut Koester, *Trajectories through Early Christianity* (Philadelphia: Fortress Press, 1971).

22. See, for example, Hans Jonas, *The Gnostic Religion*, 178–79.

23. I use the term *universal* and its cognates to refer to those theologians and communities who argued for universal access to salvation. They were ultimately to produce what we now call orthodoxy. I use this term in preference to the term *catholic* to reinforce the multiplicity of contending traditions at this point in history.

24. *Saint Irenaeus of Lugdunum against the Heresies*, trans. and annotated by Dominic J. Unger, with revisions by John J. Dillon (New York: Paulist Press, 1992).

25. Cited by Jonas, *The Gnostic Religion*, 179. See Irenaeus, *Heresies* 1.18.5.

26. Robinson, *The Nag Hammadi Library*.

27. Ibid.

28. See Pagels, *The Gnostic Gospels* (New York: Vintage, 1979).

29. See, for example, *On the Origin of the World*, in Robinson, *The Nag Hammadi Library*.

30. Jonas, *The Gnostic Religion*, 217.

31. *Anagogy* refers to the literary device and hermeneutical technique of attributing super-anthropomorphic form to the cosmos or to reality as a whole, including a deity or deities in the context of mystical experience. The poetry of William Blake exemplifies par excellence the employment of anagogy as literary technique. Jewish kabbalism, the performance of gematria, and some forms of medieval mysticism illustrate anagogic interpretations of scripture. The author of *The Gospel of Truth* employs anagogy as a technique throughout the text, as for example, when stating, "the children of the Father are his fragrance" (34.1).

32. On initiation, see *The Gospel according to Philip*; Martha Lee Turner, *The Gospel according to Philip: The Sources and Coherence of an Early Christian Collection* (New York: Brill, 1996).

33. For a classic discussion of Manichaean teachings, see Jonas, *The Gnostic Religion*, 206–37.

34. Works in which Augustine refutes the Manichaeans include minimally *De moribus ecclsiae catholicae et de moribus Manichaeorum* (388), *De Genesi contra Manichaeos* (388–90) (both in *Saint Augustine: The Catholic and Manichaean Ways of Life*, in *Fathers of the Church* 56, trans. Donald A. Gallagher and Idella J. Gallagher [Chestnut Hill: Catholic University Press, 1966]), *De vera religione* (389–91), *De utilitate credendi* (391–92), *De duabus animabus contra Manichaeos* (391–92), *Contra Adimantum Manichaei discipulum* (393–96), *Contra epistolam Manichaei quam vocant fundimenti* (397), and so on through *De haerisibus ad Quodvultdeum* (428).

35. See *Saint Augustine on Genesis: Two Books on Genesis against the Manichees* and *On the Literal Interpretation of Genesis: An Unfinished book*, in *The Fathers of the Church* 84, trans. Roland J. Teske, S.J. (Washington, D.C: The Catholic University of America Press), 1991. See also *De Genesi as litteram imperfectus liber* (393), the last three books

of the *Confessions*, *De Genesi ad litteram* (12 volumes written between 404 and 420), and book 11 of *The City of God* (417–18).

36. I am indebted to my colleague and friend Paul Capetz for this insight.

37. One could argue for a modicum of tolerance found in Augustine by referring to his *City of God*: "The heavenly city . . . calls citizens out of all nations, and gathers together a society of pilgrims of all languages, not scrupling about diversities in the manners, laws, and institutions whereby earthly peace is secured and maintained. . . . It is therefore so far from rescinding and abolishing these diversities that it even preserves and adapts them, so long as no hindrance to the worship of the one true God is thus introduced." Cited by Miner S. Ball, "Common Good in Performance," in *In Search of the Common Good*, ed. Dennis P. McCann and Patrick D. Miller (New York: T & T Clark International, 2005). The quotation appears in Augustine, *The City of God*, trans. Marcus Dodds (New York: Modern Library, 1958), 696 (19.17). Ball cites Augustine as evidence against coercive evangelism and for a relative tolerance of difference. Note, however, that the tolerance is for "diversities" in the governance and manners appearing across nations in an earthly context, differences Augustine is willing to assimilate. Insisting on the primacy of worship of the one true God, however, does not evidence a religious pluriverse.

38. See Roetzel, *Paul.*

CHAPTER 3

1. Francis Parkman, *France and England in North America*, vol. 1: *The Old Regime in Canada*, Literary Classics of the United States (New York: Viking, 1983), 1084–85.

2. See Michel Foucault, *Discipline and Punish: The Birth of the Prison*, trans. Alan Sheridan (New York: Vintage Books, 1979), and *Power/Knowledge: Selected Interviews and Other Writings, 1972–1977*, ed. and trans. Colin Gordon (New York: Pantheon Books, 1980).

3. The next four paragraphs appeared in slightly modified version in Paula M. Cooey, "Immigration, Exodus, and Exile: Academic Theology and Higher Education," *Teaching Theology and Religious Studies* 3.3 (2000), 125–32.

4. See, for instance, Asselin Charles, "Colonial Discourses since Christopher Columbus," *Journal of Black Studies* 26.2 (November 1995), 141.

5. For example, see Zwingli, "Commentary on True and False Religion," excerpted in *The Protestant Reformation*, ed. Hans J.

Hillerbrand (New York: Harper and Row, 1968). See also James S. Preus, *Explaining Religion: Criticism and Theory from Bodin to Freud* (New Haven: Yale University Press, 1987). Moreover, this something called "religion" could, according to the theologians, be judged true or false strictly on the basis of the orthodoxy of one's beliefs. Unlike the orthodoxy established by the earlier churches, Protestant orthodoxy, in turn, depended upon subordinating practice and observance to sacred text, as according to specific, but often implicit standards.

6. For a sampling of current scholarship on Erasmus, see Istvan Pieter Bejcy, *Erasmus and the Middle Ages: The Historical Consciousness of a Christian Humanist* (Boston: Brill, 2001); Manfred Hoffman, *Rhetoric and Theology: The Hermeneutic of Erasmus* (Toronto: University of Toronto Press, 1994); Leon-Ernest Halkin, *Erasmus: A Critical Biography*, trans. John Tonkin (Oxford: Blackwell, 1993); Timothy J. Wengert, *Human Freedom, Christian Righteousness: Philip Melanchthon's Exegetical Dispute with Erasmus of Rotterdam* (New York: Oxford University Press, 1998).

7. See J.N.D. Kelly, *Early Christian Creeds* (New York: D. McKay, 1960). Origen ultimately became convinced that even the devil would be forgiven and received into heaven. While this belief was considered heretical, it is also clear that church politics factored heavily into the decision to condemn him.

8. Quoted in Ernst F. Winter, ed. and trans., *Erasmus–Luther Discourse on Free Will* (New York: Frederick Ungar, 1973). Hereafter cited within the text as *Discourse*.

9. See, for examples, *Antibarborum liber* (1494–95) and *De pueris instituendis* (1529).

10. Desiderius Erasmus, *Erasmus on His Times: A Shortened Version of the "Adages" of Erasmus*, trans. Margaret Mann Phillips (Cambridge and New York: Cambridge University Press, 1967).

11. See Erasmus, *The Colloquies of Erasmus*, trans. N. Bailey (London: Reeves and Turner, 1878).

12. While the debate is fascinating in its own right, it is outside the scope of this discussion to engage it on substantive grounds.

13. Erasmus's essay and Luther's response are published together in Winter, *Discourse on Free Will*.

14. Ibid.

15. See Erasmus, *On Mending the Peace of the Church*, in *The Essential Erasmus*, ed. John P. Dolan (New York: Penguin, 1964).

16. For a relatively succinct exposition of Luther's christology, see Dietmar Lage, *Martin Luther's Christology and Ethics* (Lewiston, N.Y.: Edwin Mellen Press, 1990).

17. See George Huntston Williams, *The Radical Reformation*, 3rd ed. (Kirksville, Mo.: Sixteenth Century Journal Publishers, 1992); and Hillerbrand, *The Protestant Reformation*, 122–52.

18. See Hillerbrand, *The Protestant Reformation*, 129–52.

19. Hillerbrand, *The Protestant Reformation*, 129–36. See also John C. Wenger, "The Schleitheim Confession of Faith," *Mennonite Quarterly Review* 19 (1945): 243ff.

20. Hillerbrand, *The Protestant Reformation*, 130. While there were groups that indulged in libertine practices, they were a small minority. It was typical of both Catholic and Protestant polemic to tar all the radicals with the same brush by accusing them of excess. Protestants in particular sought to distinguish themselves from the radical sects as paragons of order for the purpose of legitimating their cause. See, for example, John Calvin's letter to Francis I at the beginning of the *Institutes of the Christian Religion*, ed. John T. McNeill, 2 vols., Library of Christian Classics 20 (Philadelphia: Westminster Press, 1960), 1:9–31.

21. Hillerbrand, *The Protestant Reformation*, 131.

22. Ibid., 132.

23. Infant baptism was a particular sticking point here. From an Anabaptist perspective, there is no scriptural example or support for the practice. For a classic Protestant statement on things indifferent, see Calvin's *Institutes of the Christian Religion*, 4.16.1324ff. For further elaboration on the Anabaptist position, see the letter to Thomas Muntzer from the Zurich Anabaptists in Hillerbrand, *The Protestant Reformation*, 124. See also George H. Williams, ed., *Spiritual and Anabaptist Writers: Documents Illustrative of the Radical Reformation* (Philadelphia: Westminster Press, 1957), 73–85.

24. For a classic overview of these events, see Williston Walker, *A History of the Christian Church*, 3rd ed. (New York: Charles Scribner's Sons, 1970), 326–32.

25. Hillerbrand includes this letter in abridged form in *The Protestant Reformation*. For the full text see Thieleman van Braght, *The Bloody Theater: or, The Martyr's Mirror of the Defenseless Christians* (Scottsdale, Penn.: Mennonite Publishing Company, 1951), 984–87.

26. There are numerous historical accounts from a variety of different perspectives on Calvin and Servetus, taken individually and together. See, for example, Roland H. Bainton, *Hunted Heretic: The Life and Death of Michael Servetus, 1511–1553* (Boston: Beacon Press, 1960); Bernard Cottret, *Calvin: A Biography*, trans. M. Wallace McDonald (Grand Rapids, Mich.: Eerdmans, 2000); Marian Hillar, *The Case of Michael Servetus (1511–1553): The Turning Point in the*

Struggle for Freedom of Conscience (Lewiston, N.Y.: Edwin Mellen Press, 1997); William G. Naphy, *Calvin and the Consolidation of the Genevan Reformation* (Louisville: Westminster John Knox, 2003); Randall C. Zachman, *The Assurance of Faith: Conscience in the Theology of Martin Luther and John Calvin* (Minneapolis: Fortress Press, 1993).

27. What we now call the Nicene Creed was not yet in final form in 325 C.E. but was modified several times into the version that became standard by 451 C.E. See Walker, *A History of the Christian Church*, and J.N.D. Kelly, *Early Christian Creeds*.

28. See Ronald B. Flowers, *That Godless Court? Supreme Court Decisions on Church-State Relationships* (Louisville: Westminster John Knox, 1994), and Stephen L. Carter, *The Culture of Disbelief: How American Law and Politics Trivialize Religious Devotion* (New York: Basic Books, 1993), as respectively representative of these two stands.

29. Raphael Patai, *The Hebrew Goddess* (New York: Ktav Publishing House, 1968). On the contemporary significance of Mary for Protestant women see *Blessed One: Protestant Perspectives on Mary*, ed. Beverly Roberts Gaventa and Cynthia L. Rigby (Louisville: Westminster John Knox, 2002).

30. Scholarship itself may inadvertently recapitulate this interaction by abstracting and reifying popular practices as if they did not migrate through the circulation of power. As an antidote, see Carlo Ginzburg, *The Cheese and the Worms: The Cosmos of a Sixteenth-Century Miller* (Baltimore: Johns Hopkins University Press, 1980).

31. See James B. Given, *Inquisition and Medieval Society: Power, Discipline, and Resistance in Languedoc* (Ithaca: Cornell University Press, 1997).

32. The association of magic with witchcraft is in itself unremarkable. This association has occurred across cultures. Outside pre-modern Europe, magic and with it witchcraft were considered and continue to be considered morally neutral, that is, they may be practiced for good or for ill, depending on the goal to be accomplished.

33. For a good example of this process see Heinrich Institoris, *The Malleus Malificarum of Heinrich Kramer and James Sprenger*, trans. Montague Summers (New York: Dover, 1971).

34. For a recent example, see Robin Briggs, *Witches and Neighbors: The Social and Cultural Context of European Witchcraft* (New York: Viking, 1996). Briggs sets witchcraft in tension with neighbor love and draws on contemporary conflicts surrounding Satanism as linked with child molestation to explore the social dynamic that produced the European witch-hunts. I think that work on the fabrication of memory would

provide a useful resource for understanding the socio-psychological dynamics at work as yet one more feature to be taken in consideration when trying to understand the phenomenon. See Elizabeth F. Loftus and Katherine Ketcham, *The Myth of Repressed Memory: False Memories and Allegations of Sexual Abuse* (New York: St. Martin's Griffin, 1996).

35. Jonathan Barry, Marianne Hester, and Gareth Roberts, eds., *Witchcraft in Early Modern Europe: Studies in Culture and Belief* (Cambridge: Cambridge University Press, 1996); Alan Charles Kors and Edward Peters, eds., *Witchcraft in Europe, 400–1700: A Documentary History*, 2nd ed. (Philadelphia: University of Pennsylvania Press, 2001).

36. For Protestants, see Martin Luther, *Commentary on Saint Paul's Epistle to the Galatians* (Philadelphia: Miller and Borlock, 1840), and *Table Talk*, in *Luther's Works 54*, ed. Theodore G. Tappert (Philadelphia: Fortress, 1967). See also John Calvin's discussions of the reality of the devil in *The Institutes of the Christian Religion*, 1.14.13–19; 2.4.1–2.

37. See Carlo Ginzburg, *The Night Battles: Witchcraft and Agrarian Cults in the Sixteenth and Seventeenth Centuries* (Baltimore: Johns Hopkins University Press, 1983).

38. The first was one Johann Weyer (1515–1588), a Lutheran and a physician who published *De praestigiis daemonum* in 1563, subsequently republished in expanded and abridged forms in German and circulated widely. Weyer flatly rejected the possibility of witchcraft as defined by the tribunals. Loos read Weyer's work. In 1584, Reginald Scot published *Discoverie of Witchcraft*, challenging not only the concept of witch but also the rules of evidence. For Loos's recantation and excerpts of Weyer's and Scot's work, see Kors and Peters, *Witchcraft in Europe*.

39. Kors and Peters, *Witchcraft in Europe*, 315–17.

40. Ibid.

41. Ibid.

42. Ibid.

43. Ibid.

44. Ibid., 310–18.

45. However, Ginzburg's works, including *The Night Battles* and *The Cheese and the Worms*, suggests the possibility of devising such strategies.

46. For one of the earliest feminist recognitions of this dynamic see Rosemary Radford Ruether, "Witches and Jews: The Demonic Alien in Christian Culture," in *New Woman, New Earth: Sexist Ideologies and Human Liberation* (New York: Seabury Press, 1975), 89–114.

47. The witch-craze is a perfect example of Foucault's conception of the relation between power and knowledge, where power circulates

diffusely as reinforced by discourses of truth. These discourses, as definitive of what constitutes truth, render thinking outside them impossible. See *Power/Knowledge*. It is striking that these are the very processes by which we have constructed "communist" in the relatively recent past and now "terrorist." Witness Jerry Falwell's description of Muhammad as a terrorist in an interview on *60 Minutes* on October 6, 2002.

48. See Ginzburg, *The Night Battles*.

49. See Given, *Inquisition and Medieval Society*, 91–165.

50. I am indebted to Calvin Roetzel for the insight that how one rears one's children may reflect intentional dissent to a dominant culture. Contemporary examples include parents who eschew regionally defined or class defined conventions of politeness that bespeak authoritarianism, parents who teach their children not to use gender-exclusive language in the home, or parents who "home school" their children in rejection of the secular humanism of public school education.

51. Katie G. Cannon, among others, discusses how secrecy becomes an ethically necessary strategy for the survival of oppressed people, in Cannon's case, specifically for African American women. See *Black Womanist Ethics* (Atlanta: Scholars Press, 1988).

52. Paul E. Capetz, *Christian Faith as Religion: A Study in the Theologies of Calvin and Schleiermacher* (Lanham: University Press of America, 1998).

CHAPTER 4

1. Cited by N. Ashimbaeva and V. Biron, *The Dostoevsky Museum in St. Petersburg: A Guidebook* (St. Petersburg: Bojanych Press, 2003), 26.

2. Ibid., 13.

3. In his famous article, "Civil Religion in America," published in *Daedalus*, 19:1 (1967): 1–21, Robert Bellah developed the concept "civil religion" to describe American appropriation of features of Protestant Christianity for national ends. The para-religious or meta-religious functions of secularism to which I refer here extend his concept of civil religion by locating religious appropriation for State purposes as central to any definition or instantiation of secularism. In other words, "civil religion" is not simply an add-on to an otherwise religiously neutral State; it lies at the very heart of secularism, as a national or imperial way of life. Secularism is religious, though its religiosity may be masked in order to support its claim to religious neutrality.

4. For a discussion of the apocalyptic Yankee Protestant milieu in which Ward-Howe was writing, see James H. Moorhead, *American*

Apocalypse: Yankee Protestants and the Civil War, 1860–1869 (New Haven: Yale University Press, 1978).

5. Jeanne Halgren Kilde, "How Did *Left Behind's* Particular Vision of the End Times Develop? A Historical Look at Millenarian Thought," in *Rapture, Revelation and the End Times: Exploring the* Left Behind *Series*, ed. Bruce Forbes and Jeanne Halgren Kilde (New York: Palgrave Macmillan, 2004).

6. Susan Friend Harding, *The Book of Jerry Falwell: Fundamentalist Language and Politics* (Princeton, N.J.: Princeton University Press, 2000).

7. Amy Johnson Frykholm, *Rapture Culture: Left Behind in Evangelical America* (Oxford: Oxford University Press, 2004).

8. Michael Duffy, "Marching Along," *Time* (September 9, 2002).

9. Rob Garver, "Leftward Christian Soldiers," from http://www.portside.org, June 24, 2005.

10. See http://www.christianalliance.org

CHAPTER 5

1. Kathryn Tanner, *Jesus, Humanity, and the Trinity: A Brief Systematic Theology* (Minneapolis: Fortress Press, 2001), and "What Does Grace Have to Do with Money?" *Harvard Divinity Bulletin* 30.4 (Spring 2002).

2. Presbyterian Church (U.S.A.), *The Constitution of the Presbyterian Church (U.S.A.), Part I, Book of Confessions* (Louisville: Office of the General Assembly, Presbyterian Church [U.S.A.], 1989).

3. This is a classic definition of one of the earliest heresies, known as Docetism, from the Greek term for "appearance."

4. For a conservative religious perspective see Ralph Reed, *Politically Incorrect: The Emerging Faith Factor in American Politics* (Dallas: Word, 1994). For environmentalist perspectives, theologically framed, see John B. Cobb, Jr., *Is It Too Late? A Theology of Ecology*, rev. ed. (Denton, Texas: Environmental Ethics Books, 1995); Sallie McFague, *The Body of God: An Ecological Theology* (Minneapolis: Fortress Press, 1993); Gordon Kaufman, *Theology for a Nuclear Age* (Manchester, U.K.: Manchester University Press, 1985); Jay B. McDaniel, *Earth, Sky, Gods, and Mortals: Developing an Ecological Spirituality* (Mystic, Conn.: Twenty-Third Publications, 1990).

5. Mark Lewis Taylor, *The Executed God: The Way of the Cross in Lockdown America* (Minneapolis: Fortress Press, 2001); Helen Prejean, *Dead Man Walking: An Eyewitness Account of the Death Penalty in the United States* (New York: Vintage Books, 1994).

6. The one contemporary theologian who in my opinion has worked through this traditional theological apparatus and re-articulated it for a contemporary time in ways that make sense is Katherine Tanner, *Jesus, Humanity, and the Trinity*, as well as *The Politics of God: Christian Theologies and Social Justice* (Minneapolis: Fortress Press, 1992). For a compelling contemporary rethinking of the anthropological implications of this apparatus in terms of justification and sanctification, see Serene Jones, *Calvin and the Rhetoric of Piety* (Louisville: Westminster John Knox, 1995), and *Feminist Theory and Christian Theology: Cartographies of Grace* (Minneapolis: Fortress Press, 2000).

7. Delores S. Williams, "Black Women's Surrogacy Experience and the Christian Notion of Redemption," in *After Patriarchy: Feminist Transformations of the World Religions*, ed. Paula M. Cooey, William R. Eakin, and Jay B. McDaniel (Maryknoll, N.Y.: Orbis Books, 1991).

8. Kelly Brown Douglas, *The Black Christ* (Maryknoll, N.Y.: Orbis Books, 1994).

9. For one of the more recent examples, see Elisabeth Schüssler Fiorenza, *Jesus: Miriam's Child, Sophia's Prophet* (New York: Continuum, 1994).

10. Sallie McFague, *Speaking in Parables: A Study in Metaphor and Theology* (London: SCM, 2002).

11. As my colleague Calvin Roetzel points out, the Greek term translated as "nations" might be better translated "gentile groups," because the concept "nation" is a relatively modern one.

12. For an example of this interpretation, see J. Andrew Overman, *Church and Community in Crisis: The Gospel according to Matthew* (Valley Forge: Trinity Press International, 1996), 339–52.

13. See related passages from the Sermon on the Mount, Matthew 5–7; becoming a child, Matthew 18:1-5; and summarizing *Torah*, the Law, Matthew 22:37-40. See also Krister Stendahl, "Matthew," in *Peake's Commentary on the Bible*, ed. M. Black and H. H. Rowley (New York: Thomas Nelson, 1962), 769–98.

14. My translation. For texts that instruct in a similar way, but from a different context, see Romans 12, especially verses 20–21. Here, however, the focus is more upon the subject of ethical action rather than the other who is the object of such action.

15. On the significance of the gift, see Jacques Derrida, *The Gift of Death*, trans. David Wills (Chicago: University of Chicago Press, 1995).

16. See Dorothee Soelle, *The Silent Cry: Mysticism and Resistance*, trans. Barbara and Martin Rumscheidt (Minneapolis: Fortress Press, 2001).

17. Kathleen Sands, "Uses of the Thea(o)logian: Sex and Theodicy in Religious Feminism," *Journal of Feminist Studies in Religion* 8 (Spring 1992): 7–33.

18. Sallie McFague, *Life Abundant: Rethinking Theology and Economy for a Planet in Peril* (Minneapolis: Fortress Press, 2001). See also Paula M. Cooey, "Eros and Intimacy in Edwards," *Journal of Religion* 69.4 (1989): 484–501.

19. See Judith Plaskow, *Sex, Sin, and Grace: Women's Experience and the Theologies of Reinhold Niebuhr and Paul Tillich* (Washington, D.C.: University Press of America, 1980).

20. See, for example the classic formulation of Anders Nygren, *Agape and Eros*, trans. Philip S. Watson (Chicago: University of Chicago Press, 1982).

21. See respectively, H. Richard Niebuhr, *The Responsible Self: An Essay in Christian Moral Philosophy* (New York: Harper and Row, 1963); Paul Louis Lehmann, *Ethics in a Christian Context* (New York: Harper and Row, 1963); Sharon Welch, *A Feminist Ethic of Risk*, rev. ed. (Minneapolis: Fortress Press, 2000).

22. One of the best theological renderings of courage ever written is Paul Tillich's *The Courage to Be* (New Haven: Yale University Press, 1952). While Tillich focuses on courage as such, however, I want to emphasize courage not only for the self who exercises it but also as a response on which meeting the need of another depends.

23. Paula M. Cooey, "That Every Child Who Wants to Might Learn to Dance," *Crosscurrents* 48.2 (Summer 1998): 185–97.

24. The school, renamed the Western Hemisphere Institute for Security Cooperation (WHINSEC), is located in Fort Benning, Georgia. The SOA was actually "closed" in 2001 and "reopened" as WHINSEC immediately; it was entirely a cosmetic change made in Congress, aimed at undermining legislation that would actually close the school and investigate the abuses. See http://www.soaw.org/new/article.php?id=110.

25. I met Rick (not his real name) in Thailand in early March 2003, while working on a research project unrelated to this book. I interviewed him in his home at great length, then corroborated as much as I could of his story through other sources. These sources included local colleagues and peers of his, a member of the mission board of his denomination who served at the time that he and the board negotiated an amicable parting of the ways over the issue of arms, websites representing the organization he has helped form and with which he presently works, and newspaper coverage of this

organization. I received his permission to use the interview in my own work.

26. I am racially marking the white people to counter the phenomenon of assuming whiteness as normative, in contrast to other ethnicities and races that go marked under the rubric of "people of color." "White" names distinctive characteristics, attitudes, and histories that are no more and no less universal than, say, "black," for example. In my mind, to name whiteness is to own up to certain configurations of power that produce white racism. This would hold for other distinctions along lines of gender, class, and sexual orientation as well. I think that these distinctions are culturally produced oversimplifications. Nevertheless, owning the legacy of whiteness, from a white Jesus to the injustice of white privilege, is something white Christians need to do.

27. For obvious reasons, I am again protecting identity here by changing the names.

Index of Proper Names

INDEX OF CONCEPTS